Yorkshire Grit

Yorkshire Grit

The Life of Ray Illingworth

Mark Peel

pitch

First published by Pitch Publishing, 2023

Pitch Publishing
9 Donnington Park,
85 Birdham Road,
Chichester,
West Sussex,
PO20 7AJ
www.pitchpublishing.co.uk
info@pitchpublishing.co.uk

A CIP catalogue record is available for this book
from the British Library.

ISBN 978 1 80150 452 2

Typesetting and origination by Pitch Publishing

Printed and bound in Great Britain by TJ Books, Padstow

Contents

Introduction

'AS A race, we Yorkshiremen are rude, boorish, stubborn, aggressive, argumentative, disruptive, intolerant and just plain, downright bloody-minded. We harbour a series of complexes ranging from inferiority to persecution, and we are violently resentful of authority in any guise.' So wrote the well-known sports journalist Don Mosey and while his depiction of his fellow Yorkshiremen is something of a generalisation, much of it applied to his good friend Raymond (Ray) Illingworth, one of Yorkshire and England's most esteemed cricketers.

According to the illustrious journalist and broadcaster John Arlott, Illingworth 'was and is entirely Yorkshire', his character and outlook shaped very much by his background. Born in the cricketing heartland of Pudsey, the town which nurtured the Yorkshire and England legends Herbert Sutcliffe and Len Hutton, Illingworth's roots were skilled working class in surroundings where civic pride and personal endeavour compensated for a lack of wealth. Imbued with a love of cricket from early childhood, he supplemented his natural talent with a fierce determination to succeed. Introduced to the unforgiving environment of the Bradford League when playing for Farsley aged 15, his progress was such that he made his debut for

Yorkshire three years later and he marked the occasion with a half-century against Hampshire.

Playing for Yorkshire in those days was the pinnacle of any Yorkshire-born cricketer's ambition given the club's revered tradition as the dominant team in the country, but that history weighed heavily on the younger players as they attempted to live up to the giants of old. With competition for places intense and expectations high, not least from their fanatical supporters, Yorkshire professionals tended to be dour, hard-bitten types contemptuous of flair and ostentation. Reared on the adage of 'Give 'em nowt', and an intolerance of failure, they played not for pleasure or entertainment but to win at all costs.

In this coercive atmosphere of players protecting their backs the dressing room wasn't always a haven of harmony, especially for any aspiring newcomer. This was particularly the case in the 1950s when gnarled old pros such as England bowlers Johnny Wardle and Bob Appleyard took their frustration out on their younger team-mates when they failed to measure up. According to Essex and England all-rounder Trevor Bailey, Yorkshire's bowlers in the 1950s reminded him of Greek guerrillas in war against the Nazis in that they were united against the common foe but divided among themselves.

Subjected to a number of barbs himself, Illingworth had the personal resolve to stick up for himself and make progress. Never short of self-confidence on the cricket field, his unyielding personality and uncompromising will to win placed him firmly in the Yorkshire tradition. With his impressive feats as an all-rounder, he made his debut for England in 1958 and was chosen for the MCC tour to Australia and New Zealand in 1962/63. The tour, managed by the Duke of Norfolk and captained by Ted Dexter, exposed cricket's class divide all too clearly as the amateurs enjoyed privileges such as single rooms and access to cars denied to the rest of the team. Affronted by such preferential treatment and the lack of organised practice, Illingworth made his views known to his superiors, gripes that cost him £50 of his £150 tour bonus.

In many ways that tour sounded the death knell of the amateur since the abolition of the distinction between amateurs and professionals in November 1962 reflected wider social changes. For the 1960s was the decade of *That Was the Week That Was*, a late-night show that lampooned establishment figures, the Beatles and Harold Wilson, the Huddersfield grammar-school boy whose premiership stood for a more meritocratic society. In this climate, professionalism in cricket gathered pace with the establishment of the Cricketers' Association in 1967 to give the players a voice and the development of a more hard-nosed ethos whereby entertainment came a distant second to winning.

At a time when Yorkshire's reactionary regime was out of step with the march of progress, the plain-speaking Illingworth used his enhanced status within the team to act as its unofficial shop steward. As a proud professional dedicated to self-improvement, he clashed with a committee that treated the players as second-class citizens by addressing them by their surnames, paying them poorly and failing to offer them contracts, the only county to lack a contracts system. By 1968 Illingworth was at the height of his powers, but, aged 36 and under some threat from Yorkshire's promising young off-spinner Geoff Cope, he asked the committee for a three-year contract to provide some security for himself and his young family. His request was brusquely rejected by chairman Brian Sellers who showed him the door, a poor reward for years of unstinting service.

Illingworth's departure proved as beneficial to him, as it was detrimental to Yorkshire. Moving to Leicestershire as captain in 1969, he instilled in them a winning ethos and took on the England captaincy in place of the injured Colin Cowdrey, who ruptured his Achilles tendon in a Sunday League match early that season. Rising to the occasion, Illingworth proved a natural leader and the following summer he beat off a challenge from Cowdrey to lead MCC in Australia and New Zealand that winter.

The decision was fully vindicated by Illingworth's triumph in regaining the Ashes after 12 years. Leading with all his customary shrewdness, he won the total confidence of his team by fighting hard for their interests and beating the Australians at their own game. At the same time his attritional approach upset the purists and his combative manner offended manager David Clark, an establishment figure with a fixed view on how England should play. Particularly galling to Clark was Illingworth's objection to playing an added Test to compensate for the complete abandonment of the Melbourne one due to bad weather, since that extra game in an already crowded schedule would disadvantage England.

There was also his heated altercation with umpire Lou Rowan in the final Test when Rowan warned England's John Snow for intimidatory bowling. If that finger-wagging confrontation in full view of the television cameras at the Sydney Cricket Ground wasn't bad enough, Illingworth's unilateral decision to take his players off the field in response to some crowd trouble caused the manager near apoplexy. A bitter row ensued in the England dressing room before Illingworth agreed to return on the assurance that order had been restored.

According to traditionalists such as the *Daily Telegraph*'s august cricket correspondent E.W. Swanton, Illingworth had crossed a line by undermining the umpire's authority, a view later endorsed by the Cricket Council, the game's governing body, but Illingworth remained unrepentant, blaming the umpire for his officious attitude throughout the series.

The following summer Illingworth again defied the game's authorities in the England–India Test at Lord's when Snow barged diminutive Indian batsman Sunil Gavaskar to the ground as Gavaskar ran a quick single. Outraged by what he'd seen, Billy Griffith, secretary of the Marylebone Cricket Club (MCC), confronted Snow in the England dressing room at the lunch interval and ordered him to apologise immediately, and when Snow took exception to Griffith's strictures, Illingworth asked Griffith to leave the dressing room. Snow did eventually apologise but Illingworth's refusal to take the matter more seriously earned him criticism from the blue-blooded elements of the press.

Attrition continued to characterise his leadership of England, his finest moment coming against Australia at Headingley in 1972 when his all-round performance ensured England retained the Ashes. His star waned against West Indies the following summer and, following a heavy defeat at Lord's, he was cast aside as captain, his proud record of played 31, won 12 and lost five one of the best among England captains.

Having transformed Leicestershire into a match-winning outfit, Illingworth returned to Yorkshire in the new role of team manager. His appointment was viewed as a move of desperation by some, since the club had struggled under the divisive leadership of Geoff Boycott and his botched dismissal as captain in September 1978 only inflamed divisions. Thrown into this cauldron of acrimony and suspected by Boycott's supporters of being behind his sacking, Illingworth chose to fight fire with fire. 'I've warned people I'm like a bull elephant', he once said. 'If you cross me, I never forget,' and it was his constant feud with Boycott, an idol to many Yorkshiremen on account of his phenomenal batting, that ultimately cost him his job.

While Illingworth was unfortunate to inherit the Boycott imbroglio (ironically, he'd wanted Boycott to succeed him as England captain), a more profound problem concerned his failure to adapt to his new role. As captain, his success had been based on his strength of personality and his tactical brilliance, but his attempt to control his captain from the pavilion sowed further conflict. After one captain, John Hampshire, resigned and a second one, Chris Old, was sacked, Illingworth stepped back into the breach as skipper, aged 50, but while his tactical expertise remained undiminished, he lacked the capacity to heal the bitter divisions engulfing the club. By the time he was dismissed in 1984, the result of the pro-Boycott uprising within the membership, he could point only to the winning of the John Player League (JPL) as the sole reward for his five years of labour.

Convinced that fate had dealt him a harsh blow at Yorkshire, he continued to pride himself on his raw honesty, not least his reservations about the modern game. Although remembered for his dogged campaign to enhance the status of his fellow professionals, he drew the line at Kerry Packer's World Series Cricket which brought untold wealth to the likes of Tony Greig, Clive Lloyd and Viv Richards. Recalling his tough initiation at Yorkshire and his failure to command a regular place in the England side until he became captain, he slated the post-Packer generation for their aversion to practice, their lack of basic skills and their celebrity lifestyles. When asked by *The Cricketer* magazine which modern player he admired, he replied, 'None.' His downbeat assessment rather encapsulated his discordant approach during his time as chairman of the England selectors between 1994 and 1996. In line with his experience as team manager of Yorkshire, he once again demanded the final say over selection and downgraded the authority of the captain in a way he would never have tolerated when he was England captain. Although the incumbent, Mike Atherton, was a tough northerner with a mind of his own, he reluctantly accepted the new realities, especially following his fine for alleged ball-tampering at Lord's in 1994, which had somewhat eroded his authority.

Priding himself at all times on his candour, Illingworth's tendency to criticise his players did little to promote team spirit. Having berated the captain and the tour management for their failure of leadership on England's tour of Australia in 1994/95, their 3-1 loss contributing to the dismissal of coach Keith Fletcher, Illingworth now assumed unprecedented powers as chairman and team manager, calling himself 'supremo'.

After drawing 2-2 with West Indies in 1995, Illingworth set off for South Africa that autumn full of hope, but the tour was bedevilled by his fractious dispute with fast bowler Devon Malcolm, who'd destroyed the South African batting at The Oval a year earlier. Frustrated by his failure to get Malcolm to alter his action to his satisfaction, Illingworth resorted to criticising him in public, behaviour that made matters worse. Embittered by his treatment, Malcolm rarely performed to standard, not least at a critical stage in the deciding Test at Cape Town. His wayward bowling so appalled Illingworth that, following England's defeat, he launched into a bitter tirade against Malcolm in front of the team.

Stung by this broadside, Malcolm, on his return home, accused Illingworth of humiliating him, a charge that Illingworth totally rejected. Aggrieved that Malcolm had escaped censure for his outburst, he exercised his right to reply in typically uncompromising terms that landed him in trouble with the game's authorities. Fined for bringing the game into disrepute, Illingworth managed to win on appeal but the spat tarnished his final months in office.

A Yorkshireman to the very end, Illingworth's success was based more on his results than his methods, which made him a controversial figure like his contemporaries Brian Close, Fred Trueman and Geoff Boycott. Given the extent of that success, it is perhaps not surprising that he never deviated from the hard professional ethos of his youth, that brought him such success as a player and captain, but his brusque management style – which was compared to that of a Victorian mill owner by the sports journalist Ian Wooldridge – proved less productive in a more egalitarian age. 'The trouble with Illy is that he always wants his own way,' reflected his good friend Close, and another ally, Jack Bannister, the former Warwickshire seamer, wrote that Illingworth was 'dogmatic and single-minded to the point of being blinkered'.

Yet it was that single-minded cussedness that had seen him overcome the poverty of his youth, the taunts of the older Yorkshire pros, Brian Sellers, the amateur establishment at Lord's, David Clark, Colin Cowdrey, Bill Lawry, umpire Lou Rowan, the Test and County Cricket Board (TCCB) and many a rival captain along the way. When Illingworth joined Leicestershire, Sellers warned their secretary, Mike Turner, that they were taking on a troublemaker, but Leicestershire welcomed him with open arms and Illingworth in turn showed Yorkshire what they were missing. According to Keith Fletcher, by no means an unqualified admirer, Illingworth rarely made the wrong decision and it was that reputation for sound judgement, especially in a crisis, that makes him such a fascinating study.

Chapter 1

'Young Illingworth'

IF THE Battle of Waterloo was won on the playing fields of Eton, the winning of the Ashes, cricket's equivalent of Waterloo, was often won on the playing fields of Pudsey, the west Yorkshire town with a great cricketing heritage. Situated on a hill between the two great industrial conurbations of Leeds and Bradford, Pudsey had grown prosperous in the 18th and 19th centuries through its manufacture of woollen cloth, a prosperity that had faded by the 1930s as the Great Depression began to bite.

It was here that Ray Illingworth was born on 8 June 1932, in Parkfield Close, in the shadow of St Lawrence Church, one of the few churches to give their name to a cricket club. He was the only child of Fred Illingworth, who ran a cabinet-making, joinery and furniture business, and Ida Wilson, a kindly housewife who took her maternal responsibilities very conscientiously. Both parents were pillars of the local Unitarian Church and were honest, down-to-earth types who worked hard, saved carefully and helped those in trouble. Devoted to their son, they ensured that he was well fed and smartly attired and impressed upon him the importance of such basic values as honesty, modesty, discipline and diligence.

In common with many northern towns at that time, when church and chapel held sway, Pudsey was a hive of communal activity with its Sunday Schools, church choirs, choral societies, brass bands, working men's clubs and cricket and football teams. From humble origins at the beginning of the 19th century, cricket in the town acquired a greater prominence when it came under the influence of the churches, manifest in its two eminent cricket clubs, Pudsey St Lawrence, formed in 1845, and Pudsey Britannia, formed in 1854. Between them they nurtured some of Yorkshire's finest: John Tunnicliffe, who represented the county between 1891 and 1907, formed a notable opening partnership with Jack Brown. Together they shared 19 stands exceeding 100 and in 1898 they established a record partnership of 554 against Derbyshire, a record subsequently broken by another Pudsey man, Herbert Sutcliffe, when he and Percy Holmes scored 555 for Yorkshire against Essex in 1932.

Major Booth (Major being his first name and not a military rank), the son of a prosperous Pudsey grocer, was a formidable all-rounder who first played for Yorkshire in 1908. In 1913/14 he made his England debut against South Africa and was on the cusp of greatness when tragedy struck. Leading his men from the West Yorkshire regiment at the Battle of the Somme on 1 July 1916, he was mortally wounded and died in the arms of Abe Waddington, later of Yorkshire and England, an experience that haunted Waddington for the rest of his life.

Herbert Sutcliffe was born in the village of Summerbridge, near Harrogate, but lived most of his life in Pudsey and played for both of its cricket clubs. War delayed his debut for Yorkshire till 1919, but he quickly established himself as a player of exceptional class and went on to form a prolific opening partnership for England with Jack Hobbs. In a career which extended until 1939 and in which he scored over 50,000 runs, few moments gave him greater pleasure than the civic reception Pudsey accorded him in April 1925 on his return from his triumphant tour of Australia when the town brass band played 'See the Conquering Hero Comes'.

Sutcliffe was to act as mentor to another Pudsey prodigy, Len Hutton, born in 1916, who first played for Pudsey St Lawrence aged 13. Making his debut for Yorkshire in 1934 and for England in 1937, Hutton achieved immortality the following year by scoring 364 against Australia at The Oval, the highest individual score in a Test until it was surpassed by the West Indian Gary Sobers in 1958. His achievement brought further renown to Pudsey and the town celebrated it with a peal of the church's bells 364 times.

Hutton survived a debilitating injury to his arm in war-time to remain England's most prominent batsman for another decade, and in 1952 he became his country's first professional captain. Unbeaten in six rubbers during his three years in charge, he regained the Ashes in 1953 and retained them in Australia in 1954/55, the prelude to his retirement and a well-merited knighthood.

Pudsey was also the birthplace of other notable Yorkshire cricketers: Harry Halliday, who played either side of the Second World War, Billy Sutcliffe, who captained the club in the mid-1950s, and Richard Hutton, who emulated his famous father by playing for Yorkshire and England. When Illingworth made his debut for Yorkshire in 1951, he was one of four Pudsey-born players in the side.

In 1935 the Illingworths moved to the textile village of Farsley, three miles from Pudsey, where Fred's business was located, living at 7 Bryan Street in rented accommodation. Ray Illingworth later wrote that living and growing up in a row of terraced houses was 'not nearly as bad as some sociologists would have us believe'. 'At least it wasn't during my childhood. There was a natural community spirit – we all knew each other intimately.'

During the 1930s, Fred's cabinet business was earning him a steady income, but the onset of war in 1939 compelled him to close it and go into munitions. Illingworth recalled him dropping a shell on his foot in an armaments factory at neighbouring Rodley and having to have the boot cut away from a broken toe. He also recalled the air-raid sirens sounding which rattled the windows of their home, given its proximity to the police station where the sirens were based, and the lights going out, but, despite this and the food shortages, life proceeded more or less as before.

When peace was restored in 1945, Fred found it difficult to re-establish his business, largely because of the shortage of timber, but he was versatile enough to turn his hand to other skills.

Content living in this self-contained community, Illingworth went to the city as little as possible because he was a terrible traveller. He recalled returning from a day in Leeds with his parents and having to get off the bus two miles from home because of travel sickness. He did, however, enjoy his trips to Bradford for the Christmas pantomime and the annual seaside holiday to Bridlington. There they stayed at Mrs Tate's lodging house, drove the dodgem cars at the funfair, played cricket on the beach and went for long walks up to Flamborough Head. Although money was tight, it wasn't a major inconvenience for Illingworth because he and his friends made their own fun. He wrote, 'My childhood was happy and comfortable and secure and I did not feel the need to ask for anything more than I had. At the pictures our imaginations were fed on the swashbuckling exploits of Errol Flynn and Tyrone Power, and then we went home and translated them into our own terms. We moved into our own world and lived our private fantasies. They were simple and harmless, giving us hours of pleasure and causing no one any disquiet or offence.'

His only scrape occurred when the local bobby caught him and his friends sledging down one of the main roads and took them off to the police station, where they remained until they were collected by their worried parents.

In a tight-knit community where everyone knew everybody else, there was never any shortage of takers for a game of football and cricket. They played in the street, in the fields or on any piece of unkempt ground, preparing their own wickets. On one occasion, a herd of cows strayed on to their pitch and they had to spend part of their precious pocket money getting it level again. Such was their commitment that on occasions Illingworth and his friends walked three miles to Calverley Park, taking with them a large roller and mower. There they cut and rolled the pitch and had a full-scale match with Fred Illingworth acting as the umpire. Later, during the war, when all the fields were ploughed up, Farsley Cricket Club had access to a horse and he could draw the cutters across the square, enabling Illingworth and his friends, including some evacuees, to play there.

Fred Illingworth had been a useful cricketer in the Pudsey Sunday School League, the competition that gave Herbert Sutcliffe his introduction to cricket, and it was he who gave his son his love of the game and his first bat at the age of three, which became his prized possession. Together with his friends, Illingworth played whenever the opportunity presented itself. Foremost among them was Donald Jones, a highly gifted sportsman and near-neighbour with whom he was almost inseparable; Billy Hudson, who introduced him to billiards and golf; and Eric Hargate. All of them went on to play for Farsley and although they later drifted apart Illingworth wrote that 'the golden days of childhood are hallowed memories and all those associated with them remain important figures in one's life. Donald Jones and Eric Hargate and Billy Hudson were part of growing up, to me; they are part of my life, a part which I remember with warmth and affection.'

During the latter part of the war, when Hutton was playing in the Bradford League, Illingworth cycled to all the grounds to follow his idol and study his technique. 'Len was an inspiration for any starry-eyed cricket lad. To see him play on a turning wicket was an education in itself. The ball never seemed to turn when he was batting. He was always in such a sound position to play his strokes.'

At Frances Street Elementary School, Illingworth monopolised the batting in the school playground where stumps were chalked on the wall of the building, so much so that one of the masters, Teddy Shepherd, bowled him leg breaks and googlies in the hope of getting the others a bat.

With his aptitude for maths, geography and woodwork and his general all-round ability, Illingworth quite enjoyed studying, but, displaying a mind of his own, unusual for someone of his age, he declined the opportunity of going to grammar school because the greater amount of homework would curtail his opportunities for sport.

He continued to perform creditably at Wesley Street School and at a time when discipline was very strict – the headmaster Mr Ingham and his colleague Mr Sutcliffe wielded six-foot canes – he remained on the right side of the law. The two exceptions to this rule were the time he was asked to pick up a new cane from a basket shop and sawed it in half so it broke when it was first used; then, on 3 July 1946, when he and his friend David Swallow, later an award-winning journalist, played truant to watch Yorkshire face the Indians at Bradford, the first time they'd been to a first-class game.

Rising early to ensure they were at the front of the queue, they were photographed by the local newspaper, which appeared in the next day's edition, and was seen by their headmaster. Fortunately for them, Mr Ingham had a sneaking regard for their nerve – they had gone to see Hutton, after all, who made 183 – and let them off with a mild rebuke. In general, he was a successful pupil, coming second out of 20 in class during his final year, excelling in school sports and winning praise from the headmaster for his care with the National Savings money contributed by the children.

Although Wesley Street lacked facilities of their own, they were able to play their home games of cricket at Farsley Cricket Club. Appointed captain at the age of 14, Illingworth dominated the organised competition between the local schools, averaging 100 with the bat and taking 30 wickets at 2.4. In a challenge match against Wyther Park School, Leeds – both schools led their respective section of the school league – he took 5-11 and scored 52 out of 64 to win by ten wickets.

Wesley Street's use of the Farsley cricket ground reinforced Illingworth's links with the club. Prior to this, he had practised at Pudsey St Lawrence, but when they refused to select him for their second XI on grounds of his youth, he joined Farsley in 1946, and was immediately placed in their third team.

Noting the enthusiasm of many youngsters at Farsley, one of their first XI, Eddie Hargrave, persuaded the committee to form an under-16 side and enter the Bradford Junior League. They duly marked their entry the following year by easily winning the trophy – Illingworth picking up the batting award – and they demonstrated their prowess by beating the league's best XI by five wickets. Hargrave, who managed the side, promised them a bag of chips each if they beat local rivals Bowling Old Lane and after the match he was talking to his opposite number when Illingworth approached him and said, 'Come on, we are all in the chip shop.' He wanted his reward.

Spending every spare minute down at the club, Illingworth joined in the Tuesday and Thursday evening ritual of rolling the pitch in preparation for the weekend game, during which he learned much about the capricious nature of pitches, knowledge that proved invaluable throughout his career. He also discussed the intricacies of the game with club veterans such as Donald Waterhouse, who took over 1,000 wickets in the Bradford League, and Harry Bailes. 'Raymond was always a mature lad,' wrote Hargrave, 'but he'd listen to advice and was never the least big-headed.' In August 1946 he made an inauspicious debut for Farsley second XI by failing to score and his progress was unspectacular the following year, because he still lacked the physical strength to get the ball away, but in 1948 he took a big step forward with his promotion to the first XI, which played in the second division of the Bradford League.

The Bradford League, formed in 1903, was one of the oldest and fiercest in the world with its galaxy of top-flight cricketers and hard-nosed ethos. During the First World War it had played host to such names as Sydney Barnes, Jack Hobbs, Herbert Sutcliffe and Wilfred Rhodes and thereafter it was the arena in which the likes of Len Hutton, Jim Laker and Bob Appleyard cut their teeth. With its proud traditions, local rivalries and large, partisan crowds, the cricket wasn't for the faint-hearted and those who survived this tough baptism were invariably men of steel.

Because of injuries, Illingworth was thrust into the Farsley first XI in May 1948 in the Whitsun derby against Pudsey St Lawrence, who ranked among the top sides in the Bradford League. In beautiful weather and in front of a large crowd of over 2,000 in deckchairs, both sides struggled with a bumpy wicket which caused a couple of injuries, but none of this deterred Illingworth. Displaying that sound temperament which so characterised his career, he impressed with both bat and ball, helping his side to a draw. The *Pudsey and Stanningley News* cricket correspondent wrote, 'Feature of the game was the performance of 15-year-old Raymond Illingworth, of 7 Bryan Street, on his debut with the senior side. He first took a hand with the bowling, when Pudsey were digging themselves in and finished with the best average on the Farsley side with 3-14 in six overs. But it was not all – young Illingworth then went on to further delight with a well-played innings that received wide commendation.' Realising a new talent in their midst, captain Harry Bailes said to him, 'Don't you go and ask to go back to the second team' – a reference to Donald Jones's request after he'd lost form. 'Don't worry,' replied Illingworth. 'There's no way I'm going to want to go back.'

As part of Farsley's youth policy, Illingworth was given every chance to establish himself, often by opening or batting at number three. After scoring 43 against Bankfoot, the local paper wrote, 'It was the promising youngster who stood firm while wickets fell around him.' This was the high point of his season, along with captaining Farsley under-16s to another triumph. When they made it three Championships in a row in 1949, Illingworth was presented with a special trophy.

In 1948 Yorkshire had invited him to the nets at Headingley where he came under the supervision of head coach Arthur Mitchell, known as 'Ticker', and his assistant Bill Bowes, both mainstays of the great Yorkshire side of the 1930s. Mitchell, a dour middle-order batsman who played six times for England, was as tough as granite and treated a net practice like a Test match. A figure of austere integrity who abhorred flamboyance both on and off the field, he unnerved many of his proteges with his acerbic tongue and reluctance to praise, designed partly to test their temperaments, but those who could withstand his jibes appreciated a coach of rare pedigree. Illingworth called Mitchell the most honest person he'd ever encountered and his perfectionist temperament reinforced his own conviction that the game should never be played frivolously. 'I don't know who this youngster is but he will play for Yorkshire,' remarked England spinner Johnny Wardle after bowling to Illingworth in the nets, and Mitchell himself remarked that if Illingworth didn't represent the county he deserved to be sacked.

In August of that year Illingworth was chosen to tour the south of England with the Yorkshire Cricket Federation, which comprised the best under-18s in the county. The team contained such names as fast bowler Fred Trueman and all-rounder Brian Close, both of whom were to become good friends of Illingworth. The ebullient Trueman led the singing as the coach headed south and drew great cheers when he dangled Illingworth out of the window to be travel sick. He and Close were the leading personalities, providing much of the entertainment and consorting with the local girls whenever the opportunity presented itself.

They also provided the fireworks on the field, not least in the game against Sussex Colts, when Close scored a century and

Trueman took four wickets. 'It was no contest,' recalled Jim Parks, the Sussex and England wicketkeeper, who played in that game. 'They were such a good side and all had played league cricket in Yorkshire. Compared to us they were hardened pros.'

While Trueman and Close made their debuts for Yorkshire the following summer, Illingworth began to turn heads at a lower level, especially in the Priestley Cup, the knockout competition of the Bradford League. Having scored 41 not out against Bankfoot to help Farsley win their second-round tie, he came of age in the third round against Pudsey St Lawrence. In a game played over successive midweek evenings, and in front of capacity crowds at Farsley, Illingworth hit an undefeated 148 out of his side's total of 394. It was the highest individual score in the competition for eight years and the photo of Illingworth celebrating his innings in front of the scoreboard occupies pride of place in the Farsley clubhouse to this day. 'Young Illingworth, the phrase has been on the lips of all local cricket enthusiasts this week,' gushed the *Pudsey and Stanningley News*, as it profiled his career to date. The *Bradford Observer* called his innings 'a wonderful display' and the *Bradford Telegraph and Argus* correspondent wrote, 'For a mere boy who has graduated through Farsley school and junior cricket … his batting was an extraordinary combination of endurance and skill and richly deserved the £21 collection to which his "political" friends contributed after close of play.' (He spent the money on kitting himself out with cricket gear.)

Farsley won by 100 runs and easily beat Lightcliffe in the semi-final to play Yeadon in the final at Bradford's Park Avenue ground. Needing only 20 runs to beat the former Nottinghamshire batsman Walter Keeton's record of runs scored in the Priestley Cup in one season, Illingworth was out for 1 as Farsley lost by five wickets.

Before the final, Illingworth had made his debut for the Yorkshire Colts (the second XI) against Northumberland and although achieving little in this game and two subsequent ones that season, he later recounted the thrill of getting paid. 'I felt I was a millionaire getting two of those big white fivers. I hadn't earned anything like that working with my dad so it seemed a lot of money to me.'

Up to the age of 17, Illingworth had wavered between a career in cricket or football. After leaving school, he played wing-half for Farsley Celtic but mainly with Pudsey Athletic, a talented side on a level with Ashley Road, Leeds United's junior side. He was invited to trials with Huddersfield Town, Bradford City and Aston Villa – their scout said he was the best two-footed player he'd seen – but he was dissuaded from pursuing a footballing career by Norman Jackson, a member of the Pudsey Athletic committee, and a Pudsey St Lawrence cricketer. He told him to stick to cricket, a line reinforced by Illingworth's father. He fretted about the risk of injury and reminded him that there was less money in football in those days compared to cricket. Accepting their advice, Illingworth contented himself with playing a high standard during National Service, when every RAF station had four or five professionals and for charity matches thereafter. 'Dickie' Bird, his Yorkshire team-mate, recalls him playing left-half for a Yorkshire XI against a Showbusiness XI at Oxford Stadium, Bradford, and performing admirably. He continued to follow the game closely – his idol being Tom Finney, the great Preston North End and England player – and he became good friends with Leeds United's manager, Don Revie, and their centre-half, Jack Charlton.

Illingworth continued to make progress in 1950, hitting 76 against Durham and 69 against Northumberland for the second

XI, and scoring more freely in the Bradford League. According to the *Bradford Telegraph and Argus*, 'A pleasant feature of the Farsley and Keighley encounter was the excellent innings played by their 18-year-old Yorkshire colt Raymond Illingworth. Batting exactly two hours, his fine effort contained 11 fours and his score of 80 runs was the highest obtained in League Cricket since he was promoted to the Farsley first team in 1948.'

He also matured as a medium-pacer who occasionally resorted to spin. When playing for Wesley Street against Wyther Park School in 1946, he suddenly sent down a slower one which turned a fair bit, prompting the opposing umpire to say, 'If you can bowl off breaks like that, lad, don't waste your time on seamers.'

Increasingly inclined to follow that advice in the nets at Farsley, his promise was noted by club professional Jackie Firth, who was soon to leave Yorkshire to become Leicestershire's wicketkeeper. On 2 September 1950, Farsley had been dismissed for 58 on a rain-affected wicket by Saltaire and with their left-arm spinner out of sorts they appeared to be heading for defeat. Recalling his off breaks at practice, Firth told Illingworth to get on and bowl his spinners. His suggestion was taken up by the captain and Illingworth duly obliged with 5-5 in his side's three-run victory. His success, and 5-13 against Lightcliffe the following weekend, proved defining moments in a year in which Yorkshire coach Bill Bowes, concerned that Illingworth lacked the necessary pace to meet the club's needs as a seamer, changed him into an off-spinner.

In October 1950 Illingworth was called up for National Service in the RAF and was posted to Cheltenham. By good fortune the posting officer, who came from Dishforth, Yorkshire, was a fanatical cricketer and he recommended Illingworth for a posting to the RAF station there, some 30 miles from Bradford. On his return, he suffered an acute attack of pneumonia and only the fervent determination of his family saved him from an operation that would have destroyed his ribcage.

Told not to apply for a specific trade which would have sent him on a course but stick to general duties, he was appointed in charge of sports stores and managed to complete his stint of service without performing guard duty. He also managed to play a lot of football for the station and cricket for the RAF and Combined Services, which he much enjoyed. Representing the former against the Army at Lord's, along with Jim Parks, Fred Titmus and Alan Moss, all future England team-mates, he bagged a pair, the only one in his career, falling to Close in the second innings, and took 4-58 in a draw very much in the Army's favour.

A chanceless 133 for the Yorkshire Colts against Nottinghamshire impressed all those who saw it and, weeks later, he was due to play for Combined Services against Warwickshire, when he was summoned to Headingley to make his first-team debut. Yorkshire were playing Hampshire and the circumstances couldn't have been more challenging when he walked to the wicket at 40/4 to join his captain, Norman Yardley. Undaunted by the threat posed by opening bowler Vic Cannings – who'd taken all four wickets – and the cluster of close fielders, he negotiated the attack with aplomb, his rock-solid defence giving way to a series of stylish cover drives which bore a resemblance to his idol Hutton. 'When I started playing cricket, I just hit everything through the covers,' Illingworth later recollected. 'That was just from watching Len, the best there's been as far as I'm concerned.'

He was fortunate to have the encouragement of his captain at the other end, although one leg-side swat which nearly went for six called for a word of caution. While the large crowd went into raptures, Yardley came down the pitch and said, 'Keep 'em on the floor, lad!' When he was finally out to Cannings for 56, Illingworth had added 148 with Yardley, who remained unbeaten on 183 in Yorkshire's total of 378/7 declared, a total that set them up for a ten-wicket victory.

His success left him totally grounded. The local reporter found him casually throwing a ball about with friends on arriving at the Farsley ground to interview him, and when asked to describe his debut, Illingworth called it his lucky date. He didn't know why he'd been given precedence over Close, by then an England player, and confirming his wish to be a professional cricketer, he said he would make a much better cricketer than cabinet-maker.

Although National Service restricted Illingworth's appearances in 1952, he was primarily available for Farsley. He began in scintillating form making 162 not out against Saltaire, hitting 23 off one eight-ball over, and 81 against Brighouse. He followed up with 5-25 against Bowling Old Lane and 84 against Lidget Green and he continued to score prodigiously in a year in which he averaged 64.92 in the league. In the return game against Lidget Green, he survived a hostile spell from Bill Copson, the former Derbyshire and England bowler, who took a hat-trick, before he and Gordon Barker, later of Essex, added 141 for the fourth wicket to earn them an honourable draw. Then, in the final game of the season, he took 6-70 and scored 91 not out in Farsley's ten-wicket victory against Windhill, which secured them promotion to the first division of the Bradford League.

He enjoyed playing for the Combined Services under Squadron Leader Alan Shirreff, representing them against the Indians at Gillingham. Despite being one of four future England players in the team – Trueman had recently made his Test debut – they lost by nine wickets, but he made useful runs in the RAF's win over the Royal Navy and took 5-32 in the draw against the Army. He also gained his first three wickets in the County Championship against Gloucestershire at Bristol, his victims including Jack Crapp, a former England player, and Arthur Milton, a future one.

At the end of his National Service, Illingworth returned to the joinery business with something less than enthusiasm. Eddie Hargrave recalled father and son coming to his house to polish a suite of furniture and Ray spending most of the time staring out of the window. Yet for all that, it was a job and his father would always give him time off to play cricket as he strove hard to make it with Yorkshire. Later he was to write, 'Frankly I couldn't have managed at that time without the help I received from my parents, who did so much in many ways, to further my ambition as a cricketer.'

Chapter 2

A Harsh Apprenticeship

'IN YORKSHIRE, cricket was one of the finer passions of life,' wrote the eminent cricket writer Sir Neville Cardus, and that passion was amply exemplified in the county's dominance over all-comers at the game. Playing with the fanatical pride and immense self-belief associated with the Yorkshire character, the team took to the field determined to emulate past glories. For ever since the illustrious 28-year captaincy of Lord Hawke between 1883 and 1910, Yorkshire had won Championships with predictable regularity, none more so than in the 1920s and 1930s with revered names such as Wilfred Rhodes, Herbert Sutcliffe, Bill Bowes, Maurice Leyland, Hedley Verity and Len Hutton. A Yorkshire cap was said to rank as a higher honour than an England one and no one better encapsulated that adage than Brian Sellers, who led Yorkshire to seven Championships between 1933 and 1947. The son of Yorkshire amateur and committee member Arthur Sellers, and educated at St Peter's York, he was a martinet of fearsome repute, used to getting his own way. Intensely competitive, he demanded total submission to the team ethic, no matter how eminent the individual, but his physical courage, tactical acumen and unshakeable commitment to Yorkshire cricket earned him the undying allegiance of his players.

Yet success on the field often cloaked deficiencies off it and this became increasingly clear throughout the 1950s when Yorkshire were overshadowed by Surrey under Stuart Surridge, a leader every bit as charismatic as Sellers. Even by the class-ridden standards of English post-war cricket, the Yorkshire committee seemed a relic from a bygone era. Many of the committee, often successful businessmen running large companies, were appointed for their social connections rather than their knowledge of the game. 'At the end of a season even after you'd won the Championship most of the committee would still not know your name,' Illingworth later complained. 'Whatever you did, they always said it had been done better before,' commented all-rounder Ken Taylor.

Even before becoming chairman of Yorkshire in 1959, Sellers was a force to be reckoned with by virtue of his membership of several influential Lord's committees and his role as an England selector. 'There's only one fellow you have to look out for round here,' Wardle informed Trueman on his Yorkshire debut in 1949. 'His name is Sellers.' Even in a more egalitarian age, Sellers continued to treat the club as his personal fiefdom, combining iron discipline with a razor-sharp tongue. 'His language was that of the navvy to his work-mate, labouring on a building site,' wrote John Hampshire, a Yorkshire stalwart of the 1960s and 1970s, 'but his attitude was that of the Commanding Officer to the humblest private.' All the players, including the cocksure Trueman, stood in awe of him (some who got to know him appreciated his kindness and loyalty) and when he arrived at the ground in his large Bentley, the tempo of the play invariably increased.

Totally dedicated to Yorkshire cricket, Sellers regarded playing for the county as a privilege and traded on the fact that most players saw it that way. In contrast to other counties, Yorkshire didn't award contracts and were ruthless in dispensing with those who didn't measure up. They also paid capped players a meagre wage out of which they had to fund their travel, accommodation and meals. (The fact that the players stayed in different hotels or guest houses hardly promoted team spirit.)

Compared to the great Yorkshire sides of the inter-war years, the one of the 1950s was barely inferior with luminaries such as skipper Norman Yardley, a former captain of England, Hutton, Willie Watson, Wardle, Appleyard, Frank Lowson, Close and Trueman, but riven by cliques and feuds it rarely played to potential, failing to win the Championship outright between 1946 and 1959. With expectations high and a host of strong-willed characters jostling for prominence, it was a harsh environment for any youngster to make the grade. They were expected to do all the menial jobs such as look after the kit when travelling by train and pay the tips with no certainty that the senior players would reimburse them. In one of his first games for Yorkshire, Illingworth hung a shirt on what he thought was a spare peg only to have it thrown across the dressing room by Wardle; and when on a subsequent occasion he offered an opinion he was told very brusquely to keep his mouth shut for a year. 'Individually, they were much better than we were,' declared Ken Taylor, a member of Yorkshire's Championship-winning side of the 1960s, 'but they played for themselves. They were batting for their averages or working to bowl at nine, ten, jack.'

Two of the most demanding members of the 1950s team were the spin duo of Appleyard and Wardle. Born in 1924 and the son of a train driver, Appleyard was seven when his mother left home and 13 when his sister died of diphtheria. His father remarried but tormented by the outbreak of war in 1939 – he'd been a traumatised veteran of the First World War – he gassed himself, his wife and his two young daughters. Moving in with his stepmother's parents and inspired by their deep Christian faith, Appleyard displayed remarkable stoicism, beginning work as an engineering apprentice and joining the Royal Navy during the closing months of the war.

Although a successful bowler in the Bradford League between 1947 and 1949, he didn't make his Yorkshire debut until 1950 at the age of 26, but from his first match he fully embraced the club's cult of invincibility. 'We didn't like to lose,' he later recalled. 'It was unforgiveable to Yorkshiremen. The first time I was on a losing side I thought the world had come to an end.' In 1951 he captured 200 wickets in his first full season, but struck down with a life-threatening tuberculosis the following May, which necessitated the part-removal of a lung, he was incapacitated for the next two years. He returned in triumph in 1954, making his England debut against Pakistan and was a valuable member of Hutton's Ashes-winning side in Australia that winter, due not least to his ability to bowl both off-cutters and off-spin.

Yet, his triumph against adversity had come at a cost since his combative personality and forthright views made him an awkward team-mate, especially to his juniors. 'My first taste of the hardness of Bob Appleyard came in that very first game,' Illingworth recalled. 'I was fielding at wide mid-on and Appleyard was hit high over midwicket. I was late picking it up against a dark background and consequently a bit late setting off and I missed the catch. Well, Appleyard gave me the biggest rollicking I had ever had in my life up to that point, and bigger than anything I was to experience in the future. Ten thousand saw me being blasted like a little schoolboy. I saw Appleyard at his toughest in my first game, and in my view he never changed.' Recalling the severity of those times, Illingworth later said, 'No word of encouragement, no helpful tips. There was no mitigation, no excuse accepted, no allowances made. You either swallowed the insults and gritted your teeth, or you went to pieces.'

On another occasion, when Illingworth was told by Yardley to replace Appleyard next over, he duly walked towards the umpire, only to find Appleyard peeling off his jersey, prepared to carry on. 'What do you want?' Appleyard inquired.

'Skipper has told me to bowl,' Illingworth replied.

'Bugger off. I'm bowling here,' said Appleyard, and that was that. Nothing was said to him, and Illingworth had to retreat in some embarrassment.

Acquainted with Illingworth's reservations about his intolerance, Appleyard later commented, 'Ray Illingworth was a nice man and very good cricketer – but people like him and Doug Padgett, they weren't coming out of the same world I'd come from. I had to learn to be hard to survive.'

Wardle, from a harsh mining background, was of a similar disposition, expecting choice of ends, objecting strenuously if taken off in favour of Close or Illingworth and berating those who dropped catches off his bowling. On one occasion when Illingworth felt the lash of Wardle's tongue he hit back, telling him that he'd always been a good fielder and the reason he was missing catches was his inconsiderate attitude. 'I was all right after that,' Illingworth later recalled. 'In fact from that point, whenever there was a slog on and the batsmen were attacking Johnny, I was sent into the outfield. I think I got 30-odd catches one season, which was a hell of a lot for an outfielder. But the others were still frightened and you can never play a team game when players are frightened.'

In this toxic atmosphere, Illingworth looked to Yardley to stand up to the hard men but, hating conflict, Yardley preferred to look the other way. 'Norman Yardley, our captain, was a nice man,' recalled Illingworth. 'Too nice. If he'd stamped it out, we would have won two of those seven titles Surrey were winning on the trot. In 1954, he only had to change the bowling to win the final game, which would have given us the title. But Wardle and Appleyard wouldn't let him take the ball away.'

Illingworth also looked to his great hero, Hutton, to help build bridges in the team, but despite being his travelling companion, he found him detached and unhelpful, not least with giving advice. 'He was a funny man, was Len – slightly sarcastic all the time. He'd hear an argument in the dressing room and he'd throw a bit of wood on the fire to keep it going.' The one occasion he did give advice wasn't music to Illingworth's ears. Having bowled a tight spell without any luck against Hampshire at Bournemouth in 1953 Illingworth was asked by John Bapty of the *Yorkshire Evening Post* afterwards whether the ball was turning. 'A little,' Illingworth replied, only to be contradicted by Hutton, who later told him, 'Never say it is turning when you have not taken any wickets.' (In the second innings, Illingworth took seven wickets.)

In 1953, in one of Yorkshire's most undistinguished seasons ever, in which they fell to 12th in the table, Illingworth displayed his real worth from the first Championship game with 146 not out against Essex at Hull. Entering at 104/5, he played confidently from the start and mastered the attack, whether of speed or spin. Adding 146 with Yardley, who made 85, he batted four and a half hours for his maiden Championship century. According to 'White Rose' in the *Bradford Telegraph and Argus*, Illingworth on this evidence seemed destined to break the heart of many a bowler. 'No other century for years by a Yorkshire Colt has surpassed in merit Illingworth's effort, which would have been an outstanding performance in any event, but was made the more notable because it came at a time when the side was in a trying situation.'

His performances thereafter rather paled in comparison but half-centuries against Northamptonshire and Somerset and figures of 6-29 against Kent and 7-22 against Hampshire confirmed his burgeoning promise. *Wisden* noted his heartening advance and England all-rounder Trevor Bailey wrote in the winter edition of *The Cricketer*: 'It looks as if Pudsey has produced yet another outstanding cricketer. Young Ray Illingworth, in his first full season of first-class cricket, gave every indication of becoming an all-rounder in the true Yorkshire tradition. He bowled his off breaks steadily, although he must improve his accuracy.

'His batting is even more promising and he could easily become a performer of real class. He has many attractive scoring strokes and when he has tightened up his defence a little, he will assuredly score many runs.'

The following year Yorkshire bounced back to challenge Surrey for the title, but the return of Appleyard after two years of chronic illness and Close from a serious knee injury restricted Illingworth's opportunities with the ball. Chosen for only a handful of games, his batting fell away and he bowled only 203 overs compared to 719.2 overs the previous year. Playing against Gloucestershire at Bristol, acting captain Hutton brought him on to bowl when Tom Graveney, their best player, came in to bat, telling him to keep it quiet for several overs. 'The runs didn't just dry up,' Illingworth recalled, 'I got him out. But as soon as we got rid of Tom, he took me off again. I wasn't very happy but that was Len's strength – he could read a game like a book.'

In early July Illingworth bowled Yorkshire to success over Surrey at The Oval with 8-69, the best analysis of his career to date, but when the two counties met again at Sheffield a week later, he wasn't even playing. Aggrieved about his lot, Illingworth didn't sit about and mope. He worked ever harder in the nets with Arthur Booth, the former Yorkshire left-arm spinner who'd headed the national averages in 1946, concentrating on bowling an immaculate line and length.

He continued to be in and out of the side during the first part of 1955, a situation which prompted interest from other counties for his services, most notably Warwickshire, who offered him £850 and expenses, a sum equivalent to what Yorkshire capped players were earning. Although flattered by Warwickshire's overtures, he had no wish to leave Yorkshire and would only go as a last resort. Back in favour by the end of June, Illingworth chipped in with useful wickets, but it was his batting that really caught the eye throughout a sunlit August. Beginning with 53 in the Roses match at Sheffield, during which he put on 188 with Willie Watson, who made 174, he then scored 61 and 29 not out against Leicestershire to help Yorkshire to a two-wicket win. Particularly impressive was the way he played the Australian slow left-armer Jack Walsh. 'He was so good that I always wanted to get him to the other end,' recounted Walsh. 'He always spotted and smothered my googly and chinaman and really hit the loose deliveries.'

Frustrated by Yorkshire's failure to award him his county cap – they hadn't awarded any for four years – Illingworth approached Yardley and asked him to inform the committee that if they didn't think him worth his cap, they should release him. His words had their desired effect because after his 63 against Derbyshire in the next game, Yardley said, 'Gather round, boys, it's my pleasure to give Ray his cap.' It proved one of the great thrills of Illingworth's life. According to Trueman, 'It was a popular choice and Ray has proved himself well worthy of it.'

'I must admit it niggled that I'd had to ask for the bloody thing!' Illingworth later declared. 'I'd been playing since 1951 and held just about every record for an uncapped player.'

He continued to show his class with a chanceless 94 against Nottinghamshire, 116 against Essex and 138 against MCC, the 1,000th recorded century in all Yorkshire matches.

That winter he took the boat to South Africa to coach at Christian Brothers' College, Kimberley, only to be dogged by a mystery illness that was diagnosed as tuberculosis. Immediately on his premature return home, he went to Leeds to see a specialist who'd operated on Appleyard. He just looked at his fingernails and teeth and said, 'You haven't got TB.' The specialist then took him to see a consultant who examined the surgery he'd undergone for an abscess and explained that he would have to have another operation. This time the operation at Leeds Infirmary went fine and he was fit for the beginning of the new season.

After eight years in charge, Yardley handed over the baton to Billy Sutcliffe, an accomplished batsman and an affable personality who laboured under the handicap of being the son of the great Herbert. In a summer of atrocious weather and damp pitches, run-scoring was never easy, as the Australians discovered every time they faced England off-spinner Jim Laker, and Hutton's retirement had left a great void in the Yorkshire batting. Having tried Padgett as Lowson's new opening partner, the committee then opted for

Illingworth, but he proved no more successful in that position, and nor did Ken Taylor, who gave way to Sutcliffe.

While Illingworth's run famine – along with Close's – was the cause of public comment by Yorkshire chairman Tom Taylor in his review of the year, the same couldn't be said for his bowling. Although still operating in the shadow of Wardle and Appleyard, he exploited the damp pitches to perfection, taking 100 wickets in a season for the first time. Once again, his most notable performances came during the closing weeks, beginning with 5-62 and 4-57 against Somerset, 5-48 against Lancashire and 4-36 and 6-26 against Worcestershire to finish second in the all-England bowling averages with 102 wickets at 13. *Wisden* complimented him on his great leap forward and *The Cricketer* wrote that 'Illingworth improved beyond all expectations as an off-spinner. He took over the supporting role to Wardle and Appleyard which had formerly been taken by Close.'

For all his frustration of playing second fiddle to Wardle, he learned a lot by bowling alongside him, especially the art of patience and precision. 'You work and work away until the batter makes a mistake,' Wardle drummed into him. 'Don't give them anything.' When bowling against Gloucestershire on a turning wicket at Cheltenham in 1957, Wardle took 6-25 and Illingworth 2-16 as the home side, requiring a mere 68 to win, scraped home by two wickets. After the game, Wardle took Illingworth out to the middle and gave him some invaluable advice, as he later recalled. 'When we were bowling in the first innings, the wicket was wet but not doing much and we both had reasonable figures. But in the second innings I had about 2-20 and Johnny had six. And he took me out and showed me the marks of the first innings. Where his marks all pitched within a yard of length, mine were more like two yards. And he said, "That's why I cashed in more second time because I knocked it about more in the right place when it was wet in the first innings." He was just proving the point of what you had to do when things weren't in your favour.'

During the next match against Warwickshire at Edgbaston, Wardle stood at mid-off and impressed on Illingworth that only total concentration would eliminate the one bad ball an over. Consequently, he never bowled better, taking 1-14 off 14 overs, and quickly established himself as one of the world's most accurate spinners.

Wardle also taught him the need to educate the rest of the side in the dressing room 'as to the way, you as a bowler, are thinking'.

'He [Wardle] was a great bowler, and I mean great,' recalled opening bowler Mike Cowan. 'And so knowledgeable. It's no fluke that Brian Close and Ray Illingworth became good captains because they used to go out to the middle with John and look at the wicket before play began. He knew the game backwards.'

Illingworth began 1957 in vintage form with the bat, hitting 80, 54 not out and 97 in three of his first four Championship innings, prompting the *Bradford Telegraph and Argus*'s Dick Williamson to call for his elevation to a place higher than number seven. No other batsman in the side had performed with greater adaptability, or in making runs when needed.

He continued to score consistently, finishing third in the Yorkshire batting averages with 1,066 runs at 33.31, but the highlight of his year was his 9-42 against Worcestershire on a slow pitch at Worcester, the season's best analysis. Commenting on his accomplishment, *The Times* wrote, 'Illingworth belongs to a small band of young professional all-rounders, one of whom may one day find a permanent place in the England side. He is a better bowler than Close, but a lesser batsman. In both departments he is the equal of Titmus and of the others … none shows more promise. His action is not unlike Laker's; the approach after a couple of crab-like steps is leisurely, and he makes good use of the ball that all successful off-spinners must master, the one that drifts away from leg to off.'

He finished the Championship with 5-31 and 4-63 against Glamorgan, helping him complete the double of 1,000 runs and 100 wickets for the first time. There would be five encores over the course of the next seven seasons.

Yorkshire's late-season resurgence took them to third place in the Championship, a rise of four places, but it didn't stop the rumblings of discontent within the broad acres. For all his geniality, Sutcliffe was no more successful than Yardley in curbing the dressing-room feuding and when a number of senior players conspired to force his removal, he resigned the captaincy and retired from the game, to Illingworth's regret. 'Billy tried hard to move things on a bit. But he was 29 and found himself up against the same seasoned professionals that Norman had found hard to captain.

'It wasn't easy for him. And it didn't help that the crowd were on his back, too. We all heard the jeers of "You're not as good as your dad!" Billy was a good bloke but it was very hard work for him.'

In order to stop the bickering, Yorkshire took the audacious step of replacing Sutcliffe with Ronnie Burnet, a 39-year-old amateur with no experience of first-class cricket. The decision shocked many but Burnet, who'd captained Baildon to honours in the Bradford League, and had led Yorkshire second XI to the Minor Counties title in 1957, nurturing a talented group of youngsters in the process, proved an inspired choice.

Rejecting the committee's choice of Vic Wilson as senior professional, Burnet specifically asked for Wardle, an astute tactician who hankered after the captaincy himself. Forced to miss the first seven Championship games of the new season because of injury, Burnet handed over the captaincy to Wardle, who much enjoyed the responsibility, so much so that returning to the ranks proved a deflating experience. Not only did Burnet ignore his advice, he also cast aspersions over his bowling; when playing Derbyshire at Chesterfield, he told him to bowl a fuller length, since he was turning the ball too much; then against Somerset at Sheffield, after Wardle's 6-46 in the first innings, he forced him to change ends to give Trueman a better foothold and when Wardle responded with an over of full tosses, Burnet accused him of not trying. Incensed by the charge, Wardle rounded on his captain in a vitriolic outburst that sealed his fate. Desperate to end the friction in the side, to which Wardle's acerbic tongue and divisive personality had contributed, the committee voted to release him at the end of the season.

Stung by his dismissal and the abrupt nature of its implementation – no reason was offered – Wardle chose to fight back, lending his name to a series of articles in the *Daily Mail* criticising the club. His fulminations caused a predictable outcry and because he was in breach of contract he was released immediately, a decision that led MCC to withdraw their invitation to him to tour Australia.

Wardle's dismissal was the most disconcerting event of a dismal season in which Yorkshire – hit by 24 blank days – fell from third to 11th in the Championship. In such atrocious conditions there were few opportunities to excel, but Illingworth boosted his reputation with England captain Peter May by bowling him with a beauty during Yorkshire's crushing victory over Surrey at Sheffield. Placed on stand-by for Laker in the second Test against New Zealand, Illingworth made his England debut in the fourth Test at Old Trafford in an experimental side now that the series had been won. Welcomed warmly into the fold by May, Illingworth bowled tidily, capturing three cheap wickets in yet another England victory, but it wasn't enough to guarantee him a further game at The Oval or win a place on the boat to Australia. (Even when reinforcements were required mid-tour, it was John Mortimore, the Gloucestershire off-spinner, who was chosen.)

Casting his disappointment to one side, he managed a productive August, taking 7-49 against Essex at Middlesbrough, 4-46 and 5-51 against Derbyshire at Headingley and 6-69 against Glamorgan at Swansea. More important, he'd enhanced his value to the team, becoming the fulcrum of the attack, a trusted adviser to Burnet and acknowledged mentor to the younger players. 'He was the brains behind the side,' recalled Dickie Bird. 'If anything went wrong at Yorkshire, you'd go to Raymond for advice.'

Although Burnet lacked playing ability and tactical acumen, he was never afraid to ask for advice, chiefly from Close and Illingworth, and usually he accepted it. More important, his geniality and encouragement, especially to those who were struggling, helped foster a great team spirit, the results of which became clearly visible the following year. Recalling his leadership, Illingworth rated him very highly. 'He made everyone believe in himself and some of our scoring feats in 1959 were incredible. We've never got near them since. He got everyone playing for each other and playing like hell for Yorkshire, and that has stuck in my mind ever since. There can be no stars in a team game. Ronnie Burnet sowed the seeds of that philosophy in my mind more than any other man, and it is a philosophy I have never forgotten.'

Chapter 3

Champions at Last!

THE SUMMER of 1959 will always be remembered as one of glorious sunshine which helped revitalise the county game, none more so than in Yorkshire, since their adventurous spirit resulted in countless victories in the closing overs. Following Watson's move to Leicestershire at the end of the 1957 season and the release of Lowson and Appleyard, along with Wardle a year later, the team had an inexperienced look with opportunities for younger players such as wicketkeeper Jimmy Binks, batsman Bryan Stott and spinner Don Wilson.

For Illingworth, the true, firm wickets allowed his batting the opportunity to blossom as he unveiled his full repertoire of shots, foremost of which was his lofted on-drive. After a quiet start to the season, he burst into full bloom at Colchester in late June with 150 against Essex, one of his sixes hitting a young boy in the crowd. (He later went to visit him in hospital.) 'It was a splendid effort and his duel with Trevor Bailey thrilled the large crowd,' reported Jim Kilburn in the *Yorkshire Post*.

A fortnight later, at Scarborough, Illingworth once again showed his partiality for the Essex bowling – all three of his Championship centuries to date were against them – by scoring

75 not out and taking valuable wickets as Yorkshire won at the last gasp.

He continued in vintage form with a career-best 162 against the Indians and 100 for the Players against the Gentlemen at Lord's, adding 184 for the seventh wicket with Close. According to *The Times* correspondent, Illingworth rode his early luck to bat with greater assurance than Close and stake a strong claim for a Test recall.

He was duly selected for the fourth Test against India. Once again, he came in at the tail-end of another one-sided series in which England had totally dominated. Their continued superiority at Old Trafford and The Oval offered Illingworth little opportunity to shine with the ball, but scores of 21, 47 not out and 50 helped him win the all-rounder's slot on the forthcoming tour to the West Indies.

Back with Yorkshire, Illingworth's match figures of 9-95 helped beat Middlesex at Scarborough, while an accomplished 74 not out proved Kent's undoing at Headingley. The match fully vindicated Burnet's enterprising approach. Declaring 134 behind Kent's first innings of 356, Yorkshire then dismissed them for 109 with Close taking a career-best 8-41. Needing 244 to win, the home side suffered early losses, but Illingworth took charge and guided his team to a two-wicket victory with two minutes to spare, much to the jubilation of the crowd, who rose to him on his return to the pavilion.

Illingworth's absence, and that of Trueman, for the final Test was keenly felt, since Yorkshire's defeats to Somerset and Gloucestershire threw the Championship wide open. He marked his return with a composed 40 not out against Worcestershire as Yorkshire inched home by five wickets with minutes to spare. 'Not for the first time in 1959, Raymond had a good match,' recalled Bryan Stott. 'He was 27 by this time and had become a very, very good cricketer. We'd been able to see him steadily improve with nearly every game.' As far as Illingworth was concerned, this improvement was down to the greater opportunities afforded him. 'The reason why it went so well with me with the bat was that all through the second half of the season I batted at number five, which was to the credit of Ronnie Burnet. Ken Taylor was a very gifted, talented sportsman, but it hadn't gone too well for him as opener and Ronnie moved him down the order. I said I was playing well at number five and Ronnie agreed to move Ken down the order below me, which was the first time a captain had done that.'

He was also to the fore in their final Championship game against Sussex at Hove, which they needed to win to be assured of the title. Entering at 38/3 in reply to the home side's first innings of 210, his 122, along with invaluable contributions from Jack Birkenshaw and Don Wilson, effected a splendid recovery, giving Yorkshire a surprising lead of 97. According to *The Times* correspondent, he'd scaled new heights with his fourth century of the season, while to Kilburn, he'd been for some weeks the most trustworthy of the Yorkshire batsmen. 'He accepted the responsibility of the current occasion and carried it with faith and unflagging attention to detail. No bowler troubled him.'

Beginning an abbreviated final day's play of four and a half hours 46 ahead and with seven wickets remaining, Sussex, with 85 from Jim Parks, made steady progress through the morning session, extending their lead to 178 at lunch with three wickets left. With time running out and opposition captain Robin Marlar in no mood to gift Yorkshire the Championship with a declaration, Close quizzed Burnet about his tactics during the interval. When

Burnet declared that all they could do was to put Trueman on downhill and downwind, Close replied, 'Fred's not bowling at all well this match, leave him out of it, let Illy have the wind and put Don Wilson on at the other end. If they can't do it, we are not going to make it.' Accepting Close's advice, Burnet placed his faith in the spinners and Illingworth took the three remaining wickets.

Needing 218 to win in 105 minutes, opener Bryan Stott set the tempo by taking 15 off Ian Thomson's first over. Although Taylor and Close went cheaply, Stott and Padgett then added 141 in an hour with some exhilarating stroke-play and spectacular running between the wickets that forced the Sussex fielders into some glaring mis-fields. By the time both were out, victory was all but assured and when they duly triumphed with seven minutes to spare Yorkshire had won the Championship outright for the first time since 1946, thereby breaking the Surrey curse. Flushed with the joy of victory, Burnet led his team down the pavilion steps to receive a thunderous ovation from the crowd, which contained a large Yorkshire contingent.

With a long journey to Scarborough for the festival ahead of them the team had to cut their celebrations short, but their homecoming was buoyed by the sight of their supporters lining the streets of Scarborough in the small hours to cheer them in. 'We were all in different cars so we arrived in penny numbers,' recalled Stott. 'But everybody was up waiting in the hotels. It will stay with me for ever.'

The reception was even more heartfelt later that morning when they took the field against MCC, a match they won by seven wickets with Illingworth contributing 105 not out and 35 not out. He signed off in style with valuable runs and wickets in Yorkshire's 66-run win against the Rest, his final tally of 1,726 runs and 110 wickets earning him the accolade of being one of *Wisden*'s Five Cricketers of the Year. Acknowledging the major part Illingworth played in Yorkshire's success with both bat and ball, Bill Bowes concluded: 'Reliable in the field, a safe catcher, a good thrower, pleasant in looks, manner and dress, Illingworth thoroughly deserved the honour of representing England in West Indies.'

Following their 4-0 reverse in Australia the previous winter, the England selectors discarded many of the stalwarts of the post-war era in favour of younger players such as Ted Dexter, Ken Barrington and Mike Smith. The current captain Peter May was a man whom Illingworth liked and respected, his courtesy and modesty in no way mitigating his steely desire to win, a trait that brought him into conflict with manager Walter Robins. Robins, a former England leg-spinner, was an amateur of the old school whose overriding mission was to mend fences with the Caribbean community after Hutton's controversial tour there in 1953/54. This he achieved to a large degree with his flair for public relations, but his attempts to persuade May to play a more enterprising style of cricket met with a stonewall response.

Up against a revitalised West Indies side that numbered Gary Sobers, Rohan Kanhai and Wes Hall among its luminaries, the tourists started very much as underdogs, a perception accentuated by their ten-wicket defeat against Barbados. An obdurate 72 from Illingworth in the second innings helped win him selection for the first Test at Bridgetown, a game that ended in a high-scoring draw. Aside from the batting of Colin Cowdrey, Dexter and Ken Barrington, England's main hope of victory centred on their famed opening attack of Trueman and Brian Statham, amply illustrated in the second Test at Port-of-Spain, when they wreaked havoc on the home batting with bowling of the highest class.

The ignominy that befell their batsmen, allied to a number of contentious decisions, prompted sections of the capacity crowd to riot, forcing the abandonment of play for the day. After a weekend of consternation and public contrition by the island authorities, the game resumed in an orderly atmosphere. England, 270 ahead on first innings, elected to bat again – Illingworth 41 not out – en route to a 256-run victory.

One up in the series, May's strategy of containment became ever more paramount. For the remaining three Tests, Illingworth, along with fellow off-spinner David Allen, wheeled away over after over bowling his off-stump line to five men on the off side, in what he called the toughest cricket of his career. On those flat pitches, he took only four wickets in the series, but he played a crucial part in England's 1-0 win by keeping the West Indies stroke-makers in check. 'It was important that we bowled our overs economically, and I was pleased that I only conceded 383 runs from 196 overs,' Illingworth later commented. 'It was not a matter of bowling defensively, but figures like those give your captain control in the field, and he can work his attacking bowlers round you. David Allen was my partner, and he bowled 197 overs for 417 runs, which is why we were never batted out of the series by a top order which included Sobers, Walcott, Worrell, Kanhai, Hunte and Nurse.'

One casualty from the tour was captain May, who was forced to return home owing to complications arising from an internal operation he'd undergone the previous summer, much to Illingworth's regret. He later wrote, 'Peter was an ideal captain, hard but fair and always ready to give his players a helpful word of advice and encouragement when it was needed.' May, in turn, rated Illingworth, describing him in his tour report as 'a very nice, sensible person and an excellent tourist'.

Despite his disappointing batting in the West Indies – 92 runs in eight innings, succumbing to Sonny Ramadhin's leg spin on four occasions – and a bowling average of 95.75, Illingworth kept his place in the England side for the first four Tests against South Africa that summer. He took six wickets in the first Test at Edgbaston, but had few opportunities with the ball thereafter as Trueman and Statham cut a swathe through the brittle South African batting. On his omission from the final Test for Lancashire leg-spinner Tommy Greenhough, the *Daily Mirror*'s Brian Chapman wrote: 'Fine player as he is, Ray's record hardly justified an extended run.'

Despite winning the Championship the previous year, Yorkshire had persuaded Burnet to give up the captaincy. 'I know he didn't want to go after winning the Championship and I can understand that,' wrote Illingworth. 'But he was beginning to struggle physically and we didn't want a skipper who was missing a week here and a week there. I didn't agree with Brian Sellers very often, but he pushed Ronnie into retiring and it was the right decision.'

With Sellers opposed to both Close and Illingworth succeeding Burnet, the crown passed unexpectedly to Vic Wilson, Yorkshire's first professional captain since Tom Emmett in 1882, following a disappointing 1959 in which he'd been dropped. Recalled for Yorkshire's final match of the season – the Champion County against the Rest – he responded with a second-innings century which turned probable defeat into unlikely victory and was rewarded with the captaincy. It proved a shrewd choice, since his firm leadership and upstanding character won him the respect of all, except Trueman, who he sent home when he turned up late for a match at Taunton in 1962. It was a decision that Illingworth fully endorsed, since to have let him off would have corroded team spirit. Admiring Wilson's unruffled determination in a tight corner and his ability to get the best out of the players, he declared, 'Vic was one of those players that you would want in the trenches. He was totally reliable, a man who gave 100 per cent and never gave up.'

Although prone to bouts of inconsistency and losing twice to runners-up Lancashire for the first time since 1893, Yorkshire finished the 1960 season strongly. They won four out of their last seven Championship games, losing only to Glamorgan at Swansea, a game in which Illingworth returned match figures of 15-123, the best-ever return by a Yorkshire off-spinner, and this on a placid wicket. A week earlier, he'd excelled against them at Bradford with 4-33 and 45 and 53 not out. Requiring 173 to win, Yorkshire had slumped to 94/6 against spinners Don Shepherd and Peter Walker before Illingworth and Don Wilson added 49 for the seventh wicket; then, after Wilson was out, Trueman gave valuable support until he was dismissed with seven needed. When Binks was run out with four still required for victory, last man Mike Cowan needed to negotiate the final two balls of Shepherd's over; somehow, he just managed to survive, leaving Illingworth to score the winning runs off Walker, a feat which he celebrated by tossing his bat in the air.

He also played a leading part in Yorkshire's penultimate Championship game against Worcestershire at Harrogate by taking 4-51 in their first innings of 139. With Lancashire losing momentum, the White Rose only needed to gain first-innings points to retain their title, a task they duly completed while Illingworth was at the crease with his captain. 'It was appropriate that Illingworth should have been with Wilson, for in the hour of need he has been the staunchest of stand-bys,' wrote *The Times* correspondent. With another four wickets in the second innings, he helped bowl Yorkshire to a nine-wicket win and during their convincing win in the Champion County versus the Rest game he once again completed the double.

That September Illingworth toured Rhodesia and South Africa with the International Cavaliers, a team of England and Australia Test players, managed by the sports journalist Ron Roberts and captained by Richie Benaud. Although the public response was disappointing, Illingworth ranked it as his most enjoyable trip and not just for the splendid hospitality. Roberts put them on a win bonus – they were undefeated – and Benaud's leadership proved inspirational. 'Richie's enthusiasm was tremendous as he made you believe you were better than you were,' he later reflected. 'Richie's attitude and enthusiasm rubbed off on everybody and I remember getting more bounce than I ever did in my life.' Many years later, when assessing the strengths and weaknesses of captains he'd known, Illingworth ranked Benaud the best, stating that he had no weaknesses.

Yorkshire began 1961 with some swagger, winning seven out of their first eight Championship matches with Illingworth taking 6-51 against Nottinghamshire, 8-50 against Lancashire and 7-54 against Warwickshire. His form earned him a call-up for the first Test against Australia, an occasion when he ran into some trouble, courtesy of Trueman, who was notoriously unpunctual. 'Fred took me to Edgbaston to play in a Test match,' he recalled. 'We had to be there at two o'clock and he said he'd pick me up at midday. At twenty past twelve I rang his wife and she said, "Don't worry, Fred is setting off shortly. He's just popped into the local garage to have a couple of tyres fitted."'

On arrival at Edgbaston about an hour late, they received a severe dressing-down from chairman of selectors Gubby Allen, no admirer of Trueman.

In a match that England were fortunate to draw, Illingworth bowled poorly and after achieving little in the defeat at Lord's, he was out of the Test side for over a year.

For most of the season Yorkshire seemed destined to be champions for a third successive campaign, but defeats against Leicestershire, Kent – despite Illingworth's nine wickets in the game – and Middlesex in August enabled Hampshire to win their first-ever title. Yorkshire slightly begrudged Hampshire their triumph, claiming that they had been the beneficiary of some generous declarations, and so beating them in their final Championship game at Bournemouth was doubly satisfying. Bowling with unerring accuracy on a worn pitch in front of a large crowd on one of his favourite grounds, Illingworth took three wickets in four balls to finish with 7-39 in Hampshire's first innings; he then followed up with 5-63 in the second innings as Yorkshire's victory by 58 runs assured them of second place in the Championship.

That they were able to go one better in 1962, seeing off a fierce challenge from the greatly improved Worcestershire, said much for the spirit in the side. With the batting once again inconsistent, they experienced mixed fortunes early on, but on good days and bad Illingworth continued to stand out, scoring 98 against Somerset and 63 and nine wickets against Gloucestershire. He followed up with 107 against Warwickshire, his first century for three years, 80 not out against Glamorgan and 7-40 against Northamptonshire, despite losing all three games. They looked set for another defeat when playing Hampshire at Bradford on 29 June, since their opponents, requiring 163 to win, had reached 156/5, but Illingworth, with four wickets, induced a dramatic collapse, as he and Trueman dismissed the last five men for one run.

Having snatched victory in these most unlikely of circumstances, Yorkshire remained undefeated thereafter, although the wet weather accounted for a substantial number of draws. In the matches won, Illingworth often proved their talisman, taking 5-63 and 4-49 against Gloucestershire at Bristol, 6-26 against Essex at Sheffield, 5-10 against Sussex at Scarborough and 5-52, coupled with two half-centuries, against Kent at Middlesbrough. According to Jim Kilburn, Illingworth's match-winning 84 not out in that game illustrated his enviable form in the strength and certainty of his stroke-play and his admirable ability to adapt his approach to the needs of the occasion.

He continued to fly high with consecutive centuries against Hampshire at Bournemouth and Surrey at The Oval and 91 against Leicestershire at Leicester. *The Times* reported that during the last few weeks of the season Illingworth was often at his best, and he batted now with the utmost skill, yet despite outplaying both Hampshire and Surrey, Yorkshire had to settle for draws, which meant they had to win their final game against Glamorgan at Harrogate. A crowd of 10,000 packed into this small, homely ground to see the visitors, inserted on a drying wicket, bowled out for 65, Don Wilson taking 6-24 and Illingworth 3-28.

Yorkshire in turn struggled and could only muster 101, 67 of which came from Ken Taylor. The next day torrential rain washed out play and only the heroics of the ground-staff who worked through the night enabled a prompt resumption on the final day. Once again, Glamorgan faltered against the spinners, leaving Yorkshire 66 to win, which they accomplished by seven wickets much to the jubilation of the capacity crowd, hundreds of whom converged in front of the pavilion to hear captain Vic Wilson, in his farewell game, call it the most memorable day of his life. In a year when his side hadn't always played like champions, their reliance on Illingworth remained undiminished, especially in the home straight. Kilburn wrote, 'Illingworth's fifth attainment of 1,000 runs and 100 wickets was less dramatically compiled but he finished the season in splendid form and with impressive self-confidence, particularly as a batsman. He was officer-of-the-watch on Yorkshire's homeward run to the Championship berth.'

Chapter 4

The Model Professional

RAY ILLINGWORTH was the ultimate professional in his devotion to the game and his rigorous commitment to self-improvement through stern endeavour. Jimmy Binks recalled him batting against Fred Trueman in the nets at Oxford and when he was bowled with a composition ball, he picked up his sweater without saying a word. He walked straight into the pavilion kitchen, asked for a carving knife and cut the ball in half.

Immaculately turned out, he took great pride in his cricket equipment and keeping it in shape. On one occasion Lancashire captain Bob Barber, when short of kit, took his bat and started bashing Trueman around, much to Illingworth's displeasure.

His attention to detail was legendary. He wore a thick flannel cloth around the small of his back to absorb sweat, he wore a robust pair of boots properly studded to prevent him slipping and wool socks to stop him blistering. He rubbed Vaseline into his fingers to keep his skin moist and Friars Balsam to stop them splitting on the inside. An early riser, he liked to get to the ground in good time to practise and to examine the pitch, carrying a ball to detect the bounce. According to Yorkshire fast bowler Bob Platt, 'Raymond was a very subtle man. He could read a pitch from the first ball and his entry into the attack often coincided with the ball beginning to turn.' Possessing an equable temperament in general, he could get riled when asked to bowl on a green top, especially when the Yorkshire batting had failed. With a photographic memory of a batsman's strengths and weaknesses, he would set his field accordingly and he could anticipate the shots of those he hadn't previously encountered by noting the nature of their grip.

A favourite Illingworth ploy against a new batsman was to bring his fielders in to save a single and have no deep midwicket or square leg, thus challenging the batsman to hit the ball in the air. On a good wicket he normally started with a slip, leg slip and three saving a single on the off side – on a turning wicket he would dispense with cover and crowd the bat with two or three short legs. Beginning with a modest angled run, Illingworth crept up to the crease with his soft-shoe shuffle, bowling with an upright action from close to the stumps. Like all Yorkshire bowlers, his outlook was essentially miserly, begrudging every run. When someone encouraged him to toss one up at a wild hitter on the grounds that he would strike one six and then get out, Illingworth retorted, 'I can get him for less than six!'

'Ray bowled such a good line,' according to Close, 'that I never felt in any danger fielding at short leg to him,' although he did suffer a nasty blow to the head when Gloucestershire's Martin Young lapped Illingworth, the ball rebounding to Sharpe at slip, who caught it. 'Brian, if that ball had struck you full on the temple, it would have killed you,' Gloucestershire's opener Arthur Milton commented afterwards. 'Yes, that's true,' replied Close, 'but it would have been caught at cover.'

Mike Smith, a superb player of spin, admitted that he was never able to dominate Illingworth and the only batsmen he saw get after him were his team-mates, John Jameson and Jim Stewart, both renowned hitters. Another batsman to get his number was Hampshire's Roy Marshall, who flayed him all over Scarborough in the final match of the 1961 season, prompting Illingworth to plead with his captain, 'Get Fred on, I'm top of the averages,' to which Trueman responded, 'Bloody keep him on. I've been bowling all summer.'

Even in festival cricket Illingworth remained highly competitive. Robin Hobbs, the Essex leg-spinner, recalled him expressing disgust when his team-mate Brian Taylor missed a stumping off him. According to fellow off-spinner Fred Titmus, 'No one could accuse Ray Illingworth of being a "fun" person exactly. If you asked him mid-season how it was going, he would rattle off exactly how many overs he had bowled for how many wickets, but small talk was not his thing.'

'Ray was very average-conscious and that's bad,' concurred Trueman. 'He was always moaning about something. If hit about, he would say, "Get me off, skipper. I can't bowl to this bugger."'

Thinking others had all the good fortune, Illingworth once humorously asked Yorkshire off-spinner Jack Birkenshaw, 'How do you get wickets with that rubbish?' 'Well, why don't you try it?' Birkenshaw replied, at which point Illingworth bowled a waist-high full toss that went sailing out of the ground.

(It was the same with Illingworth's batting. Trueman recalled him watching Phil Sharpe batting beautifully at Taunton in 1962 and saying, 'He's getting all the bad balls, they don't bowl bad 'ums to me!' On another occasion he was batting with Don Wilson against Hampshire's opening bowler Butch White in the gloaming at Portsmouth and getting very agitated by Close's refusal to declare. 'It's all right for him, he's not going to get bloody killed, is he?' he said to Wilson. When Wilson hit a six, he shouted down the wicket, 'What the hell are you doing, Wils? Pack it in and get out.')

With his low arm and flat trajectory, Illingworth relied on beating the batsman off the pitch rather than in the air, although he could give the ball a tweak to extract turn from a slow pitch. He also developed a well-disguised arm ball and because of his powerful body action, the legacy of his apprenticeship as a seamer – just like Jim Laker – he could make the odd ball leave the bat. According to Wilson, 'Raymond was mean, really top class. On a turning wicket he would bowl any side out. On bad wickets opposing batsmen thought, "My goodness, I'm not going to get anything off Raymond. My best chance is to get them off Wils." I often copped wickets on those occasions.'

'As far as I was concerned, Raymond was the best off-spinner I played with or against,' recalled Binks. 'He was one of the hardest to keep to as well, as the variations in flight were so subtle. He bowled such a good outswinger with his rather low arm and, when he wanted to be, he was a yard quicker than most.'

Leicestershire's Barry Dudleston recalls facing Illingworth for the first time in 1967 and wondering how he would ever score a run off him in the face of his unrelenting accuracy and the intimidating presence of Phil Sharpe, Close, John Hampshire and Trueman yards from the bat. Having been advised by the latter not to bother with a guard, he duly registered a pair, dismissed by Illingworth in both innings.

He brought the same unflinching commitment to his batting that he did to his bowling. Standing correctly sideways on and blessed with a good eye, he picked up the line and length of the ball quickly, knowing when to play and when to leave. A doughty fighter who had to be prised out, Illingworth was content to quietly accumulate, and if the conditions were taxing for batting, he relied on his solid technique and temperament to see him through. According to Dickie Bird, his soft hands and foot movement were the secret to his mastery of damp wickets.

Early in his career, like many Yorkshiremen, he struggled against a good leg-spinner, especially on fast pitches, because he preferred to play within the confines of the crease. On MCC's tour to West Indies in 1959/60, he fell to Ramadhin on a number of occasions and drawing on this experience he lectured Richard Hutton on how to play the Trinidadian as they waited to bat against him in the Roses match at Old Trafford in 1964. 'Whatever you do, don't play back to him,' Illingworth said more than once. Minutes later he did precisely that himself and was lbw to Ramadhin first ball. Such was his embarrassment he made his way back to the pavilion in an ever-widening radius to avoid the incoming batsman, Hutton, whose 64 helped set up a convincing Yorkshire victory.

Although his batting lacked flamboyance and could sometimes tax the patience of the crowd, not least the Yorkshire one, Illingworth, when set, could unveil a full range of shots. While his handsome cover drive, based on his idol Hutton, was the prized one in his repertoire, he also profited from his crisp square cut, the pull and the lofted on-drive. The value of his batting is best illustrated by the numerous times he made runs when they were most needed. Trevor Bailey wrote, 'I have lost count of the times, after my county had achieved a breakthrough with the new ball, that we have been unable to press home our advantage because of his arrival at the crease. He has always been exceptionally good against seam bowling and clearly relished leading a recovery.'

Bailey went on to explain that the reason Illingworth's batting was underrated lay in his lack of opportunity because of his position in the Yorkshire middle order, a point acknowledged by Trueman. 'If Raymond had played with any other county he would be going in number three or four and got 2,000 runs easy. Playing with Yorkshire many a time he had to throw his wicket away. To give him credit, he was never loath to do it for his side.'

As a fielder Illingworth lacked the pace and strength of arm to be a natural outfielder, but his safe hands made him an ideal gully and, even into his 40s, he took some highly agile catches.

Never happier than mixing with the Yorkshire side of the 1960s, Illingworth enjoyed a post-match beer and game of snooker or darts, but he left the serious socialising to the likes of Sharpe, Wilson and Hampshire. A fierce competitor at whatever game he played, Illingworth became fascinated by bridge because of the skill involved when watching the Yorkshire bridge school of Willie Watson, Johnny Wardle, Ted Lester and Vic Wilson. He formed a partnership with Close, whose casual approach created tension. On one occasion Illingworth went for a walk leaving Close with a certain four spades only to find that he had gone two down. Astounded that he'd failed to make the contract, Illingworth demanded an explanation. Close ruefully explained that he'd lost interest, to which Illingworth replied, 'Don't lose interest while you're playing with my money.' They were playing for a penny a hundred.

Given their similar age and status in the Yorkshire team, Close remained Illingworth's best friend despite their differences in character. Aside from Close's tendency to break furniture when a guest at Illingworth's home through his clumsiness, his reckless driving tested his sangfroid. 'I had a few adventures with Brian,'

Illingworth recounted. 'It was really frightening to be with him in a car, chiefly because of his lust for speed and tendency to lose concentration.' Having survived one hair-raising trip from Scarborough to Torquay that shredded his nerves, he and his wife Shirley endured an even more terrifying one following dinner at Ilkley. 'We came back over the moor,' Illingworth recalled. 'There was quite a steep drop on one side of the narrow road. Closey was driving with one hand and twiddling the knobs of the radio with the other.' Thereafter Shirley banned him from being Close's passenger.

In the days when professional cricketers often travelled long distances between matches, Illingworth normally teamed up with Doug Padgett. According to Padgett, life on the open road had its problems. 'Cars weren't what they are now and there were no motorways. Me and Raymond travelled together all our careers but our cars weren't high-powered stuff by any means. Illy had a Standard Vanguard first and then a Triumph Herald.' On one occasion Padgett was driving Illingworth's Herald back from the south and pulled up at some lights at Bawtry town centre, when a vehicle went straight into their rear, laying them both flat out on the floor of the car looking up at the roof. They survived in one piece but Illingworth thereafter blamed his stiff neck on the accident.

No sooner had Illingworth repaired the car than he was the victim of another piece of careless driving when a driver ran into the back of him in the narrow alleyway leading to the Balmoral Hotel car park at Scarborough. He wasn't best pleased.

On yet another occasion he was a passenger in Padgett's new Ford Corsair when the car caught fire underneath the bonnet. Fortunately, a lorry was passing by and the driver jumped out with a fire extinguisher and put out the blaze.

Illingworth's most notorious journey occurred on returning from Clacton to Scarborough with Richard Hutton in August 1963. Having driven the first part of the journey in his brand-new Ford Zephyr automatic, he asked Hutton to take over while he had a sleep. He wrote, 'I was awakened by a strong smell of burning rubber and Richard's dreamy voice saying, "I say, Illy, your brakes aren't very good." Looking up I found we were approaching a roundabout at about 70mph. How we got to the other side is a bit of a mystery but when we stopped, I found that Richard had driven from Clacton with the handbrake on.'

Illingworth took over and drove at a snail's pace into Grantham to find an all-night garage. He had to pay for the relining of the brakes and they reached Scarborough at about 3am, so he wasn't best pleased to lose the toss the next morning and have to field first.

According to son-in-law, Ashley Metcalfe, there were two priorities in Illingworth's life – his family and cricket, although not necessarily in that order. It was at Wesley Street School that he first met Shirley Milnes, the daughter of a cashier in a textile mill, and three years his junior. There they formed a low-level attachment before drifting apart once Illingworth left school at 14 to begin work and Shirley went to grammar school. Having barely set eyes on each other in six years, a diffident Illingworth asked his friend John Percival to contact Shirley to see if she would go out with him. She consented and on their first date at the Pudsey Feast, a biannual fair, she was surprised by how much he'd grown. He remained painfully shy, however, and could barely speak to Shirley's mother without blushing. Consequently, he bought a copy of the *Yorkshire Sports* so that when he visited her every Saturday evening, he didn't have to speak to her. For the next five years they remained a couple until Illingworth, now established in the

Yorkshire side, bought Shirley an engagement ring on her 22nd birthday. Borrowing some money from their parents and using their hard-won savings – Shirley was working in the office of the same textile mill as her father – they bought a house for £2,100 and furnished it for an additional £400 before their wedding at Farsley Parish Church on 20 September 1958. Close was best man and the honeymoon was spent at the Imperial Hotel, Blackpool.

It goes without saying that Illingworth was greatly blessed by his marriage to Shirley. A strong, unpretentious Yorkshire lady of great warmth and compassion, she proved the perfect wife and mother. A keen follower of the cricket, she was hugely popular with the other cricketers and their wives, someone in whom they could confide.

In 1961 their first child, Vicky, was born, followed by Diane in 1965. Never regretting the absence of a son, Illingworth was devoted to his daughters in the way that he and Shirley had been very close to their own parents. Missing his family intensely when on the cricketing circuit – Dickie Bird recalled him always being on the phone to Shirley – he spent as much time as possible with them. Even at the height of his fame as England captain, he shunned the celebrity lifestyle for something more homespun back in Yorkshire, tending to his garden or picnicking with his family on Ilkley Moor.

One of Illingworth's leading priorities was to provide security for his family, but this was easier said than done since professional cricketers of that era found it hard to get suitable winter employment to supplement their meagre summer's income. After working for his father, Illingworth did a variety of jobs, working in a chemical factory, selling sports goods with his old Farsley team-mate Jimmy Claughton and looking after the greens at Fulneck Golf Club, none of which he found particularly fulfilling.

In 1962 he was introduced by his Yorkshire team-mate Brian Bolus to his employer Eddie Joyce whose firm, Shaun Wilson manufacturing company, sold Christmas cards and fireworks from a base in Leeds, and Joyce agreed to employ him on a commission-only basis. Never employed as a salesman before, Illingworth lacked the confidence to accept this and asked for a minimum sum, to which Joyce agreed, but once into the job his confidence soared and he agreed the following year to work on commission. 'Then I doubled it the next two years as I worked very hard,' he later recalled. 'I used to start in Scotland and he would ring me at the end of the first week and base his whole sales for the year on what my figures were for the first week. If I was up he would order up, if I was down, he would order down. I did so well it affected the commission of the other lads as he paid them 12.5 per cent and knocked it down to ten per cent plus a little bonus! He would show my figures to the other representatives and say if I could do it, so could they. I worked for 16 years through the 1970s during the winter while I was England captain. When I was on tour others did it for me like Neil Hartley. I paid them commission, but they didn't earn as much as I did.' 'Raymond made a good business out of it, he covered the whole country,' recalled Don Wilson, who worked with him one year. 'But I didn't work that hard.'

In 1979 Illingworth ceased working for Shaun Wilson. Recalling the poverty of his youth, he always appreciated the value of money, which helps explain his frugal approach to life, the one exception being the purchase of his Jaguar, and the meticulous care he took with any business transaction. In later years, after two successful benefits, he was able to buy a small apartment in Spain, which proved a shrewd investment, given the amount of time he spent there and the pleasure it provided his family.

Chapter 5

Master Tactician

ILLINGWORTH'S EXPLOITS in 1962 won him a recall to the England side for the final Test against Pakistan and selection for the forthcoming tour to Australia and New Zealand over Tony Lock, which caused some consternation. 'Not for one moment am I suggesting that Illingworth is a rabbit, but he must rank as the luckiest cricketer in England to be making the trip,' wrote *The Mirror*'s Brian Chapman. Even Illingworth pronounced himself surprised given his understandable belief that the selectors would never pick three off-spinners, the others being Fred Titmus and David Allen, and not take one left-armer.

With the Duke of Norfolk an eccentric choice as manager in addition to Ted Dexter as captain, Colin Cowdrey vice-captain and David Sheppard as senior player, Illingworth thought there was 'a lot of Sussex, southern bias on that tour', just when the distinction between amateur and professional was abolished in November 1962. Not only did the amateurs dine exclusively, they travelled in their own cars and had wives to accompany them, a divide that provoked some resentment with the more militant professionals. Even the Duke's ability to charm Australians with his talk of brighter cricket and love of the turf left Illingworth underwhelmed. 'We would arrive in each state,' he recalled, 'and he would make a little speech about the bonding of the Commonwealth and absolutely did nothing else. Alec Bedser [the assistant manager] did all the work.'

While Illingworth liked Dexter, feeling he could talk to him man to man, the same couldn't be said of his relationship with Cowdrey. 'Cowdrey was less easy to deal with,' he commented. 'Sometimes he didn't fancy opening and he'd pick and choose where he wanted to bat. It used to annoy everyone.' They clashed twice. On the first occasion, Illingworth refused Cowdrey's order to bowl at him in the nets when the latter turned up late at the end of an exhausting session, and later on, he greatly resented acting as 12th man in the return game against Victoria when unwell, so that Cowdrey could take his wife to a film premiere.

Unsuccessful in the early matches against the states, Illingworth found some form against Victoria and the Tasmania Combined XI, which could have won him selection for the third Test on a dry surface at Sydney. The selectors, however, buoyed by their seven-wicket win at Melbourne, persisted in playing three seamers and paid the penalty because, despite Titmus's 7-79, they lost by eight wickets. 'They should have picked me or David Allen to play alongside Fred Titmus,' Illingworth later recollected. 'He needed a spinner at the other end to create pressure.'

They erred again at Adelaide by preferring Illingworth ahead of seamer Len Coldwell on an unusually grassy pitch. That said, he could count himself unlucky to finish with only one wicket. Losing the toss, Dexter introduced him after 45 minutes and with his fourth ball he bowled Bill Lawry to make Australia 16/2. In his next over he had Neil Harvey dropped off successive balls by Cowdrey and Brian Statham, errors that might have cost England the match as Harvey went on to score 154. Later, in Australia's second innings, Illingworth was confined to his hotel with a sore throat, but when England looked in some trouble on the final day, he rose from his sick bed ready to bat, only for Ken Barrington and Tom Graveney to play out time.

With the Ashes at stake in the final Test at Sydney, England took the unusual option of playing their three off-spinners, but on a dreadfully sluggish pitch neither side made any effort to seize the initiative. With time running out, Dexter approached Illingworth and asked whether he would open England's second innings in place of Cowdrey, a request that irked him, especially since he was short of batting practice. 'Ted said, "These players are so good, coming in the middle order." I told Ted, "I'll do it for you, but I think it's a disgrace."' He did his best, putting on 40 with Sheppard, England's highest opening partnership since Brisbane, before holing out to Richie Benaud. Despite half-centuries from Sheppard, Barrington and Cowdrey, Dexter felt unable to declare until lunchtime on the final day and Australia, after some early shocks, put up the shutters, much to the disillusion of the crowd.

Illingworth continued as a makeshift opener in the three Tests in New Zealand with moderate success, but *Wisden*'s end-of-tour assessment that he'd failed to justify his selection with either bat or ball was hard to refute. In addition, his propensity to speak his mind against disorganised net practices and selection policy alienated his superiors. 'The type of tourist who only does what is necessary,' wrote the Duke of Norfolk. 'Could be more cooperative and approach tasks in a happier manner. Always amenable to discipline and would conform with any definite instructions, although perhaps voicing displeasure.'

'He is selfish to a fault off the field,' concurred Dexter, and 'difficult to reprimand as it takes no tangible form … In my opinion Illingworth made only a 50 per cent contribution to team spirit,' probably alluding to the occasion at the beginning of the third Test, when, not selected, he stayed at the team hotel alone rather than support the side. The Duke's assessment of Illingworth, while fairly restrained, suggests an aversion to his habit of moaning. Dexter recalled such an occasion on the recent MCC tour to the West Indies, when they were based in Jamaica. 'We were all staying at the Courtly Manor Hotel with its colonial-looking chalet rooms ranged around a swimming pool. When we arrived in our rooms, smiling maids bustled in to take our washing, bring us towels and turn down the beds. This was luxury, we thought.

'Raymond Illingworth had other ideas, putting his head round the door. "Rooms are a bit bloody small, eh?" he opined.'

'Never happy unless he's moaning is Illy but he's a really great fellow and one of my best pals in cricket,' wrote his room-mate in Australia Ken Barrington.

With Trueman viewed as difficult and self-centred, he, like Illingworth, was docked £50 of his £150 tour bonus, a sanction they both thought to be deeply unfair. On receipt of the official letter from MCC informing him of Illingworth's fate, Yorkshire president Sir William Worsley was at a loss at the news. 'Raymond, I can't understand this,' he told him. 'I have known you for 15 years and nothing like this has ever happened.' He asked whether he would like a personal hearing to get a fuller explanation, but hard though Sir William tried to organise a meeting with the Duke of Norfolk, the latter always seemed to be engaged with other business. It was an act of discourtesy which reflected all too readily MCC's attitude towards the players, especially the professionals, and helps explain why Illingworth never felt established in the England side until becoming captain.

Back on the county circuit, Illingworth's responsibilities became ever more pronounced now that his good friend Brian Close had succeeded Vic Wilson as captain. Continuing the example of his two predecessors, Close forged a healthy team spirit by treating everyone as equals and involving them all in dressing-room discussions. With a cast of diverse characters voicing strongly held views, these discussions could get very heated, but once on the field of play they all played for each other.

'There was a strong argument about cricket,' Illingworth recalled. 'We didn't go off to nightclubs. We talked. Everyone was expected to have an opinion but the older ones said more than youngsters like Geoff [Boycott]. Yorkshire were winning and things were happy. There was nothing personal.'

'We were Yorkshire lads together and that was always a great advantage. Say what you like about overseas players, I still believe that 11 Yorkshiremen have something no other side could have.'

A tough, unselfish player who flourished in the heat of battle, Close was an inspiration to his bowlers for his blind courage at short leg and his extraordinary immunity to pain. As befitted a racing fanatic, he was a gambler who was prepared to lose a game in order to win it. An implicit believer in his ability to shape the cricketing weather, he was the past master at heaping pressure on the batsmen through his bowling and fielding changes, some of which appeared highly eccentric but invariably paid off.

Never better than when attacking, Close could lose concentration when the opposition was well set, at which point Jimmy Binks would seek out Illingworth and tell him to have a word with the captain. According to John Hampshire, Illingworth knew every opponent in the game. His genius lay in making life as hard as possible for any batsman who could dominate, compared to Close. 'Fortunately, knowing Brian so well I could say what I wanted,' recalled Illingworth. 'He would accept suggestions from me as his mate but was less receptive to Fred or others. I could give Brian a kick up the backside. He would snap back into action.

'I can still see Closey at the end of a day's play, sitting in the dressing room surrounded by the press boys. He'd be saying, "Well at that stage, I decided this or I did that." And all the lads used to look in my direction and raise their eyebrows.

'He and I made a good team as captain of Yorkshire and senior player because of differing characters and temperaments – I think we have always had a basic respect for each other in every way, and I was very happy to serve under him in the Yorkshire team of the sixties. It never occurred to me to wish I was the skipper. It was a good side; it was a happy side; it was a winning side; it was a well-led side and I was part of that leadership. I was quite content with that.'

In their lengthy close-of-play discussions, Close and Illingworth gave priority to the theory of fielding, becoming the first team to post a silly mid-off. Although the Yorkshire spinners, and Illingworth in particular, had claimed many a victim in the leg trap, the growing prominence of pad play meant that the ball was increasingly going on the off side rather than to short leg. Conscious of Colin Cowdrey's inclination for pad play against slow bowlers, especially early in his innings, Close and Illingworth conspired to upset his poise by crowding him with players in front of the wicket to stop him playing with his pad. On one occasion Close crouched so close at silly mid-off that Cowdrey complained to the umpire. He was out soon afterwards. Another time, at Dover in 1964, Close's proximity to the bat persuaded Cowdrey to give Illingworth the charge and he was stumped. 'Of course, Brian was lucky to have Illy as a sidekick,' recounted Phil Sharpe. 'Raymond was so methodical and straight down the middle whereas Closey would do something ludicrous and it would work. It was the ideal combination.'

According to Bryan Stott, 'Ray Illingworth would be the ideal for any cricketer to emulate because of his understanding of the game and his ability to discuss it. There was always a reason behind his thinking.' Bowlers, in particular, appreciated his help. 'Watching Raymond, you could see his mind on the game,' commented Bob Platt. 'If bowlers were struggling, Raymond would come and have a word with you.'

Fast bowler Mel Ryan remembered Illingworth once saying to him, 'Mel, what do you think about on that long walk back to your mark?' 'I mumbled something about looking round the ground and how I didn't really think about anything until I turned and started my run-up. He wasn't impressed. "Well, you shouldn't be looking at that bird sat in the corner, you should be thinking on where you're going to put your next ball. Nothing else. Just that one thing." He was so meticulous. He talked cricket, cricket, cricket all the time.'

Platt reckoned that Illingworth more or less ran the show right through from 1959 to 1968. 'Brian was occasionally vague and at other times so positive. He wasn't always the man you'd turn to for technical assistance. That was Raymond's province.'

All-rounder Richard Hutton felt Illingworth was rather suspicious of him at first because of his educated background, but over time they became quite close and Illingworth acted as his bowling mentor. He said, 'When I first played, I frequently went for three an over. Raymond said I should get it down to two an over with guidance and help. He was a great reader of individual strengths and weaknesses. Yet if I look back, Raymond was the one player who probably helped me more than anyone else. He was always ready to offer guidance and talk to me about the game. Over the years I took a lot of his ideas on board.' He recalled a game against Sussex at Eastbourne in 1967 when he was bowling to Tony Greig. Conscious that Greig liked to hit the ball on the up, Illingworth advised Hutton to bowl to him just short of a length three or four inches outside off stump, calculating that Greig would edge one to slip, which is precisely what occurred. Hutton reckoned that if Illingworth had fielded at mid-off when he was bowling, he would have picked up an extra 50 wickets a season.

For many years Illingworth worked in tandem with fellow spinner Don Wilson, who was indebted to him for his help. 'Ray Illingworth was the brains of the Yorkshire team. He thought about the game very deeply. I was so lucky to bowl opposite him for all those years.' On one occasion, when Wilson was bowling poorly at Swansea, Illingworth, who was bowling at the end where the ball was turning, swapped ends to help him.

In a side renowned for its brilliant fielding, few were better than Ken Taylor at cover and Wilson at midwicket. 'We worked a lot of run-outs together,' Illingworth wrote. 'I used to station my mid-on just that little bit deeper to tempt the batsman into a quick single. When he went for it, Wils would come sweeping in from midwicket, the telescopic arm would go down and the batsman would be on his way.'

Another to sound him out was Yorkshire's promising new opener Geoff Boycott, who suffered from an inferiority complex. Illingworth used to reassure him that he was the best player in the country. At Swansea in June 1965, Yorkshire lost a low-scoring match to Glamorgan because of some woeful catching. Berated by Close during one interval for dropping a catch off his bowling, Boycott had the temerity to allude to two missed chances by Close himself, at which point an enraged Close lifted Boycott's trembling body off the ground and with one hand drew a clenched fist. Only the intervention of Trueman and Illingworth saved Boycott from injury and Close from his day in court.

'The Yorkshire players of his day were often bickering among themselves,' wrote Keith Fletcher, never a great admirer of the county, when discussing Illingworth. 'The back-biting was such that when something went wrong, it was always someone else's fault. They could not stop picking each other to bits. Yet once out of the pavilion they were united and they always knew how to win.'

After beginning 1963 with a century against Warwickshire, Illingworth was incapacitated with an injured Achilles tendon, sustained by bowling on the hard Australian wickets, and was out for nearly two months. He returned against Sussex on 17 July and when captaining against Glamorgan at Cardiff in place of Close, who was playing for England, he provided proof of his tactical acumen. During the closing overs of the second day, as Glamorgan were battling hard to stay in the game, he turned to the occasional leg spin of John Hampshire, who prior to the match had taken one wicket at the cost of 134 runs. He promptly had Alan Rees caught at slip by Hutton and impressed Illingworth enough to be told that he would open the bowling the following morning. His comment raised many a doubt among the Yorkshire team but they were silenced on the morrow, since Hampshire, getting spin and bounce, polished off Glamorgan in no time to finish with 7-52.

Yorkshire's win enabled them to recover their lead at the top of the table, a position they never vacated thereafter, and they won the title with back-to-back victories against Leicestershire, games in which Illingworth returned the remarkable figures of 16-87.

For the first time in six years, Yorkshire never threatened for the Championship in 1964, primarily due to the decline of Trueman. Illingworth, however, continued to be a model of consistency and achieved the double for the sixth time. The true extent of his class was on display against Kent at Dover, one of his favourite grounds. Inserted on a rain-affected wicket, he batted superbly against Derek Underwood, a destroyer on such a surface, and the other Kent spinners, his 135 helping Yorkshire recover from 41/4 to 256. 'It was a session in which you had to watch every ball very closely indeed,' recalled Illingworth. 'You could have no idea what it might do … anything might happen. So, to score 135 gave me as much pleasure as, I think, any innings I ever played.'

The next day he finished off Kent by bowling them out twice with figures of 7-49 and 7-52, Jim Kilburn calling it 'one of the most notable all-round performances in cricket history'. The England wicketkeeper-batsman Alan Knott, then a novice in the Kent team, and on the back of three successive noughts, including a first-innings dismissal to Illingworth, recalled his anxiety facing him in the second innings. 'Inexperience suggested to me that bold measures were called for, so I charged his first ball. My straight drive was sadly mistimed but as the ball lobbed so perilously close over Ray's head I scampered down the pitch for a single and the crisis was past.' Later he was to write, '"Illy" is undoubtedly tremendous on a turner, whether it be wet or dry. He is a much bigger spinner of the ball than many people give him credit for, and he can make the ball deviate even on a perfect track. When the pitch is giving him some help, his flight is a little flatter. His ability to bowl straight and drop the ball on a perfect length means that a batsman must take risks to break out of the restraint he imposes.'

Having reached the summit of his cricket career at Dover, Illingworth continued to strut the highest peaks with 7-78 against Surrey at The Oval, a game Yorkshire lost. With a far superior batting and bowling average for the season than David Allen, he felt aggrieved to have missed out to the Gloucestershire off-spinner on the MCC tour to South Africa that winter. 'I didn't play for about four years in the 1960s when I was the leading all-rounder in the country,' he later remarked. 'Another spinner, David Allen, spoke with a plum in his mouth to M.J.K. Smith and was chosen ahead of me.

'I'd never have grumbled if Fred Titmus played in place of me. Fred and myself said whoever was in form should play, but not people in front of us. We were both better players than David Allen.'

In the selectors' defence, it is fair to point out that Allen's Test record of 918 runs at 25.50 and 122 wickets at 30.97 compared favourably with Illingworth's (23.24 batting and 31.20 bowling), especially overseas where his lavish turn benefited from the harder, bouncier wickets.

Missing out on South Africa, Illingworth derived much pleasure from Yorkshire's three-week, post-season tour of the USA, Canada and Bermuda. Beginning in New York against two West Indian sides, they then travelled to Washington – Trueman calling it 'the city of memorials' – Toronto, Calgary, where snow stopped play, and Vancouver, rated by Boycott as the most beautiful ground he'd ever seen. In Los Angeles, Illingworth scored 144 against

South California, his second century of the trip, and for the final leg in Bermuda the side was strengthened by the guest appearances of Gary Sobers. Huge crowds turned out to watch him excel as Yorkshire easily saw off the locals to remain unbeaten.

Back home, Illingworth started the new season in fine fettle, exploiting some rain-affected wickets to devastating effect, not least his 8-20 off 30 overs against the champions Worcestershire at Headingley. Impressed by what he saw, Norman Yardley wrote: 'Illingworth is way ahead of established England off-spinners Titmus and Allen in wickets taken and is probably playing better than at any time in his career.' His rich harvest of wickets earned him an England recall for the final Test against New Zealand at Headingley, a game they completely dominated. Asked to bowl seamers by captain Mike Smith, he responded by taking 4-42 in the tourists' first innings, but with Titmus taking 5-19 in the second innings, his efforts counted for little and he was omitted for the rest of that summer.

Returning to the ranks, his game lost some of its lustre in a year when Yorkshire once again didn't seriously challenge for the Championship. The county did, however, find some consolation in winning the Gillette Cup, the highly popular knockout one-day competition, now in its third year. Having easily disposed of Leicestershire and Somerset in the earlier rounds, Yorkshire narrowly beat Warwickshire in the semi-final, with Illingworth's 45 and 13 overs for 29 runs winning him the man-of-the-match award.

Facing Surrey in the final at Lord's, Yorkshire, led by a scintillating 146 from Boycott and 79 from Close, amassed a formidable 317/4 in their allotted 60 overs. In reply, Surrey suffered the worst of all starts when Trueman dismissed John Edrich, Bill Smith and Ken Barrington in one over and by the time Illingworth emulated his feat, the game had long ceased to be a contest, Yorkshire winning by 175 runs. Their success earned them an appearance on stage later that evening at the Victoria Palace, home of the Black and White Minstrels.

With the county game increasingly weighed down by a defensive mentality and falling attendances, the game's administrators resorted to any number of legislative changes to try and revive its appeal. Curing the malaise, however, proved easier said than done and the experiment of limiting first innings to 65 overs in some Championship matches, introduced in 1966, was abandoned after one year.

In another wet summer, Yorkshire overcame the constant interruptions and turgid pitches to return to winning ways. From the outset their attack of Trueman, Tony Nicholson, Illingworth and Wilson were among the wickets. At Leicester in early June, Leicestershire's new captain Tony Lock induced the groundsman to doctor the wicket to his advantage by sanding it at one end, but it was Illingworth who stole the show with 11 wickets in his side's comprehensive victory. Further success against Warwickshire at Edgbaston and Sussex at Headingley accentuated his claims for a Test recall, especially now that Titmus, England's leading all-rounder, appeared to be on the wane. Picked for the third Test against West Indies at Trent Bridge, Illingworth contributed little with either bat or ball in a game England lost and he made way for Titmus at Headingley. Once again, England were outplayed, their limp performance causing such dismay that half the team were axed, including Titmus and Cowdrey, who was replaced as captain by Close.

Close insisted on Illingworth's return for the final Test at The Oval and when told by chairman of selectors Doug Insole that

'Ray has had his chance and failed,' he replied, 'He's failed because he's never been used properly.' It took him a long time to convince the selectors that Illingworth was good enough but he prevailed in the end and to good effect. In a remarkable transformation England, under Close's dynamic leadership, won by an innings and Illingworth played his part with 2-40 and 2-22, in addition to his tactical insights, as he later recalled:

'Gary Sobers was probably at the height of his powers and had already scored 691 runs in seven knocks *[sic]*. But I'd spotted one potential weakness.

'So, on the way down to London I said to Closey, "Look Brian, the one thing about Sobers is that he'll always go for the hook shot at any stage of his innings, even right at the start. We've never really tried him out properly yet. So, when he comes in, tell midwicket to walk back ten yards instead of walking in and let him have it straight away. He'll definitely go for it."

'So, John Snow let Sobers have a bouncer first ball, Gary nicked it on to his body and Closey, who had stood his ground at forward short leg, took the catch. It worked like a treat.

'Afterwards, when I heard him telling the press how he'd devised the plan that got Sobers first ball, I thought, "Bloody hell, Brian, come on." But I didn't mind if it made the old boy happy.'

Having led the table by 40 points at the beginning of August, Yorkshire faltered thereafter, losing closely fought games to Surrey, Northamptonshire and Warwickshire, in contrast to Worcestershire who were making up lost ground. By the time both counties began their final game on 31 August, the defending champions were only six points behind. On a difficult pitch at Harrogate, Yorkshire established a first-innings lead of 91 over Kent, only then to succumb to Derek Underwood in their second innings. With Kent needing 201 for victory, they closed at 38/2 at the end of the second day.

Heavy overnight rain threatened to frustrate Yorkshire's hopes of the title, while Worcestershire, needing 183 for victory against Sussex, made steady progress in the morning session. The dismissal of top scorer Tom Graveney soon afterwards, however, dealt a severe blow to their hopes and shortly after play resumed at Harrogate news filtered through of Worcestershire's defeat by 31 runs. Their demise meant Yorkshire were champions for the 30th time and they celebrated in the appropriate manner as Illingworth and Wilson bowled them to a 24-run victory.

With Close firmly installed as England's captain and Yorkshire once again champions, Illingworth had every reason to look forward to the new season with great optimism. An automatic selection for the first Test against India at Headingley, he took seven wickets in England's convincing six-wicket win. Following on, India, led by their captain, the Nawab of Pataudi, who made 148, made a much better fist of it. In response to his successful farming of the strike with the tail, Close and Illingworth decided to cover his straight hitting with deep fielders and bring in those squarish to the wicket. This gave Pataudi greater opportunities to score in the square leg and midwicket vicinity, but to do this he would have to hit across the line. Their ploy worked to perfection because in Illingworth's next over, the Indian captain advanced down the pitch to hit him over midwicket, missed and was bowled.

Illingworth took another seven wickets in the second Test at Lord's, his 6-29 in the second innings, his best-ever Test figures, consigning India to a heavy defeat. At the end of a one-sided three-Test rubber, he topped the England bowling averages with 20 wickets at 13.3, but he lacked penetration in the first Test against Pakistan at Lord's. As the visitors played out time during the closing overs, he found himself fielding at short leg to Close's off spin when two full tosses whistled past his ear on the way to the boundary. When he sought an explanation from Close for his loose bowling, Close confessed to getting a little bored to which an enraged Illingworth spluttered, 'Well, don't get bloody bored with me standing there.'

Illingworth had further cause to be aggrieved with Close when the latter accepted the selectors' conviction that they should restore Titmus for the two remaining Tests against Pakistan. Not only was Titmus back in form, they contended, he was also more likely than Illingworth to succeed in the West Indies that winter. To add insult to injury, the selectors picked the young Surrey off-spinner Pat Pocock in preference to Illingworth for the tour, and when Titmus was forced to return home early because of injury they called up Tony Lock, then captaining Western Australia, as his replacement.

England's loss was Yorkshire's gain as they battled to preserve their crown against a formidable challenge from Kent. When the two sides met at Canterbury in early August, the game marked the reappearance of the 46-year-old Godfrey Evans eight years after his retirement in place of Alan Knott, who was making his Test debut. Bowled by Illingworth for 10 in the first innings, Evans gained a measure of revenge by catching Illingworth off Alan Dixon for nought.

Yorkshire's convincing seven-wicket victory proved a real tonic, but a week later they were back in the headlines for all the wrong reasons. Facing defeat by Warwickshire at Edgbaston, Close resorted to blatant time-wasting in a desperate effort to take the two points for a draw. Amid the volley of criticism directed at the team – Illingworth defended Close, pointing to the wet conditions – Kilburn wrote that 'Yorkshiremen expect matches to be saved by cricketing skill rather than tactics open to question.' An MCC disciplinary panel ruled that Yorkshire's delaying tactics constituted unfair play and held Close entirely responsible for their conduct, a censure that cost him the England captaincy.

Devastated by the outcome, Close found solace in leading Yorkshire to an overwhelming victory against Warwickshire at Middlesbrough in their penultimate game. Once again, Harrogate became the venue for the final denouement with Yorkshire needing four points against bottom side Gloucestershire to retain the title. On a cold autumnal day and in front of a capacity crowd, opposing captain John Mortimore, on winning the toss, inserted Yorkshire on a wet pitch, telling Close that 'you've got to work for it now'.

A marvellous exhibition of hard graft by openers Boycott and Sharpe gave their side the perfect start and when the middle order collapsed, Illingworth stood firm, batting with great assurance against the spinners.

Following a robust last-wicket stand of 64 by Wilson and Trueman the next morning that took Yorkshire to 307 all out, Gloucestershire batted quietly through to lunch. Thereafter the effects of the heavy roller began to wear off, allowing Illingworth to come into his own, turning in a performance which, according to Close, would have flummoxed the world's best batsmen. 'As he has so often done in the past, he bowled beautifully while putting Yorkshire in a winning position. He reeled off 23 overs for eight maidens, 58 runs and seven wickets.'

Compelled to follow on, Gloucestershire found him even more destructive in the second innings, as he bowled his team to a two-day innings victory, finishing with the exceptional analysis of 13 overs and seven wickets for six runs. 'Some folks reckon tha can't bowl, Ray, but tha didn't do bad today, lad,' a supporter said to Illingworth afterwards.

'Ay. Not bad,' he responded with a smile.

His 14 wickets in one day had allowed Yorkshire to seal an emphatic victory and finish ten points ahead of Kent, ensuring that the two controversial points gained at Edgbaston didn't come into the final reckoning.

The year 1968 brought two major alterations to the Championship. First, the opportunity for counties to engage overseas players without qualification and second, the introduction of bonus points for first-innings performances. While Yorkshire refused to relax their ban on players born outside the county, their strong attack benefited from the bowling bonus points, one point for every two wickets taken in the first 85 overs. In a year when the dire weather gave bowlers the upper hand, it was the spin duo of Illingworth and Wilson that proved to be Yorkshire's most potent weapon. Seldom was Illingworth mastered on a rain-affected wicket but it happened in Yorkshire's opening Championship game of the season against Hampshire at Harrogate. The latter were all out for 122, 70 of which were scored by their new South African recruit Barry Richards. According to Hampshire all-rounder, Keith Wheatley, 'Illy was bowling sharply turning offies. Barry was stepping inside the line and hitting him into the gaps on the off side. Illy was standing there, in the middle of the wicket, scratching his head in bemusement as this young South African was toying with him.' 'Only a top player can hit the off-spinner through the covers on a turner,' commented Illingworth.

Amid the gloom, he was frequently among the wickets, most notably his 4-27 and 6-44 against Warwickshire, 5-26 against

Middlesex and 6-81 against Glamorgan. He also hit his first century for four years – 100 not out against Leicestershire – and excelled in the county's historic innings win against the Australians, their first victory over them since 1902, scoring 69 not out and taking four cheap wickets in each innings. 'Illingworth is in such good form both as bowler and batsman and was so impressive in both capacities against the Australians at Sheffield,' wrote Kilburn, 'that he must play them again with an advantage in confidence.'

He was duly selected for the third Test against Australia at Edgbaston, rather to the consternation of John Woodcock in *The Times*. He wrote, 'Illingworth returns for his 27th Test match, in which time his 58 wickets have cost him 29 apiece and come at the rate of one every 16 overs. It is an unconvincing record spread over ten years. But he has just had a good deal to do with the Australians' one defeat of their tour – by Yorkshire – and he is an old hand who can exploit the turning ball as well as any.'

Although his batting continued to disappoint in the remaining three Tests, he fully vindicated his selection. At Edgbaston he took three cheap wickets in Australia's first innings in a rain-ruined draw very much in England's favour, and at Headingley he was the leading wicket-taker on either side. In a taut, unadventurous game, Australia led by 13 runs on first innings when they went in to bat again on the third afternoon. Graveney, leading England instead of the injured Cowdrey, introduced Illingworth early and he responded by having opener Bob Cowper stumped by Alan Knott, one of three stumpings off his bowling in the innings. According to Knott, it was only the second time he'd kept to Illingworth and what he hadn't appreciated was his clever variation of flight. 'Throughout the match he made his off-spinners bite and when the wicket began to turn, he really had the Australians in trouble …'

With Australia intent on keeping the Ashes at all costs, their batsmen took root at the crease, risking little. When Illingworth winkled out their lower order on the final morning to finish with 6-87 off 51 overs, England needed 326 to win at an average of 66 an hour, but hard though they tried they were forced to settle for a draw.

Illingworth was at the height of his powers, but aged 36 and with a wife and young family to support, he was taking nothing for granted. What jolted him into action was the success of his deputy Geoff Cope, who'd come second in the national averages the previous year with 40 wickets at 13.8. Frustrated by his inability to command a regular first-team place, Cope was contemplating a future elsewhere, a development which concerned chairman Brian Sellers, who rated him highly.

It should be said that, with 12 current capped players on the books at the time, Sellers was looking to cut that number and he might well have seen Illingworth as dispensable. The two had never been close. Not only had Sellers vetoed the idea of him succeeding Ronnie Burnet as captain, he'd always viewed him as something of a troublemaker. According to Peter Walker, the Glamorgan all-rounder, Illingworth was one of the leading grumblers in the Yorkshire team. 'His complaints were not of a vicious feud-making type, but the recriminations and the impression he gave that everything and everyone was against him gave Ray a reputation for negativeness and unsociability.'

Much of his ire was directed at the committee and their reputation for miserliness. 'We won seven Championships for

Yorkshire but we were never given any kind of memento,' recalled Doug Padgett. 'It was very poor really.'

'I remember Ray Illingworth and his family coming back from a Test match to Headingley,' commented Ken Taylor. 'The Test had finished early and they ate some of the sandwiches left over from tea. Do you know, they gave him a bill. Can you believe it?'

Even after their historic win over the Australians, Trueman, who was captain that game, had to fight hard to get the committee to award the players the £5 win bonus that was applicable in county games.

Illingworth's most serious clash with Sellers occurred in July 1961. Having missed Yorkshire's game against Somerset because of a rib injury, the former, after an extensive workout, pronounced himself fit for the game against Sussex at Bradford, only for the latter to inform him that he had been consigned to the second XI. While Illingworth fulminated at what he perceived to be a great injustice, Sellers discovered that one of the team had had to cry off because of injury.

'Nah then, are you fit to play?' he asked Illingworth. 'I'm bloody not,' Illingworth replied. 'I wouldn't play for you if it was the last game in the country.'

It needed the arrival of Ronnie Burnet, by then a member of the Yorkshire committee, to calm things down and Illingworth said he would play for him.

Conscious of the rumblings about Cope, and in receipt of some attractive offers from league clubs, Illingworth sought out Yorkshire's secretary John Nash to ask him whether Cope would be selected in front of him. Nash denied this but Illingworth wasn't convinced. He later wrote, 'That was Sellers's influence again after I had just taken more wickets than anyone in the country in addition to scoring 1,000 runs *[sic]* and being near the top of the batting averages – it was ridiculous.'

He wasn't prepared to be given one more year and then put on the scrapheap when he knew there were some good contracts on offer.

Illingworth thought that the question of contracts, a source of contention in Yorkshire for some time, was exacerbated by the meagre level of remuneration compared to other counties. 'What was annoying, while we were winning Championships, was the fact that some members of the opposition were paid double our earnings. We should at least have been given the equivalent of what the better players were getting elsewhere.' (That summer Illingworth earned £1,500 as a Yorkshire player, and that included three games for England.) The issue had been highlighted in the 26 July edition of *The Cricketer* that summer by Bill Bowes, who warned that low rates of pay were deterring youngsters from becoming Yorkshire cricketers. 'It used to be a comparatively highly paid profession. Nowadays it is only the equivalent of a £1,200-a-year job – well paid in terms of earnings for four months or with thoughts of a £6,000 benefit after ten years – but it is very ordinary at a time when the average earnings in the country is £20 per week.'

Under pressure from the players, the committee did come up with better terms in August 1968 and Illingworth, representing the players, wrote to them expressing their appreciation, but then added his own personal request for a contract. 'They won't offer you a contract, Raymond,' Nash informed him, and when Illingworth advised him that he would have to resign, Nash asked him to put it in writing.

Despite Close's entreaties to proceed cautiously, Illingworth, after a series of sleepless nights, went ahead with his threat during

Yorkshire's game at Bradford on 20 August, assuming that the letter would be conditional on the committee's final decision. Within an hour or so, he was astounded to be approached by the *Yorkshire Evening Post*'s Bill Bowes, who asked him whether he was leaving. Could he have a word with him about it? When Illingworth asked how he knew about it, he discovered that Nash had telephoned Sellers, who'd replied indignantly, 'If that is what he wants, he can go. Any player who wishes to go somewhere else is no use to us.' Sellers then contacted Bowes to inform him that he'd authorised Illingworth's release and asked him to handle the press. 'So, the king was ruling with his absolute authority once again,' wrote Illingworth. 'I am convinced that if my letter had been considered by the committee soberly and sensibly, before the matter was publicised as a fait accompli, I might never have left Yorkshire.

'There were obviously members of the committee who did not and would not want me to leave Yorkshire. In my heart of hearts I didn't want to leave. But since the committee were never given a chance to consider the position and I can be just as stubborn as Brian Sellers, I went.' He later described it as the best decision of his life.

Aside from Yorkshire's decision to withhold his insurance policy on which they had paid the premium, what particularly irked Illingworth was Sellers's later contention that he'd left because he wanted more money. 'That is absolutely untrue. I was, in fact, a firm believer in the principle that all capped players should be paid the same wage.'

Illingworth's departure split opinion. If he received a contract, opined the *Yorkshire Post*, then Close and Trueman would require one and to have three players approaching 40 wasn't the way to win Championships. According to Boycott, who sympathised with his wish for a contract – and who successfully negotiated team contracts on becoming captain of Yorkshire – there was a feeling among the rank and file that his departure to Leicestershire smacked of disloyalty. 'He had been given a benefit three years earlier which had raised £6,604 – a tidy sum then even if it does not look like a lot now – and there were those who were ready to see his decision purely in financial terms. The pull of Yorkshire cricket has always been strong, and many supporters could not understand how Illingworth could turn his back on the county (especially their county) that had given him a chance, helped establish his reputation in the game and so on.'

Others were more sympathetic. 'I think it's fair to say that anyone in the team understood Illy's point of view,' wrote John Hampshire in his autobiography. 'The trouble was that no one on the committee did, least of all the all-powerful chairman, Brian Sellers. And to be painfully frank about it, his thinking was that of an age long since gone by. Cricketers in the 1960s were for the most part better educated than those of the twenties and thirties. Yet their pay and standing in the community was not what it had been in relative terms in Sellers's day.'

Whatever the rights and wrongs of the case, Illingworth's departure proved to be a defining moment in Yorkshire's history. 'Illingworth, the shrewdest of cricketers, is going to be missed badly by Yorkshire,' wrote Dick Williamson. 'The players know it and I am surprised Yorkshire are so readily prepared to let him go without any apparent effort being made to hang on to him. Yorkshire cricket is not so strong that it can afford to sanction his release at a time when other members of the side are, or approaching, the veteran stage.'

Years later, the cricket journalist Derek Hodgson wrote in *The Official History of Yorkshire Cricket*, 'Illingworth's departure proved to be a total catastrophe, a move that cost Yorkshire more dearly than almost any other in the county club's history.'

Bob Platt also placed his departure in perspective. 'But if you analyse Yorkshire's history, things went downhill from the moment they lost Raymond Illingworth in 1968 because Sellers wouldn't give him the security of a long-term contract. Then Sellers sacked Brian Close in 1970. The whole character of the side went with Illy and Close. Yorkshire were left with nobody, and I mean nobody, of anything like the same stature, apart from one man, G Boycott. Geoffrey realised that. But if Closey or Raymond had not left, Boycott would not have gone on to occupy the place in the history of Yorkshire cricket that he eventually did. So, I look at that situation and say that OK, Sellers may have had his good years, particularly when he was skipper, but as chairman, he went on too long.'

While Illingworth was helping England beat Australia in the final Test at The Oval to square the series, Yorkshire lost to Worcestershire by one run and drew with Derbyshire. Consequently, they needed to win their final game against Surrey at Hull to be assured of the Championship. In bleak, miserable conditions, Illingworth's 66 helped Yorkshire to a creditable 327/9 declared after they'd been sent into bat. They remained in control of the match thereafter, but they needed a touch of good fortune to break Surrey's resistance on the final evening. Younis Ahmed, who'd batted manfully for 75, pulled a short ball from Wilson which struck Close on the shin and rebounded to Binks. Despite blood streaming out of his trousers, Close refused to leave the field and with five minutes remaining Yorkshire took the final Surrey wicket to secure victory by 60 runs.

Champions for the third successive year, Yorkshire completed their season against MCC at Scarborough, a poignant occasion since it marked the final appearances of both Trueman and Illingworth for the county (till his remarkable reappearance 14 years later). As Illingworth came on to bowl on the final afternoon, his 7-73 nearly winning the match for his side, the band played 'For He's a Jolly Good Fellow'. The crowd, taken by surprise, applauded hesitantly and then warmly. 'Illingworth stood quietly, head a little bowed,' reported *The Times*' Alan Gibson. 'It was a moving moment. It made us remember not what he might gain from leaving Yorkshire, but what he is giving up.' For Trueman, it was even more heart-rending. At the end of the game, as the players left the field, the band played the Harry Parr-Davies number 'You Wave Me Goodbye', a gesture that moved him to tears. It was truly the end of the era.

Chapter 6

Captain of England

ILLINGWORTH'S DEPARTURE from Yorkshire left him greatly in demand. 'Here comes the richest man in cricket,' chortled his England team-mates at The Oval days later and 'How much is it this time?' whenever the phone rang in the dressing room. Half a dozen counties expressed an interest in securing his services, led by Nottinghamshire, Northamptonshire, Lancashire and Leicestershire. The first two offered the best terms but Leicestershire attracted him with the offer of the captaincy straight away. 'Even so,' he later wrote, 'there is no way they would have got me there but for one seemingly irrelevant factor – they had recently completed new dressing room accommodation. I had spent years walking apprehensively down two flights of rickety steps, collecting splinters in my feet on the way to take a shower, and I absolutely would not have contemplated doing that in every home game! But Leicestershire had built this new accommodation, Mike Turner was clearly an ambitious young secretary, and the club seemed as though it was keen to go places. All in all there seemed a better chance of my doing something there than with most of the others.'

He was persuaded in his thinking by England's top umpire Syd Buller who told him, 'Leicester's the place to go. You'll get a free hand there and you can do something.' After talks with the club at their Grace Road ground in October – during which Mike Turner's wife, Patricia, entertained Shirley and the family to tea in her garden – he signed a three-year contract and had his special registration approved by MCC in December. His terms, while less generous than those offered by Northamptonshire and Nottinghamshire, were still some 50 per cent better than what he was earning at Yorkshire.

Having opted out of the MCC tour to Pakistan because of his winter employment, Illingworth had plenty of time to prepare for his new challenge. His all-round contribution helped Leicestershire to a five-wicket win in their inaugural game of the 1969 season in the John Player League (JPL), the new 40-over competition, and he marked his first Championship game for his new county by taking 7-27 against Warwickshire. Although bad weather interrupted their progress, Leicestershire were riding high when opportunity came knocking at his door.

On Sunday, 25 May, the day he had been appointed captain of England for the summer, Cowdrey snapped his Achilles tendon when playing for Kent, putting him out of the game for over three months. While some pundits backed Roger Prideaux, the captain of Northamptonshire, to take over against West Indies, the favourite appeared to be England vice-captain Tom Graveney, who'd led them against Australia at Headingley the previous year. The selectors, however, demurred, for aside from upsetting the management in Pakistan months earlier with his agitation about player safety, his record as captain was ambiguous. 'Nothing in his terms at Gloucester or Worcester indicated high strategic awareness,' wrote Graveney's biographer, Christopher Sandford. 'He was solid, not spectacular. Illingworth in this respect had the advantage. In his first month at Leicester he was hailed as a genius. … Faced with a choice between sombre Graveney and gambling Illingworth the selectors opted for the latter.'

Sandford's view was echoed later by chairman of selectors Alec Bedser. He wrote, 'It was no secret in the game that Ray had been an invaluable tactical adviser to Yorkshire captains and had a good cricket brain. Within weeks of taking over at Leicester the grapevine was alive with commendations of his skills as a captain. His personal form was also good, and with Cowdrey on the sidelines the need for strong leadership was made all the more necessary by the loss of the heart of England's batting.' (Ken Barrington had been forced into retirement because of a heart attack and Colin Milburn had recently lost an eye in a car accident.)

Having made their choice, Bedser rang Headingley, where Illingworth had been playing for Leicestershire against Yorkshire, only to discover that he'd just left for Brighton. He remained out of communication on a journey that comprised a stopover in Northampton to visit Milburn in hospital and by the time he arrived at the Imperial Hotel, Brighton, at 8pm, he was greeted with a posse of photographers who informed him of his appointment. Naturally delighted with the news, he felt confident of stepping up successfully based on his feeling 'that the players knew enough about me to trust me to make the right decisions'.

He quickly established his authority over an experienced England side unbeaten in their previous five series, whereas West Indies in contrast were a side in transition, a shadow of their 1966 predecessors despite the presence of stalwarts such as Gary Sobers, Lance Gibbs and Basil Butcher.

Winning the toss on an easy-paced Old Trafford wicket, England made 413 before fast bowlers David Brown and John

Snow skittled West Indies for 147. Following on, the tourists performed slightly better, but still lost by ten wickets.

At Lord's, West Indies batted first on another true wicket and played with greater conviction to score 380. They then made inroads into the England upper order on the second evening and when Phil Sharpe left early the next morning, they were reeling at 61/5. A defiant sixth-wicket partnership of 128 between debutant John Hampshire and Alan Knott entertained the capacity crowd and when Illingworth marched out to replace the latter at 189/6, he continued the fightback with the former, who hit 107. Although Barry Knight and Brown didn't last long, Illingworth, fresh from 153 not out against Essex, found a reliable partner in last man Snow and together they added 72 that evening, of which Illingworth made 69.

Dropped by Lance Gibbs on 64, he otherwise batted with great fluency, especially off his legs, and at the end of the day he was mobbed by youngsters as he returned to the pavilion, undefeated on 97.

On Monday he completed his century, greatly exceeding his previous highest Test score of 50 and when he was finally out for 113, which equalled his overall aggregate in his previous 11 Test match innings, England trailed by only 36. According to *Wisden*, 'His was a grand innings, full of bold strokes and notable for forward play,' while BBC cricket commentator Jim Laker declared that he'd never seen Illingworth bat so well.

West Indies made 295/9 in their second innings before Sobers declared, leaving England to score 332 in five hours. A scintillating fourth-wicket partnership of 129 between Boycott and Sharpe put them on course for victory, but their dismissals, and that of Hampshire, run out by Illingworth, forced England to play out time.

In the decider at Headingley, batting proved a taxing business until the pitch dried out on the fourth day, when West Indies appeared to be cruising towards their victory target of 303 before Butcher was out for 91. With Sobers now at the wicket, Illingworth, believing him vulnerable to a half-volley outside his off stump early on, immediately brought back seamer Barry Knight, who'd dismissed him twice in the series. He now repeated the trick by getting him to play on to a wide half-volley without scoring. Illingworth then replaced Derek Underwood with himself, reasoning that he was better equipped to bowl at left-handers and having induced Clive Lloyd to edge to the wicketkeeper he turned back to Underwood, who promptly dismissed John Shepherd. Four wickets had fallen for nine runs and the game had swung irrevocably in the home side's favour. 'That England, coolly led by Illingworth, turned back a West Indian side in full spate was a triumph for them,' reported John Woodcock that evening.

On the morrow, with West Indies needing another 73 to win, Illingworth opted to take the new ball and his pacemen cleaned up the tail, giving England victory by 30 runs and the series 2-0. His leadership, impressive throughout, excelled at Headingley and his reward was the captaincy for the three-Test series against New Zealand. Irked by the failure of Snow to carry out his instructions by giving his all in the final stages at Headingley, Illingworth asked that he be left out of the next game. While the media were informed that he was being rested, Illingworth rang Snow to explain his thinking, a gesture that Snow appreciated even though he disagreed with the decision. He later wrote, 'From that moment I was to know exactly where I stood with him as did every other player who came under his captaincy. He spoke his mind. Just as important, I learned that he was a man of his word.

'Ray and I still had our differences after that sacking but they were always out in the open. He was never slow to criticise. At the same time he would always listen and take into account my point of view.'

Up against a New Zealand side that looked stronger than some of its predecessors, Illingworth was taking nothing for granted. Faced with a green wicket at Lord's, he was unsure what to do should he win the toss. Geoff Boycott wrote, 'Illingworth asked me what I thought and I told him that I hoped he would put New Zealand in if he won the toss – but that if I were making the decision I would bat first because Underwood would bowl them out in the second innings.'

Illingworth duly won the toss and batted, explaining to his team the logic of his decision. Boycott was out without scoring but was thanked by Illingworth for his advice, acknowledging there was an element of self-sacrifice involved.

Having been 63/5 at lunch, England's total of 190 owed much to Illingworth's fighting 53. He and Underwood then took four wickets each and following a second-innings century from John Edrich, Underwood with 7-32 bowled them to an easy victory.

After rain robbed England of a probable win at Trent Bridge, they triumphed at The Oval by eight wickets with Underwood taking six wickets in both innings. Reviewing their summer of success, John Woodcock wrote, 'Illingworth has done his job as everyone knew he would – with the professionalism which for better or worse is the symbol of his age. In outlook Illingworth and Cowdrey are much alike. Both believe in the attritional way of doing things. With this reservation, Illingworth's performance has confirmed a shrewd cricketing brain and the England team have liked playing for him.'

With no tour that winter, Illingworth's hopes of retaining the captaincy against the touring South Africans seemed remote now that Cowdrey had returned to full fitness. In the event the tour was called off following protests by the anti-apartheid movement and the government's fear of civil unrest, much to Illingworth's disappointment, who thought it another triumph for politicians over sportsmen. Yet, with Cowdrey in dire form, and unavailable for the first unofficial Test against the Rest of the World, the all-star team cobbled together to replace South Africa, Illingworth remained in charge. With a tour of Australia and New Zealand on the horizon, he did his leadership prospects no harm with his stupendous batting against a top-flight attack comprising Sobers, Mike Procter, Eddie Barlow, Lance Gibbs and Intikhab Alam. At Lord's in the first Test, he was the only England batsman to withstand Sobers, his 63 accounting for almost half his side's total of 127. After lunch Illingworth batted astonishingly well, reported Woodcock. 'His driving and forcing put the others to shame.'

He was again dominant in the second innings, his resolute 94 providing an element of respectability in England's crushing defeat. 'By any yardstick it was a fine performance,' wrote *The Mirror*'s Peter Laker. 'But in terms of strength of the opposition I rate it truly terrific. It proved again that temperament can conquer all at the top.'

Illingworth continued as captain for the Trent Bridge Test, even though Cowdrey was recalled to the side, and when England slumped to 195/9 in reply to their opponents' first-innings score of 276, he once again came to the rescue. Finding sterling support from Snow, he batted superbly to make 97, top-scoring for the third time in succession, and give his side a lead of three, which they converted into an eight-wicket victory.

England's win gave Illingworth another game at the helm, a five-wicket defeat at Edgbaston in which he dismissed Sobers twice. While he was making a confident 43 in the second innings, the selectors went into conclave to choose the captain for Australia. Given the unfortunate circumstances of his accident the previous year when he was very much in charge, natural justice seemed to point to Cowdrey. He was the doyen of four previous Ashes tours, three of which he'd been vice-captain, a victor in the Caribbean and a natural diplomat who would charm Australia. Illingworth, in contrast, was a blunt Yorkshireman and had achieved little on his two overseas tours, but he'd excelled as a leader since becoming England captain and his batting had been a revelation. Even Ted Dexter felt compelled to write, 'From a nervous fidgeting prodder, he was transformed into a dashing stroke-player prepared to carry the fight to such aggressive operators as Peter Pollock – an amazing change of outlook.'

Taking all these matters into consideration, the four selectors, Alec Bedser, A.C. Smith, Billy Sutcliffe and Don Kenyon, faced a hard choice. Ultimately, they plumped for Illingworth on the grounds that his assertive nature made him a more effective leader. Bedser wrote, 'To my mind, unlucky as it was for Colin, it would have been a rank injustice if at that point Illingworth had been asked to move aside as he had done everything the selectors had asked of him. In two summers, he had shown an unmistakable flair for sensible and firm captaincy with a high degree of tactical skill and awareness.'

'I thought that Colin Cowdrey was automatically being lined up to take the side to Australia that winter,' recalled Illingworth, 'but as the series went on, it became clear that most of the selectors wanted me to captain. The thing about Cowdrey was that the pros didn't trust him. He was a funny bloke. He'd promise you the moon and then nothing would happen.'

Illingworth's reservations about Cowdrey weren't shared by establishment correspondents such as E.W. Swanton and John Woodcock, who thought that he merited his lifelong ambition to captain in Australia. As for Cowdrey, his natural distress at missing out on such an illustrious prize was compounded by Illingworth being the beneficiary of his misfortune. The two men had never been close – Illingworth felt Cowdrey hadn't treated him fairly when captain of England in his early Tests – and their frosty relationship was further exacerbated by events in Australia in 1962/63. Resentful of the privileged position assigned to the amateurs on that tour and on other ones, Illingworth felt deeply offended by Cowdrey's high-handed treatment of him at net practice and 12th man duties. He didn't rate him as a captain, partly because of his indecision and partly his predilection for having favourites, and he wasn't slow in criticising him to his face, a trait that affronted the sensitive Cowdrey.

For his part, Cowdrey disparaged Illingworth's discomfort against the West Indian quicks in 1959/60 and he wasn't amused when Illingworth once belittled him by walking out to bat before he led Kent on to the field. He asked Bedser to be given time to consider his position as vice-captain elect, a request to which Bedser acceded.

As Cowdrey continued to procrastinate, the selectors encouraged Illingworth to write him a letter to draw a line under past differences in the interest of English cricket. Illingworth, who actually wanted Boycott as vice-captain, reluctantly obliged, but this prickly olive branch had drawn no response by the time Cowdrey met Bedser before the fourth Test at Headingley. Conscious, however, that rejection might be interpreted as sour grapes and keen to assist his good friend David Clark, who'd been appointed manager, Cowdrey finally fell in with the selectors' wishes. 'Having taken so long to decide, I think his misgivings were such that he ought to have said "no",' Illingworth later wrote. 'Quite obviously he didn't like the idea of serving under me, and it might have been better for both of us if he had declined to do so.'

While Cowdrey failed in both innings at Headingley, Illingworth contributed substantially in England's two-wicket defeat with two fifties and 3-41 in the second innings when he'd bowled beautifully to Sobers. Over a drink afterwards Basil D'Oliveira told Sobers he'd never seen him play and miss so much against Illingworth, to which Sobers replied, 'You must get it right, Bas. I didn't play – he missed me.' 'Only a genius with great self-belief could talk that way,' wrote D'Oliveira.

Illingworth scored his sixth half-century in eight innings at The Oval before signing off with a duck. Although England lost by four wickets, they once again gave a good account of themselves against superb opposition, boosting confidence for Australia. 'There'd never been a side like it,' Illingworth observed. 'They had everything – but it was much closer than the 4-1 result suggests. We dropped two catches at Edgbaston that turned the game and at Headingley [umpire] Arthur Fagg gave a couple of terrible decisions that cost us. We could have been going to The Oval at 2-2.'

Chapter 7
The Pinnacle

THERE WERE few surprises in the side for Australia although Illingworth had to pull rank in support of D'Oliveira. Already assured by Bedser that he would be chosen for the tour, a concession in return for his omission for the final Rest of the World Test, he faced strong opposition from Cowdrey, whose involvement in the selection process as vice-captain was highly unusual. As captain in the West Indies three years earlier, Cowdrey had struggled to control D'Oliveira's colourful nightlife and his misgivings, and those of manager Les Ames, had been primarily responsible for D'Oliveira's original omission from the tour to South Africa the following year.

Now with Cowdrey leading the charge against him once again, Illingworth intervened in D'Oliveira's defence, disclosing his past pact with Bedser and threatening resignation if D'Oliveira wasn't chosen. After the meeting Illingworth took D'Oliveira aside. 'I didn't muck about with Basil,' Illingworth recalled. 'I said, "You know that Cowdrey had problems with you in the West Indies. You know I stuck my neck out for you to go to Australia." I said, "Don't you let me down." And you can ask him that. And he said, "Don't worry, I won't" – and he didn't. I never had a problem with him out there.'

Later Illingworth was slightly to modify his line. 'Mostly, he was fine in Australia. I liked Basil. Mind, I did get Basil's finger jabbed in my chest more than once. And he did wreck his room on one occasion after he'd had a few. We got it paid for out of team funds we had from appearances and so on. I gave him a severe rollicking and kept him on the phone for a long time.'

Illingworth's and Cowdrey's contrasting views about D'Oliveira were the first inkling of the bad blood that existed between them throughout the tour. The man tasked with bridging the gap was manager David Clark, a staunch upholder of the amateur tradition and a former captain of Kent, who had nurtured the young Cowdrey. A genial and conscientious man, Clark had formed a harmonious partnership with Mike Smith in India in 1963/64, but now saddled with a very different type of captain, he soon found his authority questioned, since Illingworth insisted on having sole charge of playing matters. 'I started off the tour with Mr Clark with a perfectly open mind,' he later wrote. 'By the end of it I was forced to tell him that I honestly believed he was working more for the Australians than for us. He was, I told him, there as the team's manager, not as an ambassador of goodwill on behalf of MCC.' With the majority of the British press unreconciled to Illingworth's appointment and with a number of players sympathetic to Cowdrey's plight, a rift developed in the touring party, especially at first. Keith Fletcher, who thought the squad lacked the camaraderie of the Essex side or the MCC party to India in 1972/73, increasingly realised that Illingworth and Cowdrey would never settle their differences. 'They were total opposites and now there was the added needle between them of the captaincy issue.' Reluctant to fully participate in team practices from the outset, Cowdrey grew ever more detached from the Test side, and he spent much time consorting with Australian friends or playing golf with the manager's wife. He did, however, continue to fly the flag at social functions when others opted out of their responsibilities.

Despite being written off by the Australian press as 'Dad's Army' with three players nearing 40, Illingworth remained bullish about his side's prospects, chiefly because of his superior pace attack and the solid temperament of his men. When challenged about the call for brighter cricket by the press – a leading mantra of the MCC management on the previous two tours to Australia – he questioned the meaning of the phrase. 'If it means you throw caution to the winds, and lose a game to please the crowd, then that is not the way we are going to play.'

With an unprecedented six-Test series in front of them, MCC had only four first-class fixtures before the first Test at Brisbane instead of the usual seven. In the opening game against South Australia Boycott immediately found form, finishing the first day undefeated on 173, but his hope of accumulating many more were dented when Illingworth asked him to sacrifice his wicket on reaching 200 to give the others a bat. It was a request that dismayed Boycott, who wanted as much practice as possible at that stage of the tour and angry words were exchanged between them before he came into line.

Illingworth also had to admonish Snow for his lacklustre approach as South Australia easily surpassed MCC's total of 451/9 declared by making 649/8 declared, of which the brilliant South African opener Barry Richards scored 224. While accepting that his strike bowler needed to pace himself in the state matches, he drew the line at his sloppy fielding which alienated his team-mates who were vying for Test places.

Illingworth put his case so reasonably that Snow accepted the plausibility of his point of view and proved more than accommodating from then on.

MCC's undistinguished draw in Adelaide was followed by defeat against Victoria, their batsmen undone by fast bowler Alan 'Froggy' Thomson, who bowled off the wrong foot like Procter. They then suffered the indignity of following on against New South Wales and were only saved by centuries from Boycott and Brian Luckhurst. Boycott hit another century in the draw against Queensland and while this time he willingly retired on 124 it didn't stop press stories of a bust-up with Illingworth in the dressing room, allegations quickly scotched in an official statement.

Another setback was the loss of Alan Ward, whose shin splints forced him to fly home. Requiring another quick man as a replacement, Illingworth accepted John Edrich's recommendation to send for Surrey's 21-year-old tearaway Bob Willis. Given England's traditional caution in favouring youth, it proved to be an inspired choice, since Willis ably supported the opening pair of Snow and Peter Lever, chipping in with useful wickets, and taking some spectacular catches close in.

Although disappointed by the performance of the side so far, Illingworth entered the first Test in positive mood convinced that his players would rise to the occasion. Consigned to fielding first on a lifeless wicket, England not only surpassed Australia's first-innings total of 433, they ended up getting the better of the draw.

From Brisbane to Perth and a drawn game against Western Australia which drew barbs from opposing captain Tony Lock. Not only did he decry MCC's failure to press for victory after a sporting declaration, he also lamented their unwillingness to mix with the opposition. Firmly of the view that leading a national team on tour wasn't simply about winning a few cricket matches, it was about representing England and establishing friendly relations with the host country, he commented, 'Illingworth never got near to doing his job on this side of the tour in my opinion. Frankly I wouldn't have enjoyed being a member of his side on this particular tour. I have never known a more unsociable party of international cricketers.'

The mood wasn't helped by Snow's increasingly frayed relationship with the manager. Rested for the Western Australia game after bowling 50 eight-ball overs at Brisbane, he was irked when Clark told him to go and bowl in the nets. Snow protested vigorously, leaving Illingworth to pour oil on troubled waters.

Yet despite any rifts off the field, the side were fiercely united behind Illingworth in their determination to beat Australia. With another easy-paced wicket awaiting them for Perth's inaugural Test, England received an early Christmas present from opposing captain Bill Lawry when he asked them to bat first. Normally the curator approached the captain of the batting side and asked him whether he would like the pitch to be rolled before play and which roller he would like to be used. Here it didn't happen and when Illingworth found the curator, he proved unhelpful, claiming that no roller was allowed before play. Illingworth then confronted umpire Lou Rowan who sided with the curator, but, convinced he was right the England captain showed Rowan the rules at lunch to prove his case.

Given a dream start by Boycott and Luckhurst, England twice allowed Australia back into the game, so much so that they were beholden to a second-innings century from Edrich to see them to safety. A token declaration gave Snow the opportunity to land a few blows on the Australian upper order before he was cautioned by Rowan for intimidatory bowling, a decision Illingworth labelled unfair, given Snow's ability to make the ball rear off a length. It was yet another saga in the ongoing feud that simmered all series between bowler and umpire and which boiled over in the final Test.

Another problem concerned the relationship between captain and manager, which Willis later described as easily the worst that he'd ever seen. Responding to a request from the Australian media for an impression of the series so far, Clark chastised both sides for their negative cricket and said he would rather see Australia win the rubber 3-1 than have all the Tests drawn. His comments, delivered without informing his captain or the players, caused ripples when they read them on the plane to Adelaide the next day. Nobody denied that the first two Tests had been fairly tedious, but, in his justifiable crusade to promote brighter play, the manager seemed not to appreciate the intensity of modern Test cricket. 'At best this was a tactless putdown of players who had been sweating buckets for their country,' wrote Willis. 'At worst, it could have been thought an incitement to further conflict between Clark and Illingworth who, it now became clear to me, might as well have come from different planets.' 'At the time Ray and I sat with the manager in the stands at Adelaide trying to put our point of view about his statement,' recalled Snow, 'but after an hour, we were no nearer a mutual understanding and just gave up.' As far as Boycott was concerned, Clark was a Cowdrey man, out to undermine Illingworth. 'Another Establishment man trying to retain the Establishment hold on a changing game.'

The gulf between manager and players was again exposed at Melbourne over New Year, when torrential rain caused the third Test to be abandoned after three blank days. With the weather causing a body blow to the finances of the Australian Board of Control, they were desperate to recoup their losses. In consultation with MCC president Sir Cyril Hawker, treasurer Gubby Allen and Clark, they wrote off the Test and not only arranged a one-day international, the first of its kind, and won by Australia in front of 46,000 at Melbourne, but also rescheduled the Test. Though this would mean four Tests inside six weeks during the hottest months of the year, the MCC delegation agreed to the revised itinerary in the interests of Anglo-Australian relations.

Their good intentions, however, found little favour with Illingworth and his team when presented with a fait accompli. Swanton recalled running into one of them in the foyer of the Windsor Hotel and being told that it was a disgrace that the players hadn't been consulted, and that the sooner these things were managed by the professionals, the better. Such truculence had been fuelled by the team's parsimonious meal allowance, the formal dress code and the number of receptions they were expected to attend, especially on days when they were tired from travelling. At a team meeting organised in their hotel, these grievances were given full voice. Illingworth objected to the revised schedule on the grounds that, by placing too much pressure on them, it jeopardised their chances of winning the rubber, and without any hint of additional renumeration. His line was fully endorsed by everyone present (Cowdrey refused to attend) except Derek Underwood, who maintained that playing for England was an honour in itself, and it was conveyed to Clark. Clark then rang MCC secretary Billy Griffith with their demands and he agreed to pay the team an additional £50, small beer compared to what their Australian counterparts were earning and to the Australian board's profit of £70,000 from the additional Test.

For the fourth Test at Sydney, Illingworth's favourite ground, England took the uncomfortable decision to drop the out-of-form Cowdrey and give a first cap to Willis. On a grassy wicket more suited to their style of cricket, the tourists, led by an imperious 77 from Boycott, made 332, but Australia fought back, finishing the second day on 189/4. During the final session D'Oliveira suggested to Illingworth that he would get the ball to swing and the next morning Illingworth, sensing that he could be on to something, asked him to open the bowling. It proved a masterstroke, since he promptly dismissed Australia's top scorer, Ian Redpath, first ball, allowing Underwood to mop up the tail.

With a valuable lead of 96, Boycott went one better with a magnificent 142 not out before Snow was let loose on a wearing pitch. Bowling with raw pace and hostility, he decimated the Australian batting with 7-40, sending them crashing to a 299-run defeat. 'Snow bowled as well as any fast bowler I have ever seen,' Illingworth was to later write. 'I don't think any batsman in the world could have played John with that new ball. He had a superb tour. He got chest-high bounce from only just short of a length, he got movement off the pitch but above all he bowled a beautiful line: fractionally outside the off stump, so that if the ball did even just a little bit, he had every batsman in trouble.'

For the additional Melbourne Test, England recalled Cowdrey but his fragile confidence infected his slip catching, twice dropping Ian Chappell, on 0 and 14. They proved expensive misses as Chappell scored 111, his century prompting a large pitch invasion that drew fierce condemnation from Illingworth, who lodged a complaint with the ground authorities.

Australia held the upper hand but centuries from Luckhurst, despite nursing a broken finger, and D'Oliveira, along with 41 from Illingworth, kept England in the game. In Australia's second innings, the England captain found himself in contention with umpire Max O'Connell following the latter's warning to Snow for bowling bouncers at Redpath. He maintained that Australia's Alan 'Froggy' Thomson was transgressing just as much as Snow and yet he hadn't been cautioned.

Uninterested in Lawry's declaration, Boycott and Edrich, opening for the injured Luckhurst, played out time much to the indignation of the rowdy crowd. Having slated the Melbourne authorities for their inadequate practice facilities prior to the game, Illingworth didn't endear himself afterwards when he questioned the legality of wrist-spinner Kerry O'Keefe's action. Not surprisingly, he received a rowdy reception at Adelaide, the worst for an England captain since Douglas Jardine during the Bodyline series.

There was further controversy involving umpire O'Connell on the opening day of the Adelaide Test. Batting first on an excellent batting strip, Boycott and Edrich put on 107 for the first wicket until Boycott was adjudged run out for 58 going for a quick single. Convinced that he'd made his ground, he dropped his bat and stood hands on hips glaring at the umpire before returning to the pavilion to loud derision from the crowd. Despite the furore caused by his petulant reaction, Boycott was reluctant to apologise to the umpire and Illingworth felt obliged to do so on his behalf.

Led by Edrich's 130, England amassed 470 and bowled Australia out for 235, posing Illingworth a conundrum as to whether he enforced the follow-on. Consulting with Snow and Lever, both of whom were tired and carrying minor injuries, and conscious of the enormous workload they'd undergone over the previous month, he chose to bat again. His decision, perfectly understandable from a modern perspective, was greeted with amazement by the demoralised Australians. 'Illy has helped keep the series alive,' chortled Lawry, who'd already put his pads back on, and according to his opening partner Keith Stackpole, it was the England captain's only tactical error of the rubber. The fact that Australia easily saved the game helped give credence to the English press's contention that Illingworth had let his opponents off the hook, placing added pressure on him in the final Test at Sydney. While Australia dropped a bombshell by omitting their captain Lawry, England were without Boycott, who'd sustained a broken arm on an under-prepared wicket in a meaningless one-day game against Western Australia.

Winning the toss, the new captain Ian Chappell sent England into bat on a rain-affected wicket and pressurising them with attacking fields, his bowlers struck early blows before Illingworth came to the rescue. Entering to a chorus of jeers at 69/4, he showed no concern, and, resorting to the pull, he was the only batsman to break up the close fields. While wickets continued to fall at frequent intervals, Illingworth battled on to make 42 out of his team's paltry total of 184.

England struck back with two quick wickets that evening and the next day they continued to keep Australia in check until a stubborn eighth-wicket stand between Greg Chappell and leg-spinner Terry Jenner gave them a narrow advantage. At 195/7 Illingworth took the new ball and, with the seventh ball of his second over, Snow hit Jenner on the head as he ducked into a ball that barely rose above stump height. Jenner collapsed on the pitch and the bowler's cursory concern for his victim, a tail-ender, incensed the 29,000 crowd, who had seen Snow pepper their batsmen all summer. As Jenner was led off the field with blood streaming from his face, umpire Rowan chose to warn Snow for intimidating bowling, a warning that caused Snow to see red.

A detective sergeant in the Queensland drugs squad, Rowan had established a reputation as one of the world's leading umpires in partnership with Colin Egar over the previous decade. Now with Egar retired, Rowan appeared to have lost his touch, and in a series where most of the marginal decisions went against England – not one Australian was given out lbw in six Tests – he came across as unduly officious. 'In 15 seasons of first-class cricket, performing in front of umpires all over the cricket-playing world, I can safely say that I have never come across another umpire so full of his importance,' Snow later wrote. The two had clashed previously during the series over their different interpretations of what constituted a bouncer, although according to John Woodcock, Rowan's caution hadn't come a moment too soon, since earlier that day he had allowed Snow to bowl five bouncers in one over to Ian Chappell.

Aggrieved that he'd been warned for bowling one bouncer, although the over had previously contained two short-pitched balls, Snow protested vehemently and was supported by Illingworth, who both in word and gesture, holding up one finger, disputed the umpire's action. According to Richie Benaud, it wasn't behaviour becoming of an England cricket captain, rather that of a prima donna of a South American football side arguing with the referee.

The altercation did little to cool emotions. Having bowled the final ball of the over to the new batsman Dennis Lillee to a crescendo of boos, an indignant Snow snatched his hat from the umpire and walked down to his position in front of the Paddington Hill. His walk provoked a hail of beer cans, prompting Illingworth to call him back to the middle while the debris was cleared. 'Better go to third man,' Illingworth told Snow, but Snow insisted on returning to fine leg. He stationed himself beneath the picket fence on the boundary to a tirade of taunts interspersed with sympathetic applause. As he tried to greet several well-wishers, he was manhandled by a middle-aged drunk. With the help of his supporters, Snow wriggled free and walked 15 yards infield when a second wave of beer cans landed around him. It was at this point that Illingworth, fearing for the safety of his players, led them off the field, the first time this had ever happened in 209 Tests.

Accepting that he should have consulted the umpires before heading for the pavilion, Illingworth's initiative divided opinion. Many commentators, including a slew of former Australian captains, sympathised with his plight, as did Alan Knott who recalled England staying on the field in the Kingston Test riot of 1968 and becoming targets for the bottles hurled at them. In contrast, the Australian players, who'd been subjected to a full-scale riot in Calcutta in 1969, and Fletcher, who'd seen something similar with England in Pakistan that year, thought he'd over-reacted.

On reaching the dressing room, Illingworth was ordered to return by Clark, but he stuck to his guns, berating Clark for constantly siding with the Australians and neglecting the interests of his players. He told him that he wasn't going back until the playing area had been cleared. It was a similar message he gave to the umpires when they visited the dressing room to warn him that a failure to return would mean his side forfeiting the match.

After a seven-minute delay during which the ground was cleared, the team returned to a mixed reception, and in the remaining overs that evening Australia added a further 40 runs without losing another wicket. The next morning, they extended their lead to 80 and chipped away at the England upper order before a resolute stand of 69 between D'Oliveira and Illingworth evened things up. In the closing overs, Illingworth was struck on the knee by fast bowler Tony Dell and he hobbled off the field in some pain. An x-ray revealed no break and a weekend of ultrasound treatment from physiotherapist Bernard Thomas enabled him to resume batting on Monday without a runner. Neither he nor D'Oliveira lasted long, but with the lower order in defiant mood England closed on 302.

Needing 223 to win, Australia lost opener Ken Eastwood in Snow's first over before the latter withdrew from the match shortly afterwards with a broken hand as he collided with the boundary pickets attempting to catch Stackpole. Fortunately, the other bowlers, ably marshalled by Illingworth, rose to the occasion. Coming on at 58/2, the captain used the breeze well to vary his flight and picked up two vital wickets that evening, the first being Redpath, smartly caught in the leg trap by Hampshire. The Australian cricket journalist and author Ray Robinson wrote, 'In his gentle, wide-trousered jogtrot of eight steps Illy looks innocent as a backyard trundler in slippers, but not to batsmen who have to cope with his on-the-dot length plus deceptive drift that sways some balls outward when inward turn is expected.

'When Stackpole, attempting a sweep, was bowled behind his meaty legs for 67, top score, eight fieldsmen crowded to pat the broad back of the skipper whose guile had removed the biggest obstacle to an English victory.'

Recalling his vital spell, Illingworth commented, 'Peter Lever said to me, "You haven't bowled much. I wasn't sure you could do it." But I'd bowled that much in my career that, to be honest, I could nearly bowl with my eyes shut and I knew it.'

Illingworth could have had another wicket soon afterwards, but Knott missed a sharp leg-side chance to stump Rod Marsh, his first real blemish in the rubber. At the end of the over he approached his wicketkeeper and with a wry smile commented, 'Well, at least you proved you're human.'

With Australia closing the day at 123/5 and the match finely balanced, Illingworth said to D'Oliveira on their return journey to their hotel, 'Do you know, Bas, I'd give anything to win tomorrow, absolutely anything.' 'It was the first time I'd seen him show emotion,' D'Oliveira wrote. 'I realised then the pressure he'd been taking over the past three months.'

When the match resumed on the morrow, Illingworth led from the front by opening the bowling himself and after Underwood bowled Marsh he claimed the vital wicket of Greg Chappell, stumped by Knott as he was lured down the pitch by his floater. Thereafter D'Oliveira and Underwood made light work of the tail and when the latter had Jenner caught close in by Fletcher, England had triumphed by 62 runs to win the series 2-0. As Illingworth was chaired off by his team, he could rest content that he'd emulated his great hero Hutton by winning the Ashes in Australia and becoming the first England captain since Jardine in 1933 to regain the Ashes there. (He remains to this day the only England captain to have never lost a Test in Australia in a five-match series.) Amid the champagne reception in the dressing room, he remarked that nothing in his 20 years in the game had given him so much pleasure. 'We beat Australia in Australia. We did it with a team which was very much a team in every sense of the word. We did it in spite of a lot of problems which we could well have done without, but we did it and I shall always be very, very proud of that.'

Illingworth's sense of satisfaction is quite understandable. Not only had he been the soul of consistency with bat and ball – only once in ten innings had he been dismissed for less than 20 – he'd led his side superbly. Whatever personal differences might have existed off the field, the challenge of playing Australia brought them closer together. Illingworth encouraged them to congregate in the captain's suite where they could share a beer and relax, so that even the reserves were made to feel important, and he imposed no limits on a player's socialising, provided he performed the next day. On the penultimate evening of the final Test with the game finely balanced, D'Oliveira sought Illingworth's permission to attend a concert by the popular Puerto Rican guitarist Jose Feliciano. Illingworth left the decision up to him, but warned him about the potential pitfalls of a late night on the town before such a crucial day's play. D'Oliveira accepted his advice and opted to stay in and watch television instead.

According to D'Oliveira, Illingworth was the best captain under whom he ever played because he backed his players to the hilt. 'No skipper got more out of his side than Ray,' he wrote in his autobiography, an assessment that his team-mates shared. According to Knott, Illingworth was superb under pressure and, as a very honest and understanding person, won the allegiance of his players. 'He gave me the feeling that we could win under his leadership in any situation. He was always prepared to fight on, convinced that you had to give everything until the game was won or lost. … You could be losing a game but he could still get the best out of everybody and transform it, as the opposition might start to panic or play badly.'

The team greatly respected his concern for their welfare, so that even Underwood, never his greatest admirer, wrote, 'Illingworth looked after his players' interests. He was always willing to tackle the authorities on their behalf and insisted on the best for his team. He was not the ideal choice of captain in the eyes of many people, particularly when it came to handling the social duties [but] his mission was to beat the Australians, not to perform as an after-dinner speaker.'

Illingworth allowed Snow to take it easy in state games to keep himself fresh for the Tests and he encouraged Boycott to play a few more shots, with the result that Boycott played the best cricket of his career. 'Geoffrey would always look after himself as a batsman and knowing that, you had to use him as best you could in a team effort,' Illingworth recalled. 'I got through to Geoffrey on that tour better than anyone else has ever got through to him.'

When Underwood was jeered by the Hill at Sydney for dropping a catch, Illingworth moved him to another position away from his detractors. Willis recalled him being very kind to him, bowling him in short spells, while according to Lever, his help and advice meant that he returned home a better bowler.

Tactically, Illingworth was a shrewd psychologist who conveyed his plans to his players and left them in no doubt as to what he required. Those who failed to deliver, such as paceman Ken Shuttleworth bowling the wrong line to Greg Chappell at Perth, were rebuked, but always in private and with no lasting recriminations. 'Illy was great,' recalled Snow. 'He was a good, down-to-earth professional captain; the man he is in real life. It was very necessary. You have to be hard-nosed as a captain playing away in Australia. There is not much quarter given. We knew Illy had that.'

As a fast bowler, Snow appreciated Illingworth's understanding of his mentality and whether or not he was in rhythm. If he was struggling, he would take him off and try him again later. He also appreciated his ability to sum up a batsman's strengths and weaknesses and set his field accordingly. In the fourth Test at Sydney, Illingworth placed Underwood at fly slip, since Ian Chappell liked to slash at the short fast one and Underwood soon caught him there off Snow. The ploy impressed John Woodcock, who called it 'a tactical triumph for England'.

According to Boycott, Illingworth's great ability was to read a game. 'He was a brilliant tactical captain. Ray did not follow the ball or wait for things to happen, he tried to work out the opposition beforehand and stay two steps ahead of the game.

'His finest decision was to play five bowlers in all the Tests, even though it left us with only five recognised batsmen. It was risky, as we could be short of runs, but he wanted as many bowling options as possible to control the opposition batsmen. If you do that well in the field you will not need to score as many runs.

'His field placings were excellent. For example, Doug Walters used to duck with his bat in the air like a periscope, so Ray put a fielder at third man, three-quarters of the way to the fence, and we caught Doug there in one innings.'

From an Australian perspective, Ian Chappell considered Illingworth the finest captain he encountered, while according to his brother Greg, 'Illingworth's side in 1970/71 were, mentally, the toughest England side I played against. He subjected us to mental intimidation by aggressive field placings and physical intimidation by constant use of his pace attack. Winning to Illingworth was something he expected of himself and demanded of his team.'

In contrast to the grudging respect that Illingworth's uncompromising ethos generated in Australia, the manner of his victory troubled the English cricketing establishment, none more so than the venerable E.W. Swanton. He wrote that the Ashes had been retaken at a heavy and totally unnecessary cost in terms of sportsmanship. Shortly after returning from Australia, Illingworth appeared on BBC Radio 4's *It's Your Line*, hosted by Robin Day, and made some dismissive comments about Swanton's remoteness from the players.

Swanton happened to be listening and rang in to challenge Illingworth's depiction of him. Illingworth then conveyed his unhappiness with Swanton's end-of-tour assessment that MCC had helped lower standards, comments that Swanton stood by. 'Yes, I did say that, Ray, with very great reluctance. I thought I'd never hope to see an England captain threatening or seeming to threaten by wagging his finger at an Australian umpire with twenty or thirty thousand Australians looking on. If the game is going to come to this sort of pass where the umpire is going to be openly challenged on the field, I think that the end of cricket in the Test match sense is really pretty near.'

When Illingworth asked him whether he thought the umpire was right on that occasion, Swanton replied, 'Well, I think that the umpire must always be right, and he must always be respected by the players.'

Swanton repeated his comments at the official tour dinner at Lord's, a distinctly funereal affair when Illingworth was all but shunned by the MCC hierarchy, and the Cricket Council, cricket's new governing body in the UK, having absorbed the official tour report, warned all players that dissent towards umpiring decisions would not be tolerated. (In 1974 Illingworth and Knott won undisclosed damages from Beaverbrook Newspapers Limited, publishers of the *Sunday Express*, for an article Denis Compton wrote at the end of the Australian tour accusing them of cheating for applying undue pressure on the umpires.) A decade later, Willis noted that, compared with the conduct of certain sides at the end of the 1970s, Illingworth's side was a paragon of virtue, but for the moment they were tainted in the eyes of those who clung to the amateur ethos in an age of growing professional egalitarianism.

Chapter 8

The Ashes Retained

FOLLOWING FOUR months in Australia the weary tourists proceeded to New Zealand, denuded of much of their cricket kit, as Illingworth recalled. 'We had to go with a team bag with five bats and five pairs of pads. "Bloody hell," I said, "We're playing Sunday School cricket here."'

As a reward for his impeccable team spirit in Australia, the tour management wanted to give reserve wicketkeeper Bob Taylor a game in the first Test at Christchurch, but their gesture upset Knott. Although a good friend of Taylor's, he thought that Test teams should always be picked on merit and not sentiment. He conveyed his views to Illingworth who agreed, only then to go along with his fellow selectors' contention that Taylor should get a game. 'I was amazed that Illingworth should have changed his mind or have had it changed for him,' Knott later wrote. 'It was a very rare occasion when I had found Illingworth to be inconsistent.'

Having acted as 12th man for the first Test, which England won comfortably, Knott returned for the second Test when his 101 and 96 saved his side from probable defeat.

Although the cricket authorities afforded the team a tepid welcome on their return, others were more generous. They were entertained at 10 Downing Street by prime minister Ted Heath and Illingworth was given a civic reception and dinner jointly by Leicester City Council and Leicestershire County Council in the Lord Mayor's Rooms, where he was presented with a fox silver goblet donated by readers of the *Leicester Daily Mercury*. He was also given a standing ovation at the annual banquet of Leicestershire's 200 Club, granted life membership of Leicestershire CCC, who commissioned a portrait of him to be hung in the Members' Long Room, and elected the Lord's Taverners' Cricketer of the Year.

After the euphoria of regaining the Ashes, the summer's Tests against Pakistan and India proved something of an anticlimax. Played for the most part in unseasonal weather, in front of sparse crowds, the cricket lacked inspiration despite both countries offering stiffer resistance than on previous visits. With Snow unavailable because of injury, the England attack toiled long and hard in the first Test at Edgbaston, a game which Pakistan totally dominated only for bad weather to deprive them of victory.

With the Lord's Test consigned to a draw because of incessant rain, everything depended on the final Test at Headingley. In a tense, fluctuating game, England were struggling in their second innings at 142/5, a mere 108 ahead, when an out-of-form Illingworth came to the wicket. Had he been caught in the gully on 1 by Asif Iqbal, they would almost certainly have lost. As it was, he survived this chance, and another one on 22, to add 106 with D'Oliveira.

Set 233 to win, Pakistan began the last day at 25/0. 'Talk about pressure,' Boycott wrote in his diary. 'This is when your captain needs a cool head and to be seen to be quietly in control. Raymond sometimes asked my opinion, and when he came to me that fifth morning he had a clear idea that the ball was still hard, the pitch was turning and he fancied a bowl straight away before the batsmen could get in. He wanted a little reassurance that his thinking was on the right track. Many times for Yorkshire, I had watched when Raymond had to bowl a side out and he rarely failed. He could handle the pressure and I had seen for myself when he read the pitch correctly and fancied a bowl he usually got wickets. I said go for it.'

Illingworth duly opened the bowling at the Football Stand End and in his first over he dismissed Aftab Gul and Zaheer Abbas in consecutive balls before having Mushtaq Mohammad caught at short leg off one that turned.

A fine 91 from opener Sadiq Mohammad restored Pakistan's morale and put them in sight of victory, but Illingworth continued to apply the pressure. At 184/5, he turned to D'Oliveira, who responded by removing Sadiq and Intikhab Alam in one over, before calling up Lever to take the new ball and he finished off the innings by taking three wickets in four balls. As England celebrated victory by 25 runs, Peter Laker wrote: 'Illingworth confirmed yesterday that he is out on his own both as a cricketer and a tactician. All day he marshalled his bowling resources with a quiet brilliance.'

Amid the general acclaim there was one dissenter. Robin Hobbs, the Essex leg-spinner who'd made his England debut against India in 1967, resented his omission from the 1970/71 tour to Australia on the grounds that Illingworth thought his bowling too expensive. Never an admirer of Illingworth, he told him on the eve of the Headingley Test that he shouldn't be playing because of the sluggish nature of the wicket, concerns that Illingworth brushed aside.

Having bowled respectably in the first innings, Hobbs felt under great pressure when brought on at a critical stage in the second innings and, consequently, he bowled poorly, conceding 22 runs in four overs. Convinced that he'd played his final Test, a dejected Hobbs drove himself home afterwards in his whites and wrote disparaging comments about Illingworth on the walls of his lounge that he was painting. While honest enough to accept that he'd let Illingworth down with his temperamental approach, he wrote, 'Ray Illingworth was a bloody good cricketer but as a captain he was selfish, most of the top sportsmen are. I've got nothing against him that way. I just didn't like him that much and the feeling was mutual.'

The Pakistan series had exposed the fragility of England's batting and that fragility was just as glaring against India, fresh from a historic series win against West Indies in the Caribbean. Rain brought the first Test at Lord's to a premature end with India needing 38 to win with two wickets left, but the match will always be remembered for an unseemly incident in India's second innings. In the last over before lunch, Snow was bowling to Farokh Engineer, who pushed a ball on the leg side and went for a quick single. In his efforts to field the ball, the hefty Snow barged into the non-striker, the diminutive Sunil Gavaskar, and sent him flying to the ground with no bat in hand. As Gavaskar reached his crease, Snow picked up his bat and casually tossed it back to him with no air of contrition.

The incident, replayed extensively on television, shocked onlookers and when the players came off for lunch Snow was asked to apologise to Gavaskar by chairman of selectors Alec Bedser, which he agreed to do once he'd changed his shirt. While he was changing, MCC secretary Billy Griffith entered the dressing room with Illingworth's permission and started shouting at Snow. The conversation became so heated that Illingworth had to ask Griffith to leave, since he didn't want his players distracted at a crucial stage of the game. Although Snow did apologise to Gavaskar, the critics were in an unforgiving mood, especially in light of the side's conduct in Australia. Both Swanton and Woodcock not only castigated Snow for his breach of sportsmanship, they also criticised Illingworth for not intervening and offering an apology of his own. As it was, Snow was dropped for the next Test as a disciplinary measure, despite undying support from Illingworth. He later wrote, 'I suppose it can be argued that, because he was left out for reasons other than cricket, the captain's arguments did not carry the same weight as usual, but I still think it was an unwarranted over-reaction.' With Boycott missing for the rest of the series because of injury, England were once again deprived of their best two players.

In dank conditions at Old Trafford, England made an uncertain start against a little-known seamer called Abid Ali and were once again indebted to Illingworth, who scored his second Test century, putting on 168 for the eighth wicket with Peter Lever, who scored a career-best 88 not out. Thereafter they dominated the game and seemed destined for a decisive victory before rain washed out play on the final day.

England also seemed in control of the final Test at The Oval, where Illingworth's 5-70 helped gain them a first-innings lead of 71, only then for their batsmen to throw away their advantage. On a slow turner, they were bowled out for 101 by wrist-spinner Chandrasekhar to lose by four wickets, India's first Test win in England, a victory that gave them the rubber.

Although critical of the authorities at The Oval for preparing a subcontinent type of wicket, Illingworth was magnanimous in defeat, his first as England captain, and one of the biggest disappointments of his career. He admitted that his team had deserved their fate because they had batted badly in both innings. Several of the leading players looked jaded and a winter at home seemed to be in everyone's interest, especially with the Australians due the following summer.

Although Ian Chappell's side was dismissed as one of the worst Australian teams ever to tour England, Illingworth knew better. Not only did he admire the batting prowess of the Chappell brothers and the budding potential of pace bowler Dennis Lillee, he also rated Chappell's positive leadership, evident to him when he captained MCC against the Australians. 'I was leading MCC and there was a lot of swearing going on,' he later recalled. 'Even John Inverarity said a few words and I burst out laughing because that wasn't his go, was it? Ian was all about trying to toughen up his men. He did that and even though the umpires made reports in the match, things settled down. But the Aussies got tougher and a whole lot better as the series wore on.' Alarmed about the potential threat posed by off-spinner Ashley Mallett, who took five wickets in MCC's first innings, Illingworth wrote how a new type of blow-up cover had allowed moisture to settle and enabled him to extract an abnormal amount of turn. 'It's amazing what sort of comment a shrewd captain can come up with when an opposing player starts to pose a real threat,' wrote Mallett, who was unaccountably omitted from the side for the first three Tests.

On 8 June 1972, the first day of the first Test against Australia, Illingworth celebrated his 40th birthday. In contrast to Australia's accent on youth, England continued to rely on experience, even recalling Mike Smith for the first three Tests and Peter Parfitt for the final three. Their one concession to youth came with the selection of the charismatic South African all-rounder Tony Greig, who, despite several appearances against the Rest of the World in 1970, was making his official debut. A tough competitor in the Australian mould, he made an immediate impact in the low-scoring first Test at Old Trafford with two half-centuries and valuable wickets.

In dank conditions ideal for seam bowling, Illingworth, on winning the toss, took a gamble by batting first. His concern that he'd made the correct decision was accentuated by the brief pre-lunch session in which Boycott took a painful blow on the elbow from Lillee. Unable to grip his bat properly, he didn't resume after lunch, but with England soon in some trouble, Illingworth decreed that he should bat again that day. 'He was showing some stress at our perilous position,' Boycott later wrote. 'It was no good arguing with Raymond when he had made up his mind, and he was the captain. I had to get on with it.'

Resuming at 118/4, Boycott didn't last long and it was mainly down to Greig's 57 that England made 249. They then embarrassed themselves with some woeful slip catching, as Greig later recalled: 'We all turned up at the ground and realised there were no first and second slips. They'd just completely overlooked it. I was one candidate, John Snow was a fast bowler who always wanted to come in from the outfield and go in the slips, so he was another. In order to work out who should play there, Illingworth said, "Come on, let's have some deflections and we'll work it out." Snow was great in the practice: everything stuck. So, he was put at first slip and I went at second.'

When England went out to field on the second afternoon, conditions were ideal for seamer Geoff Arnold. In his second over

Australia opener Keith Stackpole edged successive balls into the slips; the first was dropped by Greig and the second by Snow.

'By now Arnold's looking over in disbelief and Illingworth can't bear to look at us,' commented Greig. 'We could hear him whinge all morning *[sic]* about dropped catches. Then, in late afternoon, the ball went straight to third slip, hit Illy on the chest and bounced off. It saved the day for all of us.

'He went on air that evening and said, "This is the worst seeing ground in the whole world. How can you expect to catch catches here when you've got all these red brick buildings? It's ridiculous."'

Despite their frailties in the slip cordon, Arnold and Snow still managed to bowl Australia out for 142. Knowing that Ian Chappell was prone to the hook, Illingworth instructed his pace bowlers to bounce him early and when Greig dropped short with his first ball to him, Chappell hit it straight to Mike Smith on the fine leg boundary. As he retreated to the pavilion, Chappell heard Illingworth say, 'Bloody good shot for nowt as I have seen.'

Holding a first-innings lead of 107, England scored 234 in their second innings and Australia, needing 342 to win, were all out for 252, the only serious resistance coming from Rod Marsh, his swashbuckling 91 including a sustained assault on spinner Norman Gifford. According to Greig, the assault should never have occurred. 'Ray Illingworth should have bowled himself instead of Norman Gifford. He was an off-spinner and would have turned the ball away from the left-hander. He would have been much harder to hit or would have at least induced a mishit before long. Every time the ball sailed into the crowd I thought, "Illy, why aren't you bowling?"'

Throughout his time as England captain, Illingworth was constantly badgering the cricket establishment to get better treatment for his players who, he thought, had been downtrodden for too long. Once he was upset to find himself travelling to London second class when a county club official was travelling first class on the same train to attend the same committee meeting. He reasoned that because they were both serving on the same committee, they should be accorded the same treatment. On another occasion, he was embarrassed when, as England captain, he invited several guests to the team hotel for dinner and was told by the waiter that his choice from the menu exceeded the team meal allowance. A similar slight occurred during the Old Trafford Test, as he later recalled: 'We were having a meal in the hotel restaurant and the bill came to £2.75 a head. Our meal allowance was then £2 and Donald Carr, who was then in charge, said we would have to pay the difference but I said no, we were playing for England, we had eaten the meal we required and we didn't intend paying the 75p excess. After a long debate and several consultations with officials, I won my point. I know that impressed Tony [Greig].'

At Lord's, Australia gave a first cap to seamer Bob Massie and in one of the most sensational Test debuts in cricket history, Massie, exploiting the humid atmosphere to perfection, sent England crashing to defeat. Astounded by his match figures of 16-137, a world record for a debutant, Illingworth was later asked by the *Daily Mail*'s Brian Scovell whether the Australians were using an illegal substance to shine one side of the ball. Illingworth thought this was quite possible and while asking not to be quoted he could write it as definite. He threatened to alert the umpires if it happened again, which it didn't.

Fortunate to get away with a draw at Trent Bridge, the England selectors made several changes for Headingley, the most notable of which was Underwood for Gifford. It was perhaps one of Illingworth's few errors in selection that he didn't play the former more often, mainly because he doubted his effectiveness on a flat wicket, but while there was some truth in his analysis, Underwood's record was superior to Gifford's or that of any other rival. At Headingley, on a grassless, mottled pitch infected by a fungus called fusarium and highly conducive to spin, Australia, on winning the toss, batted first. Overcoming the early loss of Ross Edwards to Snow, they lunched at 79/1, but afterwards the game changed dramatically as Underwood and Illingworth, who bowled Doug Walters with a beauty, made Australia look like novices.

Bowled out for 146, Australia fought back through off-spinner Mallett and, with England struggling at 128/7, the game seemed wide open, before Illingworth and Snow added 104 for the eighth wicket. Used to grafting on slow Yorkshire turners, the former batted flawlessly, mixing solid defence with an effective dispatch of the loose ball. Just before the close, he shimmied down the wicket to hit Mallett high over long-on for six to bring up his half-century, a milestone that won him a standing ovation from the Yorkshire faithful.

When Illingworth was last out for 57, England led by 117 and with Underwood near unplayable in their second innings, Australia could only muster 136. Requiring a mere 20 for victory, England won by nine wickets to retain the Ashes. According to Woodcock, 'Illingworth's handling of the whole operation was shrewd and effective. His batting, bowling, fielding and field placing all showed him for what he is – an outstanding competitor on the big day.' Although unhappy with the Headingley pitch, Australia kept their counsel and were rewarded with a superb one at The Oval, one that lasted for six days, since an additional day had been allocated to the game to help get a result.

In a classic Test, England struggled throughout against Lillee and were indebted to Knott, who followed his late flurry of 92 in the first innings with 63 in the second. Had they had Boycott back after injury it might well have been different, but having ruled himself out because of his injured finger, he then riled Illingworth by scoring a double century for Yorkshire against Leicestershire on the Saturday of the Test. Expressing his anger in public, Illingworth accused Boycott of lacking patriotism. 'I was furious and made my feelings clear to Bedser [chairman of selectors] when the Test match ended,' Boycott wrote. 'Illy was quickly on the phone, presumably at Bedser's suggestion, but there was no hint that he regretted what he had said. He was dismissive and quite unrepentant.'

The row continued to fester. When Boycott joined up with the England players to play in the one-day internationals that followed the final Test, he tried to explain to Illingworth that his finger was still healing, but Illingworth wouldn't listen to his explanation. Too angry to talk, his fury reminded Boycott of Ken Taylor's advice to him as a Yorkshire newcomer, 'Never argue with Raymond. You cannot win and he will always hold a grudge.'

Australia required 242 to win and were making solid progress against the spinners when, at 100/1, Illingworth fell heavily in the bowler's footmarks and twisted his ankle. Helped off in agony, he was unable to play any further part in the match, a serious loss to a side that regarded him as something of a cult figure. According to Woodcock, 'He means so much to this particular side that as its inspiration he was inevitably missed. On Tuesday evening after he had left the field with his ankle sprained it was as though the rest of the side kept looking round for him, unable to come to terms with his absence.'

England were also deprived of the services of Snow and D'Oliveira on the final morning and although Greig and Underwood caused a few early shocks, an unbeaten sixth-wicket partnership of 71 by Paul Sheahan and Rod Marsh saw them safely home. While regretting his lack of opportunity to bowl on a sixth-day pitch, Illingworth acknowledged that Australia merited a share of the rubber, a tribute to the positive leadership of his opposite number. 'I loved pitting my wits against Chappelli,' he later recalled. 'He was always a step ahead, the hallmark of a good captain. He didn't allow the game to meander along. He made things happen. I noticed a huge difference with the Australian side once Ian took over from Bill Lawry.'

In his review of the series, John Arlott wrote: 'Illingworth performed admirably in every department. His captaincy was as calmly thoughtful and determined as ever. He batted coolly and played Lillee as consistently soundly as any member of the team; upon opportunity he bowled effectively; and when he argued that he wanted to bowl at The Oval, he meant that he believed he could have won the match; and he does not lightly make such claims. He also took one or two catches which would have been a credit to a younger man.'

Even before his injury, which kept him out of the rest of the season, Illingworth announced that he would be unavailable for MCC's tour of India and Pakistan that winter. Aside from the physical demands of the eight-Test itinerary for a man aged 40, Illingworth fretted about the conditions out there. Four years earlier he'd written in his autobiography *Spinner's Wicket*, 'India is one place I would never tour. I have known quite a few players, English and Australian who have toured there, and have never been one hundred per cent fit afterwards. Frank Lowson, who played for Yorkshire and England in the 1950s, used to tell me that he was never the same player after touring India. Every MCC tour of India and Pakistan is bedevilled by illness. The hygiene and sanitation in these countries is still many years behind our own standards.'

Years later, when managing England during the 1996 World Cup in Pakistan and driving through Lahore, Illingworth was asked by one of his players, Robin Smith, whether he'd ever previously toured there. 'No,' he replied. 'I was picked but made myself unavailable. It wasn't like it is now, no nice hotels. We would have to stay in places like that,' pointing at some shacks at the roadside.

'Anyhow, I had started a business selling Christmas cards and I could make more money in a week in Scotland than I would playing for England. I mean, you can get someone else to work for you, but they never work as hard as you, do they?'

Having relinquished the captaincy, Illingworth fully appreciated that he might not be reinstated the following season, especially if his successor, Tony Lewis, took to high office. As it was, Lewis proved a highly popular leader without quite suggesting that his batting was international standard and after a Test trial match at Hove, in which Illingworth out-manoeuvred him, the selectors resorted to a classic British compromise – Illingworth would captain the side and Lewis would be his deputy. It was an arrangement that lasted for only one match because Lewis had to withdraw due to chronic knee trouble, an ailment which led to his retirement from the game the following year.

Back in charge, Illingworth, granted a CBE in the New Year Honours List, did little in the first two Tests against New Zealand in which England narrowly won the first and had the worst of a draw in the second, but that didn't diminish his authority. Following his success as an opener in Pakistan, Dennis Amiss maintained this position against New Zealand, but his century in the second innings of the first Test was tainted by his running-out of Boycott. 'He was obviously upset about it,' wrote Amiss. 'He threatened to run me out in the next Test match. So I had to go to Ray Illingworth our captain and say, "You've got to sort this out. Boycs seems to think I'd done it on purpose but it was just one of those things." Ray called us together after the dinner at the next Test, took us outside. Ray handled it superbly. After Boycs had been going on a bit, Ray turned to him and said, "Hang on, it's just bad luck. Dennis has apologised. Now, you stay here and sort this out, otherwise you'll never play for England again while I'm captain." I liked Ray for that. Here he was, telling a Yorkshireman that there were other people just as important in the team.'

England's innings victory in the third Test at Headingley coincided with Illingworth's return to form. His 65 helped ensure his reappointment for the three-Test series against West Indies, a side on the cusp of greatness. After a heavy defeat at The Oval and an ill-tempered draw at Edgbaston, England were trounced at Lord's. Losing the toss in ideal batting conditions, Illingworth for the first time looked powerless to stop the carnage as West Indies piled on the runs with Rohan Kanhai, Sobers and Bernard Julien all hitting centuries. Declaring at 652/8, they inflicted early losses on England on the second evening and the next day they made light work of the rest of the order, not least Illingworth, out first ball, beautifully caught by Sobers at leg slip off Lance Gibbs.

Dismissed for 233 on the third day, they were forced to follow on and lost Amiss and Boycott that evening, the latter in the final over to an irresponsible hook to deep square leg. Manhandled by West Indian supporters as he returned to the pavilion, he was livid by the time he reached the dressing room and he vented his indignation at his partner Brian Luckhurst for refusing an easy single earlier that over. The argument became so heated that Illingworth intervened and when Boycott continued to let fly, he brought in selector Brian Taylor to calm them down. Later that night at 3am, Boycott woke with a nosebleed so severe that he was admitted to hospital to have it cauterised. That visit to hospital gave rise to rumours that Illingworth had punched Boycott in the dressing room, an allegation entirely without substance.

With English spirits crushed, it's hardly surprising that they capitulated thereafter, all out for 193, to lose by an innings and 226 runs, their second-heaviest defeat ever. Even Illingworth, so often the retriever of lost causes, failed to rise to the occasion, caught Kanhai bowled Gibbs for 13. It was to be his final Test innings.

Although his captaincy had never lacked critics within the MCC hierarchy, Illingworth entered the Lord's Test as favourite to captain England in the West Indies that winter, but both the margin of defeat and the manner of it gave ammunition to those who wanted him out. (Illingworth was convinced he was the victim of political intervention by someone from outside the selectors.) Now that some of the shine had come off his leadership, his age and his fading powers as an international all-rounder – 181 runs in nine innings and six wickets for 450 runs that summer – came into the reckoning. Perhaps more damning was the defensive cricket that England had played that year, especially in comparison with West Indies, and the need for something more dynamic in the Caribbean. John Woodcock wrote: 'He will be remembered for his single-minded pursuit of the attritional style. Always a resolute cricketer himself, particularly in a crisis, he made the England side a hard one to beat rather than an easy one to watch.

'For various reasons Illingworth will be a difficult man to follow. For one thing, he has become over the last two or three years a cult figure. He aroused very strong feelings both of support and opposition.'

Middlesex captain Mike Brearley offered a more positive assessment, believing that his virtues extended way beyond his attritional style. 'He is very open, a lover of argument; he will have a dispute out with anyone, face to face. He supports his players, but expects 100 per cent at all times. He is a devoted captain, never losing concentration, confident in his own ways; he has done marvellously at critical moments. He respects hard work in others, having worked hard himself. He has been a symbol for many cricketers and cricket followers in a still class-infected game.'

Given the choice as his successor, Illingworth would have plumped for Boycott. He wrote, 'Boycs should have been my vice-captain on the 1970/71 Ashes tour and, tactically, he was the closest thing to me at that time. If I sounded him out, he would give an honest and forthright opinion. A captain should have one man he can bounce things off. For me it was Boycott. He read the game very well. Even with my own bowling, I would go up to him and before I'd asked a question, he had told me the answer. He thought on the same lines as me.'

The man appointed to succeed Illingworth was Kent captain Mike Denness, who led his side to two one-day trophies that year and who'd been vice-captain to Lewis in India and Pakistan. By a quirk of the fixture list Kent were due to host Leicestershire at Folkestone on the day of his appointment and the press were out in force to witness the two captains tossing up in the middle.

Denness recalled Illingworth being very sad although he offered his congratulations. At the end of the day, they had a drink together in one of the hospitality marquees where Illingworth talked openly and helpfully about the England set-up. The next day he received a warm reception from the Kent crowd when he came out to bat and, defiant to the last, he hit 79 not out, his highest score of the season.

Although Illingworth never played for England again, his ghost continued to stalk the side for the next three years as his two immediate successors struggled to impose their authority. During the MCC tour of the West Indies, where he was writing for *The Sun* and the *News of the World*, he spent much time in the England dressing room with many players who thought that he should still be in charge. When Denness asked Boycott whether he would bat at number four in the third Test to help bolster the middle order, Boycott confided in Illingworth. Illingworth said that it would be good for him to be seen to be helping the team's needs by complying, advice that Boycott reluctantly accepted.

Before that Test, Tony Greig also consulted Illingworth about his bowling. Illingworth told him that the swing he used back home would never work in the Caribbean and advised him to bowl his off-cutters. He thought that Greig with his enormous height could get bounce and turn, especially against the West Indian left-handers, of which there were four in their top six, and his hunch was fully vindicated by Greig's remarkable match figures of 13-156 in the final Test, which England narrowly won to help them square the series.

That result, which was hardly merited, helped Denness to cling on to the captaincy, much to Boycott's chagrin, but after England's crushing defeat in Australia the following winter, there were calls for Illingworth to replace him. Even when Greig took over from Denness in the wake of England's heavy defeat in the first Test against Australia in July 1975, Illingworth, in fine form for Leicestershire, was being touted as a player. Up against the formidable opening attack of Dennis Lillee and Jeff Thomson, Greig asked Close, 'Where are the players who can stand up to these Aussies?' Close replied, 'Well, there's me and Illy.'

Close gained his chance against West Indies the following summer and as England slumped to a 3-0 defeat, the demands for Illingworth's return as captain continued, demands that he was only too happy to consider. At 44, he'd lost none of his enthusiasm for the challenge, but age aside, the selectors decided to stick with Greig, who later excelled on the tour to India, and when they ditched him in May 1977 following his involvement with the rebel World Series Cricket, they now had a ready replacement in vice-captain Brearley. The Illingworth era was well and truly over.

Chapter 9

'Wise Old Fox'

ILLINGWORTH USED to say that his ten years at Leicestershire were the happiest of his career and it is easy to see why. For not only did he transform an unfashionable club into a power in the land, he flourished in an atmosphere that was much more accommodating than anything he'd ever experienced at Yorkshire. The players were invited into the Leicestershire committee room – Illingworth never entered the Yorkshire one – and the committee mixed easily with the players and their wives, so that Shirley and the girls greatly enjoyed staying in Leicester during the summer holidays. More important, the committee allowed Mike Turner and him to get on with running the playing side without constant meddling.

The key to his success at Leicestershire was his productive partnership with secretary/manager Turner. A former cricketer himself, Turner played a few games for the club before swapping the playing side for administration, becoming the youngest secretary, aged 25. Enthusiastic and innovative in his approach, he pioneered the Midland Knockout Competition in 1962, and its popularity was the harbinger for the Gillette Cup the following year. He also developed a winter football competition for members similar to the football pools, which enabled the club to purchase their ground, Grace Road, from the local authority in 1965 and oversee its renovation.

Despite the club's small membership – the size of the county population was 600,000 compared to Yorkshire's five million – and the difficulties attracting sponsorship in a city which played second fiddle to football and rugby – he drew on his wide range of contacts to keep the club in profit for 20 successive years.

Continuing Leicestershire's traditional policy of recruiting players from other counties – Yorkshire in particular – to boost their staff, Turner signed ex-Surrey and England spinner Tony Lock in 1965. Appointed captain the following season, Lock revitalised a club that had fallen on hard times with his infectious enthusiasm and charismatic personality, taking them from 14th to third in the Championship in two years. Unwilling to commit himself to another year in 1968 – he was now living in Australia – the club reverted to type under its previous captain Maurice Hallam, posing a challenge to Illingworth on his arrival in 1969.

After a month of pre-season training which promoted a great team spirit, that spirit was carried into the early games and at the end of May Leicestershire stood second in the Championship, but the loss of Illingworth and all-rounder Barry Knight to England duty upset their momentum. The new sense of purpose began to wither under Hallam's leadership and Leicestershire won only two more Championship matches that season – both under Illingworth, who headed both the county batting and bowling averages.

There was little improvement in 1970 when Illingworth was again absent because of Test calls and Knight had emigrated to Australia, but the following year brought an improvement in both the Championship and the JPL. Opener Mick Norman recalls

Illingworth playing cards with team-mates Peter Marner, Clive Inman and John Cotton in a break for bad weather during his first year in charge. When the three of them reacted negatively to the announcement that play was about to resume, Illingworth exclaimed, 'What are you talking about? We're professional players and should be playing.' It is perhaps no coincidence that all three were gone within a couple of years as Turner and Illingworth looked to strengthen the staff with players who shared their winning mentality. The club had already signed Australian fast bowler Graham McKenzie in 1969 and he was followed by Rhodesian batsman Brian Davison, Yorkshire all-rounder Chris Balderstone, former England pace bowler Ken Higgs and Warwickshire seamer Norman McVicker. 'Ray Illingworth took me to Leicestershire,' Balderstone later recounted. 'I might be a decent bloke on the outside but he knew I was mentally hard through football. Cricketers might think they're pretty hard but they're not compared to footballers.'

Autocratic in his approach and bolstered by his aura as a renowned England captain, Illingworth galvanised his team to greater heights, giving them fresh belief in themselves. 'On the field he had this permanent air of being in control,' recalled England batsman David Gower, who made his Leicestershire debut in 1975. 'Even in times of trouble he always gave the impression that he knew just what he was doing and that everything was in hand.' Committed to the highest standards of dress, punctuality and practice, he fashioned the team very much in his own image. 'At the outset, when Ray Illingworth had been appointed club captain, we had introduced strict disciplinary procedures relating to the conduct of players on and off the field and there were also strict dress codes,' recalled Mike Turner.

'I have particularly mentioned discipline and dress codes because Brian Davison was one of the young players who had matured and became established in the side by 1970. On the first day of training, Brian arrived at Grace Road looking like a 1960s hippy, wearing an army khaki overcoat which went down to his ankles. He was unshaven. Brian also had a reputation for living life to the full – and he did!

'Illingworth and I decided that, because Davison had a residential qualification to serve, we would not add his name to the list of Leicestershire's registered cricketers until we were satisfied that he had completely accepted the need to conform.

'In fact, he matured into a top-class player, an excellent clubman and one of the mainstays of the team throughout the 70s.'

One day in his pomp when Davison was running late and had to make an expensive dash from Leicester to Northampton by taxi, Illingworth refused to refund his expenses, knowing that the younger players would be influenced by the fact that a senior professional was subject to the same treatment as everyone else.

Illingworth rarely shirked tough decisions, especially when it came to team selection. Among his most contentious was the omission of all-rounder Jack Birkenshaw from the Benson and Hedges Cup finals of 1972, 1974 and 1975. 'It was one of the most disappointing moments of my life,' the latter recalled, alluding to the 1972 game. 'I had been a regular in the side up to the final, bowling well and doing okay with the bat. But for the final Illy decided to drop me because he wanted a lively fielder at midwicket.

'I was so down I refused to do 12th man duties. I don't think Illy was too happy about that.' (Fielding aside, Illingworth justified the inclusion of Paul Haywood by the vital runs he scored in his match-winning partnership with Balderstone.)

In 1975 Illingworth took the rare step of involving the committee in the dropping of Graham McKenzie for loss of form, but, ever the perfect gentleman, McKenzie accepted his lot, admitting that he'd been struggling for wickets. Thankfully, he was soon restored to favour in his final season and was able to play an invaluable part in the side's Championship success.

One of the more unusual omissions was that of opener Barry Dudleston in 1977 after a run of low scores. Illingworth told him that he'd lost the knack of hitting hundreds and that he should get a game that weekend to play himself back into form. Dudleston turned out for Market Harborough second XI and scored a hundred and when Illingworth heard about this, he duly reinstated him without even asking what team he'd played for.

Praise, in line with his tough upbringing, was given out lightly. Mick Norman recalls Davison scoring a magnificent 158 against Warwickshire in the Benson and Hedges Cup in 1972 and Illingworth barely complimenting him. 'There was no sympathy with Illy,' commented Roger Tolchard. 'Everything was always expected. There were never any well-dones. I used to give him an earful about that. I also used to have a go at him for not caring. During the Championship season, we were seven down against Warwickshire at tea on the last day, with more than 100 to get, and I noticed Illy had his bag packed and was heading for the car. I was 50-odd not out. "You off, Illy?" I said. "Thanks." In the end, I made a hundred and we won by one wicket. Illy's strength was his logical thinking, his down-to-earth character.'

'Something happened to Ray the moment he walked in to a ground,' wrote Tony Lewis. 'His nose twitched, he could smell the wind and this was only in the car park. Before he had reached the middle, he could sense that it was damp two yards in from the far end or that "the ball will be moving off them tufts". He could spot a new cut of annual meadow grass from 100 yards.'

'Ray possessed as good a cricket brain as there ever has been,' wrote David Lloyd. 'When it came to the tactical side of the game, he was a clinical thinker. Forensic with his preparation – he would look at the length of the boundary, consider the direction and the strength of the wind, and was a great reader of the pitch both in terms of how much grass was on it and how much moisture was in it. If he didn't like the dimensions of a ground, he would ask the home side to alter them!'

In one Middlesex–Leicestershire encounter at Lord's, where the wicket was placed very close to the Tavern boundary, Illingworth paced 45 yards to the rope, five yards fewer than the regulations stipulated, and he refused to play on it. Another one was prepared. A particular gripe was the intrusion of hospitality marquees on to the outfield, reducing the size of the boundaries. (When he went to Leicestershire, he asked the groundsman to extend the size of the playing area and shave the outfield to help take the shine off the ball.) Once when hit into the Bostik tent at Leicester by a tail-ender, he strode over to the committee balcony and berated them for making a mockery of his spin attack.

Most serious of all, he clashed with umpire Bill Alley over a short boundary at Dean Park, Bournemouth when leading Leicestershire against Hampshire. Alley wrote, 'Ray seemed to me the sort of guy who always had to have everything absolutely in the correct order. He was a perfectionist who, quite rightly in my view, was not prepared to accept any half measures. The groundsman, in his wisdom, had marked out a wicket on the far edge of the square, making one boundary very much shorter than the other. While it was noticeably lop-sided, I was prepared to overlook it. After all, the conditions were the same for both sides. But not Ray. He was hopping mad. "How dare they ruin the game by putting the wicket in the wrong place," he fumed. He told me there was only one way around this mess. I was to order the president's tent and a little fence enclosure which surrounded it to be taken down and re-sited elsewhere. "If you don't get it moved, I'll do it myself," he said. I suddenly realised he meant business, and I had to stop him. I was forced to give him a lecture. "Be sensible, Ray," I pleaded. "There is no way I am going to get the tent taken down. It stays where it is." "Bugger the president," was his sullen reply. Eventually he saw sense and wandered back to the Leicestershire dressing room in a foul mood.'

Illingworth commanded the dressing room, as was his wont. According to Gower, while he came in for some micky-taking, he had this amazing knack of being able to switch them all on to serious business at a moment's notice. 'The five-minute bell would go; Illy clapped his hands and would unveil some masterful tactical plan.' Dudleston spoke for many when he said that without doubt Illingworth was the best cricket brain he ever played with; however well or badly the team performed he could never remember them being outmanoeuvred. 'He kept it so simple. When you went out to field you knew where to go, then subtle changes would occur as to how the opposition played. He gave people their say but most suggestions he'd already thought about. He knew his players very well and everything about the team.'

Dudleston reckoned that the great advantage of a team lacking stars was the onus it placed on all-round team effort. He recalled the Gloucestershire all-rounder Mike Procter saying to him, 'We hate playing you because we never know which player is going to perform.'

'We had a very competitive side,' recalled Higgs. 'We batted all the way down the order and there were a lot of bowlers, too, with off-spinners, two left-armers and pace.

'We knew we had the ability and if we were bowled out for a low score, we knew we could bowl out the opposition, too. We had bowlers for every type of wicket.'

Although often described as a defensive captain, Illingworth could be surprisingly adventurous, offering generous declarations on the premise that an early closure gave his bowlers more time to dismiss the opposition. A past master at keeping them interested in the chase, he would go for the kill once he'd breached their defences.

A supreme tactician also, he preyed on the vulnerabilities of opposition batsmen with deadly effect. He exposed Dennis Amiss's frailty against the short ball and persuaded the nervous Derek Randall to hole out against the spinners by crowding him with close fielders; he also saw off Basil D'Oliveira, predominantly a back-foot player, by bowling him between bat and pad with his quicker delivery.

Fast bowler Jonathan Agnew recalled Illingworth bringing himself on to bowl against Lancashire's Clive Lloyd at Grace Road in 1978 and moving Balderstone round two yards at deep square leg. A few balls later, Lloyd hit one down his throat.

Not everyone fell for Illingworth's tactics. Hampshire's Andrew Murtagh recalls an exchange when playing against him in 1975:

> I first spoke to him while he was resetting the field. He was captain of Leicestershire and he believed – he certainly announced it loudly to all and sundry – that he had spotted

> a weakness in my technique. 'We won't 'ave you there, son,' he said to one of his team. 'E won't hit it there in a moonth of Soondays.' No doubt he was right but the point was he was standing right in front of me, slap bang on the 'business area' of the pitch, just short of a length. He should not have been there. Players – bowlers, batsmen and fielders – are supposed to keep off the pitch as much as humanly possible and if they do not, they risk stern admonition from the umpires. Illingworth knew this, I knew it, and as soon as the umpires spotted it, he would be moved on. But the umpires were distracted and oblivious. The purpose of his provocative stance was unknown to me. Perhaps he was attempting to rough up the pitch. Perhaps he was attempting to intimidate me. Perhaps he was testing me out, trying to upset my concentration. There was nothing for it, I decided. I had to say something.
>
> 'Excuse me, Captain.'
>
> He frowned and looked down at his feet as if irritated they had led him to such a position while he had much more pressing matters to address. Wordlessly, he moved. Nothing said. No glowering looks. No muttered curses. The really good players do not need to say much. Their record, their reputation speaks for itself.

Illingworth's astute leadership was recognised across the circuit. Brearley rated him the shrewdest captain he knew and often bought him a drink after play to pick his brain; Sussex's Johnny Barclay, noting his ruthless outlook and his composure under pressure, thought him a tougher adversary than Brian Close; and D'Oliveira used to tell Illingworth, 'You always beat us and I'd take only two players from your side. The only difference is, you,' jabbing his finger into his chest. 'You as captain,' a comment which Illingworth took as a great compliment.

Remarkably fit for his age, although running ones and twos in the one-day matches became increasingly onerous, he would prepare for each day's play by doing some stretching exercises to loosen the muscles and have a net. With his classical action, tactical acumen and a Grace Road pitch that helped spinners in the later stages, Illingworth, while no longer an 800- or 900-overs-a-season bowler, partly because of his bad back, still proved a formidable adversary. 'I hated Illingworth; his bowling that is,' wrote Barclay, who found him as hard to face as anyone because of his relentless accuracy. 'He trotted in gently, silent, always craggy and with wily thoughts permeating his brain.' On smaller grounds and on flat pitches he would let his fellow spinners shoulder the bulk of the bowling, while reserving himself for more helpful conditions. Barclay recalls playing against Leicestershire at Hove in 1978 and not having to face his nemesis once during an innings of 94. 'His presence with the ball had a mesmeric effect. Doubtless the tinge of grass in the pitch had put him off; he felt the seamers could do the job for him. John Steele and Chris Balderstone too, but they were not in the same class as the cunning old fox himself. He let me get away with it which, for a man of his astuteness, was a rare mistake, for which I have always been grateful.'

Brearley once asked Dudleston why Illingworth's reluctance to bowl himself in favourable batting conditions hadn't undermined his respect among his team-mates. 'Dudleston's reply revealed much of Illingworth's strength as a captain,' wrote Brearley. 'In the first place, he told me, Illingworth had grown up in a hard school, in the Yorkshire side of the '50s, when you earned the right to bowl in helpful conditions only by unrelenting achievement in a competitive environment where four Test match bowlers would all be itching to get their hands on the ball. Second, Birkenshaw was a fine good-wicket bowler, a master of flight, but hardly relentless enough to run through sides cheaply. Third, Illingworth almost never failed to take wickets on a turning pitch. Dudleston told me of a match against Glamorgan at the end of May, 1976: until then Illingworth had bowled only 53 overs without taking a single wicket *[sic]*, but on the drying pitch at Swansea he took 8-38.'

Dudleston's assessment was fully supported by Birkenshaw and Tolchard. The latter told Murtagh that by now Illingworth was well into his forties, the season was long, and, as captain, he would want to play in every match without rest. On top of this, there was no better off-spinner in the country if there was a bit of turn in the pitch. 'I will always remember him, above all, for his bowling,' commented Tolchard. 'He was just magnificent.'

Competitive as ever, Illingworth lashed out at those who ruined his bowling figures. On one occasion, Somerset's Mervyn Kitchen advanced down the wicket to him and mis-hit the ball to Mick Norman, who dropped it, much to Illingworth's irritation. 'You know why you dropped it?' he said. 'Your hair got in your eyes. Get your bloody hair cut.'

Playing against Lancashire at Blackpool in 1975, Illingworth was indignant when Tolchard missed stumping opener David Lloyd off his bowling because he was standing back too far. Later, when Tolchard was injured and Dudleston replaced him as wicketkeeper, he gave Lloyd another life off Illingworth because he didn't take the bails off and this time the latter couldn't contain himself, mouthing profanities at both his wicketkeepers. (He later told Lloyd that it was the worst hundred he'd ever seen.)

On another occasion, Gower was delighted to catch Derbyshire's Ashley Harvey-Walker in the deep off Illingworth and threw the ball up in triumph, only to hear his captain screaming at him to get the ball in because it was a no-ball. Unfortunately, his flat throw hit the stumps and went for overthrows – much to everyone's amusement, except Illingworth who accused Gower of being a show pony. Recalling one of Illingworth's favourite lines, 'We'd never have got away with that when Brian Sellers was captain of Yorkshire,' Gower recounted his refusal to compromise on his impeccably high standards. 'He would hold sessions in which he crucified us for being casual and took us back to what he called the ABCs of cricket. They included using two hands to pick up the ball whenever possible – at school it had seemed "flash" to use only one hand, and I carried that attitude on to Leicester where Illy dropped it out of me.' Gower later credited him with being the greatest influence on his career.

Until his last year or so, Illingworth's batting continued to be invaluable, not least in times of trouble, and because his downfall was always down to extraneous forces, he was never out of form. Following a duck at Leicester when he received the only ball that misbehaved all day, he went straight round to the groundsman to raise concerns about the pitch. Whatever the circumstance of his dismissal, he always had an excuse whether it be the failure of the umpire to give him the right guard, the inadequacy of the sightscreen or the dazzle of the sunlight reflecting off the car windscreens. On one occasion, having missed a horrible slog, he returned to the dressing room and claimed that the bowler's grunt in his delivery stride made him think the umpire was calling no-ball. In 1980 he captained Leicestershire on a light-hearted trip to Antigua in aid of Dudleston's benefit and when compelled to bat on a damp wicket, Gower and Davison exchanged bets as to what excuse he would employ for his dismissal. Gower reckoned that he would hold the state of the wicket culpable while Davison thought he would blame the oversized hat that he'd borrowed to protect him against the sun. Both were proved right as Illingworth returned complaining bitterly that he hadn't come 5,000 miles to bat on such an impossible surface and how that ridiculous hat had restricted his vision.

A creature of habit, he didn't like to have his routine upset. Barclay recalled Gower being out just before the lunch interval against Sussex and Illingworth coming to the middle denouncing Gower for spoiling his lunch. 'Whenever he set his mind to it Illingworth could win gold medals for incessant grumbling,' Barclay wrote.

He liked to have salmon sandwiches specially made for him at home teas. When he was late one day Brian Davison scoffed the lot, much to his indignation. 'I'll have you dropped for this,' he fulminated. Few thought he was joking.

In those days county sides stayed in some notoriously shabby hotels and Illingworth would quickly be on to the manager if the food and service didn't come up to standard. On one occasion he negotiated 10 per cent off the entire team bill after being told at the breakfast table that they'd run out of sausages.

Martin Johnson, the cricket correspondent of the *Leicester Daily Mercury*, recalled the time Illingworth met his match in the proprietor of the Victoria Hotel, Canterbury, an ex-merchant seaman who ran the establishment like a ship. Having refused the team a nightcap on their arrival from Leicester, claiming it was too late, and woken them early the next morning to inquire whether they wanted their eggs boiled or poached, he then delivered his final rebuff. Fancying an aperitif before dinner, Illingworth rang several times and the proprietor finally arrived with a napkin round his neck. 'Not now, I'm having my dinner,' he told the England captain. 'In his career, it was only the second recorded instance of Ray being rendered speechless,' wrote Johnson.

Johnson was perhaps unaware of an earlier confrontation at Hull, where Leicestershire were playing Yorkshire in the JPL in 1971. Mick Norman recalled some of the team drawing up at the docks in the morning to look around. The gateman told them that visitors were forbidden on Sunday, only then to recognise Brian Booth, a fellow Lancastrian whom he knew from a shared interest in greyhound racing at Blackburn. He duly let them in. Several minutes later Illingworth pulled up in his Jaguar with Graham McKenzie and Ken Higgs and was told, 'Sorry, sir, no visitors on Sunday.'

'Wait a minute,' protested Illingworth. 'You let them in.'

'Ah yes, but they're on official business,' responded the gateman.

'But I'm Ray Illingworth,' the Leicestershire captain exclaimed.

'I don't care who you are, sir. I'm very sorry.'

Illingworth's firm belief in his own rectitude – a trait he shared with Close and Trueman – landed him in trouble on occasions, but, paradoxically, his foibles made him a more sympathetic figure among his team-mates, adding to the harmony within the Leicestershire dressing room. 'Whether he had mellowed a good deal by the time I came to know him, I could not say,' wrote Gower, 'but I certainly enjoyed his dry humour. He accepted the micky-taking, and indulged a fair amount himself.'

Leicestershire's encouraging progress in 1971, strengthened by the forceful batting of Davison, and the variety of their attack, aided by the shrewd acquisition of Higgs, augured well for the new season. They began 1972 in prime form, excelling in the Benson and Hedges Cup, the new 55-over knockout competition. Having topped the Midland zone with four wins out of four, they beat the mighty Lancashire in front of a 7,000 crowd at Grace Road with Illingworth claiming the prize wicket of Clive Lloyd in his 3-30 spell. According to John Woodcock, this was the best cricket he'd seen from Leicestershire for many years.

They went one better in the semi-final against Warwickshire where, in front of 10,000 home spectators, they again won by seven wickets. On a turning pitch, Illingworth strangled his opponents' formidable batting line-up with what *Wisden* called brilliant captaincy, and accounted for Kanhai, Mike Smith and Deryck Murray, his spell of 3-19 winning him the gold award from Len Hutton. One of his shrewdest moves on the day had been to move Higgs from mid-on to slip, where, two balls later, he caught Murray.

With Leicestershire due to play Yorkshire in the final, 36 coachloads of their supporters descended on Lord's on 22 July to witness history in the making. Admitting to unprecedented nerves before a match given the significance of the occasion, Illingworth counted his blessings when Yorkshire chose to bat first on a damp pitch and without the injured Boycott, they struggled against the Leicestershire attack. Their one ray of hope was the 11 runs they scored off Davison's first over, but Illingworth kept faith in his bowler and Davison responded by giving away a mere 11 runs in his next ten overs. A total of 136/9 was all they could muster from their allotted 55 overs and although Leicestershire were toiling at 97/5 when Illingworth was out, an undefeated sixth-wicket partnership between Balderstone and Paul Haywood saw them safely home. Delayed at the ground after the game with television and press interviews, Illingworth asked Shirley and Patricia Turner to take the gold Benson and Hedges trophy back to the team hotel in a cardboard box prior to their celebration dinner.

Later that summer Leicestershire very nearly emulated their Benson and Hedges triumph by winning the JPL, but having led the table from June they slipped up in their final game, losing by three runs to Yorkshire, while their nearest rivals, Kent, beat Worcestershire two weeks later to become champions. It might well have been different had Leicestershire not suffered a crop of injuries including Illingworth, who had damaged his ankle in the final Test at The Oval. According to *Wisden*, 'Illingworth's call to England duty has always been a problem that the county has had difficulty in overcoming – as would any other – but they were lucky to have his undivided services for the early part of the season during the Benson and Hedges competition. His influence on the field, whether for country or county, was decisive. Under him the younger players responded keenly and thrived on the unorthodox.'

The 1973 season was disappointing for Leicestershire but they were back to their best in 1974 now that Illingworth could devote all his time to his county. He began the season in prime form with the ball, taking 6-28 against Derbyshire, 5-63 against Gloucestershire and 7-18 against Nottinghamshire.

He was also to the fore in the Benson and Hedges Cup. After easing through the zonal round, Leicestershire won an epic quarter-final against the holders Kent at Canterbury by eight runs and overwhelmed Somerset at home in the semi-final. On a crumbling wicket that attracted bitter criticism from opposing captain Brian Close, Illingworth proved close to unplayable with 5-20, his victims including the brilliant Antiguan batsman Viv Richards and future England all-rounder Ian Botham.

Appearing in the final for the second time in three years, Leicestershire took the early honours against Surrey, where, on a good pitch, they bowled them out for 170, Higgs finishing the innings with a hat-trick to record figures of 4-10.

Surrey struck back immediately by dismissing Dudleston first ball and, following two controversial lbw decisions by umpire Bill Alley, they never fully recovered against an attack unerring in its accuracy. Illingworth, nursing a bruised thigh, kept fighting but he couldn't adequately accelerate and his dismissal in the final over gave Surrey victory by 27 runs.

Ten days later Kent revenged their Benson and Hedges Cup defeat by beating Leicestershire in the third round of the Gillette Cup at Canterbury. Brian Luckhurst, a centurion in the previous game, repeated his feat in a magnificent partnership of 149 with captain Mike Denness before Alan Ealham led an onslaught on Illingworth, hitting him for 18 in an over which yielded 23 runs. (The latter's final figures of 0-76 from his 12 overs were among his most profligate in a one-day game.)

Kent scored 295/8 in their 60 overs and although Davison led a spirited resistance, Leicestershire went down to the eventual Gillette winners by 66 runs. They did, however, win the JPL, losing only to Kent in their second game. In contrast to many sides, Illingworth favoured a more orthodox approach to the 40-over game, getting his bowlers to bowl at the stumps, posting slips and employing his spinners to the full, believing that they had the ability to contain.

In the same way he encouraged his openers, Dudleston and Norman, to play carefully during the first 10–15 overs to give them a solid start, knowing that he had the likes of Davison and Tolchard to accelerate in the closing stages. Later, however, he did experiment with an opening partnership of Gower and Birkenshaw, fathoming that two left-handers would put the bowlers off their line.

Having tied their penultimate game against Sussex at Hove, they met their nearest rivals, Somerset, six points behind with a game in hand, in their final one at Grace Road. In front of a 15,000 crowd, the occasion descended into acrimony when Somerset's last man Allan Jones took nearly three minutes to get to the crease to face the second ball of the 38th over, his excuse being that he'd fallen down the pavilion steps. The delay meant that Leicestershire could only bowl 39 overs and thus would lose one over in their reply, a situation that riled Illingworth enough to complain to the umpire, throw away his gum at the end of the Somerset innings and extract an apology of sorts from Close.

The controversy, however, was soon overtaken by the heavy rain which washed out further play and the two points awarded to each side were enough to guarantee Leicestershire their second title in two years. 'Leicestershire are worthy winners of this competition,' wrote Woodcock. 'They are a thoroughly good one-day side, and they do it without excessive use of medium pace. … They have a wise old fox to lead them in Illingworth, one marvellously dashing batsman in Davison, three utterly reliable faster bowlers in McKenzie, Higgs and McVicker and a telling contributor in Roger Tolchard.'

As a reward for winning the JPL, the team received a pre-season trip to Paris the following spring. Mick Norman, a devout Catholic, recalls going to Easter Mass at Notre Dame Cathedral with his wife and the Illingworths and Ray's interest in the cardinal celebrating the Mass. He was less impressed by several people walking up and down the aisles and said to Norman, 'You should have a word with your senior pro; these people shouldn't be moving around.'

Although Leicestershire slipped to 11th in the JPL in 1975, Illingworth enjoyed an unexpected triumph over Close's Somerset at Yeovil. In front of a large crowd, they appeared doomed when, with two balls left and with nine men patrolling the boundary, they needed ten to win. Close took his fast bowler Allan Jones to one side and warned him against pitching the ball up on this small ground, whereupon Jones bowled two half-volleys, both of which were gratefully dispatched for six by McVicker to win the match. Somerset's defeat and the manner of it infuriated Close and there were loud recriminations afterwards. 'Tell Brian cheerio,' Illingworth said to one of his team-mates when the Somerset captain failed to emerge from the dressing room.

Having finished fourth in the Championship in 1974, Illingworth believed that Leicestershire could win the title the following year, especially given their absence of Test calls compared to other Championship contenders. Their start, however, was lacklustre, drawing six of their first seven games, and in mid-June only Gloucestershire stood between them and bottom. At a team meeting called to discuss their plight, the players accepted that they had under-performed and they reinvigorated their efforts to win 11 of their final 14 matches. The turn of the tide came with a 116-run victory against Somerset in mid-June, followed by further home wins against Hampshire and Glamorgan. They then endured their one Championship reverse when they lost a remarkable game against Surrey at The Oval. Bowled out for 68 in reply to Surrey's first innings of 259, they followed on 191 behind and led by a dogged 71 from John Steele and 41 not out from Illingworth, they staged a spirited fightback by making 283.

They then stunned the Surrey dressing room by reducing them to 65/9 with Illingworth claiming the first hat-trick of his career, before an unbroken stand of 28 between Intikhab Alam and Pat Pocock saw them home by one wicket.

They returned to winning ways against Essex at Leicester as their opponents wilted against their quartet of spinners, a common occurrence in a summer of perpetual sunshine and turning pitches, and Warwickshire at Coventry. In another game of fluctuating fortune, they had vice-captain Tolchard to thank for turning likely defeat into a one-wicket win in the final over with a superb 103 not out.

Before they resumed business, they had the small matter of another Lord's final to occupy them. Despite losing to Warwickshire in the zonal round, Leicestershire had little difficulty qualifying for the quarter-finals. As in 1972, they hosted Lancashire, winners of the Gillette Cup that year, and in a close-fought game they were made to fight all the way for their two-wicket win. Restricting their opponents to 180/8 in their 55 overs, Leicestershire found batting no easier and at 132/7 they appeared doomed, but a combination of a wet ball caused by a sharp shower and Tolchard's exhilarating stroke-play saw them home.

They now faced an equally testing home semi-final against Hampshire, a side that contained the legendary opening pair of Barry Richards and Gordon Greenidge and the explosive pace of Andy Roberts, one of the great West Indian fast bowlers. Before taking the field, Mick Norman recalls Illingworth slamming shut the dressing-room door and saying that even if one or both openers scored centuries, Leicestershire could still win. As it was, McKenzie bowled Richards in the first over and Greenidge hit a brilliant 111 out of Hampshire's total of 216, and although Roberts bowled a mean opening spell, a fine undefeated 101 from Balderstone guided them to victory in the final over.

Back at Lord's for the third time in four years, on this occasion against Mike Brearley's Middlesex, Illingworth stifled the opposition with his astute field placings and with McVicker exploiting the overcast conditions to take 4-20, they were dismissed for 146. Leicestershire, in turn, made heavy weather of their target, but an undefeated stand of 29 between Tolchard and Illingworth carried them to a five-wicket triumph, the latter making the winning hit. According to Martin Johnson in the *Leicester Daily Mercury*, 'It was perhaps fitting in a way. His leadership has been an inspiration, the conductor of a fine orchestra, although he may never have been seen again had not his legs still been nimble enough to help him reach the pavilion cordon before the avalanche of spectators. There's not much in cricket that Illy hasn't achieved – but no one's smile was broader when he collected the trophy.'

Leicestershire followed this triumph with another one – their first win against the Australians since 1888. On a benign pitch, Illingworth was able to declare twice, the second time setting the tourists 275 to win in nearly five hours and despite a not-out century from Doug Walters, he and his fellow spinners bowled them to a 31-run victory.

After draws against Lancashire and Derbyshire in the Championship, Leicestershire beat Nottinghamshire at home before disposing of Northamptonshire by nine wickets. Having rescued his side from the depths of 65/7 in their first innings with an unbeaten 73, Illingworth then took 5-20 in Northamptonshire's second innings, leaving his batsmen with an easy target to negotiate.

Illingworth, back row, second left, playing for Yorkshire, 1954.

Close, Illingworth, Trueman, Wilson and Sharpe celebrate the winning of the County Championship, Harrogate, 1966.

The England XI against India, Headingley, 1967, a three-Test series in which Illingworth took 20 wickets.

Illingworth leads the Yorkshire side off the field at Sheffield after beating the Australians, 1968.

Illingworth captaining England against West Indies, Lord's, 1969.

Illingworth returns from tossing up with rival captain Gary Sobers, England versus the Rest of the World, Lord's, 1970.

Illingworth with rival captain Ian Chappell, England versus Australia, Lord's, 1972.

Illingworth hits Australia's Ashley Mallett for six during his match-winning 57 in the fourth Test, Headingley, 1972.

Illingworth catches John Inverarity off Derek Underwood, England versus Australia, Headingley, 1972.

Illingworth with his successor as England captain, Mike Denness, Folkestone, 1973.

Illingworth leading Leicestershire to victory in the Benson and Hedges Cup Final against Middlesex, Lord's, 1975.

Illingworth and Boycott arrive at Headingley to discuss their respective futures following the former's suspension of the latter, September 1981.

Illingworth, aged 50, taking evasive action from Middlesex's Roland Butcher, Lord's, 1982.

Illingworth conversing with Mike Atherton, England's captain throughout his time as chairman of selectors from 1994–96.

Illingworth inspects Devon Malcolm's action on the 1995/96 tour of South Africa, an issue that caused a great rift between the two of them.

Illingworth with his great friend Brian Close.

'Growing old gracefully'. Illingworth remained an avid cricket watcher to the end of his life.

He also played a leading role in the return fixture against Nottinghamshire with 4-48 in their second innings, along with opener Dudleston who stroked them to an eight-wicket victory with a sublime undefeated century.

They won again against title challengers Kent at Tunbridge Wells in one of their most keenly contested games of the summer. On a sporting pitch Kent, set 202 to win, appeared favourites at 160/4, but Illingworth kept his cool, seeing off the tail himself to steer his side to an 18-run victory. *The Times*' Nicholas Keith wrote, 'Illingworth was their inspiration and architect, both as captain and bowler. He shuffled his bowling pack cleverly and each change was rewarded with a wicket.'

Back on home turf, Leicestershire gained a narrow first-innings lead over Middlesex before the spinners came in to their own. Led by Illingworth with 4-23, his opponents could only manage 179 in their second innings and his side romped home.

With Lancashire still in the chase for the Championship, Leicestershire needed seven points from their final game against Derbyshire at Chesterfield. On a green wicket and in autumnal conditions, they slipped to 77/6 before an undefeated 44 from McKenzie, playing his final match for the county, helped them recover to 226 to gain two batting points. On Monday, 15 September, Leicestershire made history by bowling Derbyshire out for 211 to take four bowling points and win the Championship. (Lancashire had failed to get four batting points against Sussex.) As Illingworth sipped champagne with his wife Shirley in the dressing room, he revealed that it was his most satisfying moment in county cricket since Yorkshire's Championship win in 1959. 'This is the one that matters most to cricketers in this country. One-day cricket has its glamour and its final showpiece, but the

Championship is the one which calls for the greatest skill, is the hardest to win, and therefore gives more satisfaction.'

Placing Leicestershire's Championship win in context and considering Illingworth's all-round contribution that summer – 963 runs at an average of 45.85 and 48 wickets at 19.97 – Woodcock wrote, 'There will be some red faces in Yorkshire this morning when they read of Leicestershire's triumph. Since they let Illingworth go, he has won many honours as a captain, having led England to victory in Australia and Leicestershire to the John Player League, the Benson and Hedges (twice) and now the Championship. As an all-round cricketer Illingworth has retained his form wonderfully well; as a tactician, he is undeniably astute. He has kept himself fit, too, for a man of 43; as fit, anyway, as a troublesome back will allow.'

While his team-mates celebrated at the Chesterfield Hotel, not-out batsman Balderstone hurried from the ground to play football for Doncaster Rovers, the first time it was thought that anyone had played county cricket and League football on the same day. The next day he duly completed his century and helped dismiss Derbyshire for 140, ensuring that Leicestershire won the Championship by 16 points. 'That was one of the happiest seasons I have ever spent in cricket, and not merely because of the results but because of the spirit,' Illingworth later wrote. 'Everyone was willing to give everything, even when he was injured – always provided that the injury was not serious enough to result in his letting the side down. The side was what mattered to everyone and when you get that attitude cricket can be a very happy game.'

With hopes raised high for another victorious year, Illingworth began 1976 with a century against Nottinghamshire, his first in five years, in the opening Championship game, rescuing his side from 28/5; then weeks later, he exploited a rain-affected wicket at Swansea to take 8-38 against Glamorgan. Winning only one of their first six Championship games, Leicestershire started inauspiciously, but as the summer drought wore on and their spinners came into their own on turning wickets, their fortunes began to improve.

One of their most eye-catching victories came against Gloucestershire in late July. During Gloucestershire's first innings, Illingworth had clashed with Mike Procter after Jack Birkenshaw recalled Procter for a caught and bowled, saying that it was a bump ball. Illingworth then admonished Birkenshaw, telling him that he should leave such decisions to the umpires and bemoaning the malign influence of overseas players on the English game. Procter didn't take kindly to Illingworth's intervention and took his ire out on the Leicestershire upper order that evening, reducing them to 31/6. In gloomy light, he found an additional yard of pace for Illingworth, peppering him with bouncers, but Illingworth, as firm as a rock, stood his ground and pulled him for several boundaries. He didn't last long the next day, but Birkenshaw and Rhodesian all-rounder Paddy Clift, taking advantage of Procter's injured knee which forced him to bowl off spin, added 92 for the eighth wicket and helped Leicestershire to a respectable 208 all out, 91 behind their opponents. Then, on a wearing wicket, Illingworth and his fellow spinners routed Gloucestershire for 130 and with Birkenshaw again excelling with the bat, Leicestershire won by four wickets.

Unbeaten in July and August, Illingworth's men chalked up comprehensive victories over Sussex, Yorkshire, Hampshire, Kent, Nottinghamshire and Middlesex, champions that year, by 303 runs at Lord's. By the end of August, Leicestershire were in second place, one point ahead of Northamptonshire when the two sides met in a rain-ruined match at Grace Road. With the visitors beginning the final day at 131/3 in their first innings, a delayed start and the failure of the two captains to agree to a manufactured finish meant that the game then became nothing more than a battle for bonus points. In response to Northamptonshire's declaration at 202/7, Leicestershire, caught on a bad pitch, closed their innings at 22/2 in order to deprive their opponents of any bowling points, and following on were 46/3 at the close. Amid mutual recriminations Leicestershire remained in second place but any hopes of them remaining there were shattered by their defeat to Somerset in their final game, one of the few occasions that Close had the better of Illingworth in their fierce rivalries post-Yorkshire.

Leicestershire's late surge in the Championship was replicated in the JPL, and by winning five of their last six games they finished joint third with Somerset and Sussex behind the champions Kent who, despite having the same number of points, won on a faster run rate.

In May 1977 the cricket world was rocked to its foundations by the launch of Australian media magnate Kerry Packer's rebel World Series Cricket (WSC). Since time immemorial cricketers had been poorly remunerated and relations between them and their governing bodies remained frayed. Their cause was taken up by Packer following the refusal of the Australian board to give the television rights of Test cricket to his Channel Nine Network. Used to getting his own way, Packer retaliated by signing up 35 of the world's top players for his WSC enterprise by offering them salaries far in excess of anything they'd previously earned.

One of Packer's leading agents had been England captain Tony Greig and when news broke of the enterprise his clandestine role in the recruitment of players was deemed serious enough to lose him the England captaincy. The decision of the Cricket Council was fully supported by Illingworth, who'd been seriously considered as captain of the Rest of the World XI, only then to be discounted on grounds of age. He wrote, 'I don't blame Greig for trying to further his own career. I have always got on well with him and I quite like him as a person. But I am bound to agree with the general feeling throughout the game that it was not quite "on" to use his position as England captain to negotiate with players on behalf of another boss. Like a lot of my fellow professionals, I was disappointed with Greig's lack of integrity.'

Recognising the modest rewards of professional cricketers, Illingworth understood the rush to join Packer, but he supported the attempt of the International Cricket Conference (ICC) and the TCCB to ban them from first-class and international cricket on the premise that they couldn't serve two masters. At the meeting of the Cricketers' Association that September, he seconded a motion in favour of the ban and spoke forcefully for it. 'Without such a ban, our county game would be a breeding ground and a creaming-off centre for future circuses.'

The Association voted for the ban but Packer wouldn't be cowed and he launched legal proceedings against the ICC and TCCB. Appearing as one of 12 witnesses for the establishment, Illingworth was questioned by Packer's advocate, Robert Alexander QC about Mike Procter's position, since as a South African he was excluded from Test cricket because of the sporting boycott of his country. Dressed in England blazer and tie, Illingworth accepted that Procter was a special case but one couldn't make exceptions. 'I think he is very unlucky but I think he has to go along with the rule.'

When asked about his own position, Illingworth admitted that he would have considered Packer's offer very carefully. 'But if I had been offered a contract and had accepted it, I would have expected to be banned from Test and county matches. I think the two games – Mr Packer's and conventional cricket – will be in direct conflict.' He thought it would be difficult to foster a healthy team spirit if Packer players were allowed to play in county cricket.

With the courts finding in favour of Packer on the vital question of breach of trade, WSC duly went ahead and introduced the novelty of floodlit cricket, coloured clothing and white balls. It proved a defining moment in cricketing history because, when the two sides finally settled their differences in May 1979, Packer's Channel Nine was granted exclusive rights to broadcast and promote the game in Australia for ten years. Writing in the aftermath of that agreement, Illingworth, while welcoming the better remuneration for Test cricketers, broadly disliked the Packer legacy of coloured clothing, aggressive marketing and growing partisanship. 'I fervently hope that as the Packer contract expires the Australian Board of Control will, in fact, get back control and that aluminium bats, coloured shirts and large-scale histrionics will be buried for ever. The damage that he [Packer] has done to international cricket has been devastating but not quite irreparable – yet.'

Frustrated to have missed out on a trophy the previous year, Leicestershire rectified this in 1977, despite a string of injuries to leading players. In one of the most dismal summers for years, bad weather accounted for the county's preponderance of draws and, when the sun did shine, undue caution played its part. Irked by Sussex's failure to make a game of it, Illingworth registered his protest by bowling an over underarm and branded their belated declaration a disgrace as the match ended in stalemate.

It was a year in which he did little of note, manifest in an early encounter with Oxford University. Dismissed cheaply, he then found he was bludgeoned around the Parks by their captain, Vic Marks. 'Keep doing that,' snarled Illingworth, 'and I'll have to bring back the quicks.' Yet, as was so often the case, he reserved his best until last with a hundred in the penultimate match of the season against Northamptonshire and six cheap wickets in the final one against Nottinghamshire. Any satisfaction Leicestershire had drawn from dismissing Northamptonshire for 172 soon vanished as Pakistan fast bowler Sarfraz Nawaz blew away their upper order. 'We had finished bowling,' commented Higgs, 'and I'd had my shower and was walking out of the ground to go to my hotel when one of the crowd shouted to me that dinner would have to wait!' Striding to the wicket the next morning at 45/9 to join his captain, Higgs displayed few nerves, befitting a man who shared a last-wicket partnership of 128 with John Snow for England against West Indies at The Oval in 1966.

Taking advantage of an improving pitch, he and Illingworth proceeded untroubled, staying together for over four hours. While Illingworth drove and pulled imperiously, Higgs employed his trademark sweep with some success and together they added 228 for the last wicket. Their stand easily beat the previous Leicestershire record for the last wicket of 157 between Ewart Astill and William Marlow and was only seven short of the highest ever in the Championship by Kent's Frank Woolley and Arthur Fielder against Worcestershire in 1909. Illingworth hit his only century of the season and Higgs was on the cusp of his maiden one when he was run out for 98. 'He was getting a bit tired by then,' declared Illingworth. 'I don't know how he'll get on when he gets to my age.'

Alluding to Illingworth's barren season with the bat, Martin Johnson wrote, 'At 10p per run, his testimonial sponsors had been thinking of a postal order rather than a cheque until yesterday. Illingworth, as he can be, was superb.'

Leicestershire drew with Northamptonshire and in their final match Illingworth led them to a resounding win against Nottinghamshire, during which he collected his 2,000th first-class wicket when he bowled Kevin Cooper.

Determined to improve on their dire record in the Gillette Cup, their time appeared to have come with a semi-final against lowly Glamorgan at Swansea. The match, however, was hampered by bad weather and Leicestershire were well beaten by five wickets. Disappointed by their defeat, they found consolation by becoming JPL champions for the second time by securing one more win than Essex, who had the same number of points. Aside from the traditional accuracy of their attack, they benefited greatly from the scintillating stroke-play of David Gower, whose development Illingworth ranked as one of the most exciting transitions of his career.

He wrote, 'My first glimpse of him came when the players assembled for the start of the 1975 season. Gower was barely 18 and right away I knew that here was something very special.' Rating him as the best timer of the ball he'd seen for 25 years, he opened with him in the JPL to give him the chance to play his shots, and Gower responded with some vintage cameos. In the Championship, however, his impetuosity often proved his undoing, much to Illingworth's frustration. 'These pretty 20s and 30s are all very nice, Gower,' he would reproach him, 'but if you could possibly manage the occasional hundred, we'd be obliged.' Acknowledging his tendency to self-destruct, Gower appreciated Illingworth's measured response. He later wrote that 'whereas some captains would unhesitantly come down like a ton of bricks, Raymond would more often give me a few moments alone, then just come to me quietly and say something like "What are you?" It was enough to make the point – I took a lot from Ray. He was very good for me and to me. He instilled the basic attitudes, turning the public schoolboy into a professional cricketer.'

Detecting Gower's early troubles against spin, Illingworth and Birkenshaw worked on his technique in the nets and, learning quickly, Gower improved beyond all recognition. He later recalled that the most important lesson Illingworth taught him was the need to be decisive against the spinners, to either play completely forward or to go back on the stumps. Anything hesitant and halfway was disastrous against a bowler of his class.

Gower also recalled the way Illingworth made his presence felt off the field. 'He would periodically have a purge on the way we dressed. Quite rightly, he had very proper ideas on the appearance of his players and would never stand for tee-shirts and jeans or anything sloppy.

'At the start of the 1977 season, he was being particularly firm about clothes, and actually issued warnings to some of us about the way we were dressing to come to games and during our first away trip of the season, I decided I would come down to breakfast in full evening dress. I put on dinner jacket, dress shirt, bow tie and smart strides and swanned into the dining room of our hotel in Taunton looking the picture of elegance. It stunned Ray for all of ten seconds before he came out with the perfect retort – "Have you just come in, Gower?"'

When Gower was on song, Leicestershire appeared invincible, except for the game against Kent in mid-July. Despite his 78, and 77 from Balderstone, their total of 247/4 looked extremely vulnerable as Alan Ealham and Bernard Julien lashed them to all parts of Grace Road. With only 15 required in six overs and six wickets in hand, Illingworth said to Birkenshaw, 'The game's gone, you may as well have a bowl.' Encouraged by Illingworth to toss the ball up, Birkenshaw duly obliged and despite being hit for six by Julien, he kept his nerve and had Julien caught at long-on before dismissing Ealham, Graham Johnson and Charles Rowe in three overs to help his side to a two-run win.

Unbeaten in the JPL until 21 August, Leicestershire then lost a ten-over game against Northamptonshire by one run. The result upset Illingworth chiefly because of Jamaican umpire Douglas Sang Hue's failure to call several bouncers from Sarfraz Nawaz wides, in line with TCCB guidelines.

Undaunted by this setback, they returned to winning ways with an overwhelming victory against Warwickshire, Gower gracing Illingworth's benefit match with a spectacular 135 not out. Needing to win their final game to remain on top ahead of Essex, they thrilled their 10,000 supporters with a comfortable win over Glamorgan. Deflated by their defeat in the Gillette Cup Final the day before, Glamorgan offered little resistance and their total of 117 was easily surpassed by Leicestershire, Illingworth scoring the winning run, to general acclaim. 'Illy was mobbed and rightly so,' wrote Brian Scovell. 'No cricketer has done more for his county than Raymond Illingworth. He didn't bowl too many overs and he didn't play too many big innings, but he thought a lot and thinking and planning are what win matches in limited-overs competitions. It was Leicester's fourth one-day success in five seasons and their total of 13 wins equalled the John Player record.' Reckoning that Illingworth playing one-day cricket at 45 must be equivalent to Jack Hobbs and W.G. Grace scoring centuries in three-day matches after 50, Scovell concluded, 'And he is still not out! Is there a finer cricket brain in the country, or indeed, the world? If there was, Kerry Packer would soon be in to sign him.'

Ironically enough it was his native county that was soon after his signature. In contrast to Leicestershire's decade of success in the 1970s, Yorkshire had endured a barren time, failing to win anything since 1969. Although the team had been severely weakened by the departure of many great players such as Trueman, Illingworth, Binks and Close, Boycott's captaincy had come in for much criticism. While no one doubted his tactical shrewdness and his prowess as a batsman, his obsession with his own game and his failure to motivate many of the younger players had bred disillusion in the dressing room. This in turn encouraged the anti-Boycott faction on the committee to remove him from the captaincy. Their resolve was strengthened by Yorkshire's disappointing results in 1977, the year of Boycott's triumphant return to England colours against Australia, when they finished 12th in the Championship and 13th in the JPL. The first committeeman to break cover was Don Brennan, the former Yorkshire wicketkeeper, who, in an interview with BBC Radio Leeds on 30 September, said that Boycott's captaincy didn't inspire confidence and that he should be replaced by Geoff Cope.

Brennan's broadside provoked outrage from many members to whom Boycott was a hero – Yorkshire's one great player – and led to the establishment of the Reform Group to support his interests. The furore also galvanised the committee into action. Weeks earlier, the chairman Arthur Connell and the president

Sir Kenneth Parkinson had met Boycott and other senior players in secret at Scarborough and were made aware of the low esteem in which the committee was held by the team. Determined to bridge the gap between committee and players, they decided to appoint a manager, a post then relatively unknown in cricket. With Illingworth their favoured choice, the treasurer Michael Crawford rang him to ascertain his interest and asking whether they could meet. As far as Illingworth was concerned, the approach came more or less out of the blue 'and when it did come, I had to do an awful lot of heart-searching'. Not only had he enjoyed nine highly fulfilling years at Leicestershire, his wife and family liked it there, forming many close friendships. That said, he found the opportunity to return to his native Yorkshire an enticing one, especially on a salary of £15,000 a year, and after discussing the matter thoroughly with Shirley, he decided to accept the offer in principle.

On 31 October Illingworth met Connell, Crawford and Norman Shuttleworth, the chairman of the finance committee, in strict secrecy – both Illingworth and Yorkshire's negotiators insisted on this – to iron out the details of his three-year contract for the start of the 1979 season. So clandestine were the negotiations that neither Boycott nor the rest of the Yorkshire committee nor Leicestershire were aware of what was afoot until the Yorkshire committee met on 10 November, an oversight that affronted all concerned, not least Mike Turner. He called the appointment breathtaking, and he criticised Yorkshire for failing to observe the basic proprieties between counties before such an appointment. He also felt somewhat miffed at Illingworth's decision to leave him in the dark over the negotiations, especially following his record-breaking benefit of £38,134, his sentiments reflecting the growing rift between the two men as Illingworth's star shone ever brighter in the club's firmament than his own. Unconvinced by Leicestershire's offer of a new three-year contract or the apparent desire to employ him in a managerial capacity when he ceased playing – Turner never put anything to the committee – Illingworth remained defiant. He told the local paper that the following year he would be 46 and there was no job for him at Leicestershire apart from playing.

'But at my time of life it would have been stupid to turn this offer down. I can't go on playing for ever, and I think the Leicestershire public will understand that, and also agree that I've given them value for money in my years here.'

Following Illingworth's impending move to Yorkshire, his last season for Leicestershire was something of an anti-climax. Only in the JPL did they challenge for honours and he suffered the indignity of being dropped for three matches in the Championship because of lack of form – a decision which probably owed something to his breach with Mike Turner over his return to Yorkshire. Although unhappy with his demotion, Illingworth kept his own counsel and on his return to the side he took 5-44 against Lancashire and 6-38 in his final Championship game against Nottinghamshire. Days later he signed off with a convincing six-wicket win against Derbyshire in the JPL, which guaranteed them third place, the same number of points as the winners Hampshire, who had a superior run rate. As Illingworth received a tea-time presentation from the club on the pavilion balcony, spectators jostled with the press to capture footage of his final game. 'Illingworth has become something of a legendary figure over the past decade, regarded among contemporary captains as an Olivier on a stage full of bit-part repertory actors,' wrote Martin Johnson. Admiring his down-to-earth personality and wry humour, he concluded, 'Illingworth was by no means infallible, and he made himself unpopular at times along the way, but when it comes to cricketing judgements, he's not often wrong. He's not irreplaceable but Leicestershire will surely miss him.'

Chapter 10

Unhappy Homecoming

ILLINGWORTH'S RETURN to Yorkshire and the surreptitious circumstances surrounding his appointment unnerved Boycott. Protocol aside, what particularly vexed him about the new set-up was the potential erosion of his own authority. A meeting with Illingworth and senior members of the committee failed to allay his concerns because while the chairman talked about the need for cooperation, there was no question of him refuting Illingworth's public assertion that he would be *alpha* and *omega*. 'Geoff will be ultimately responsible to me,' he commented. 'If it comes to the crunch, I have the final say – but neither of us will be looking for confrontations. I'm still not sure how Geoff will react, perhaps he won't be too happy about it at first. But I don't think he'll quit,' he added rather ominously.

Conscious of the continued sniping about his leadership, Boycott wrote a long letter to the committee on 21 November 1977 warning that Illingworth's appointment would intensify these divisions rather than ameliorate them. During the 1978 season he asked him how he would have felt if Leicestershire had made an appointment that diminished his authority as captain. 'My reply didn't take much working out,' wrote Illingworth. '"Geoff," I said, "considering that for the past six or seven seasons Leicestershire have been one of the most successful sides in the country, there was no question of such a situation arising. Now if I had been captain for eight seasons during which the county won nothing and only very rarely looked to be in a position to win anything, I would not have been surprised at all in a new appointment. Why should you be?"'

While Illingworth played out his final season with Leicestershire, Boycott's position was further weakened when a finger injury sustained against Pakistan in a one-day international forced him to miss a month of cricket. In his absence, Yorkshire flourished under the captaincy of his deputy John Hampshire, whose relaxed approach won over the dressing room. Hampshire was in charge when Yorkshire played Leicestershire in mid-June and he spent much time in discussion with Illingworth about the future. While never close to Boycott, he'd refrained from undermining him – indeed, he'd often defended him – and so he was deeply affronted when Illingworth told him over dinner that Boycott didn't trust him, a comment that the latter was alleged to have made four years earlier. 'To be told that I was untrustworthy represented a vicious insult to me and I was not going to stand for it,' wrote Hampshire. 'I told him [Boycott] exactly what I thought of him and reported the matter to the chairman.' It seemed Illingworth was out to undermine Boycott because he publicly questioned his credentials to lead England following his brief, unhappy stint earlier that year when deputising for the injured Mike Brearley, in contrast to his advocacy of Hampshire for the same position.

The growing rift between Boycott and Hampshire formed the backdrop to the latter's extraordinary protest at Northampton in July. Reacting petulantly to a painstaking Boycott century, the in-form Hampshire and his junior partner, Colin Johnson, staged a 'go slow' during which they scored 11 runs off the final ten overs, thereby depriving Yorkshire of a final bonus point. Although Hampshire had been guilty of brazen insubordination in front of the Yorkshire president, the disciplinary committee of John Temple, Billy Sutcliffe and Ronnie Burnet, increasingly tiring of Boycott's leadership, sympathised with him and let him off with a mild private reprimand. The fact that they also censured Boycott for slow scoring suggested that the captain was living on borrowed time. With Hampshire enjoying one of his most prolific seasons – he even beat Boycott in the averages – it was no surprise that at the meeting of the cricket committee on 29 September they voted ten to one to relieve Boycott of the captaincy, the dissenter being the president Sir Kenneth Parkinson, who thought Boycott should be given a chance to work with Illingworth in line with the committee's original intentions.

In his autobiography, Boycott claims that Illingworth, who was present the day before at the meeting of the selection committee, called for his dismissal and that his opinion helped influence the cricket committee. It was a charge vehemently denied by Illingworth, who wrote that 'he was not directly involved in any way with the change of captaincy'. He did, however, later acknowledge that Yorkshire were right to sack Boycott chiefly because he placed his own personal ambition above the interests of the team.

The defenestration of Boycott two days after the death of his mother and without adequate explanation helped rouse large swathes of the Yorkshire public to fury. Drawing on a well of sympathy for the deposed captain, the Reform Group compelled the committee to hold a special meeting at Harrogate on 9

December, although motions of no confidence in the committee and the reinstatement of Boycott as captain were defeated.

Central to the committee's case was the backing they received from Illingworth in a letter dated 10 November. He wrote, 'As you know, when I was first offered the job of Manager I said I would serve with any Captain who might be appointed and in particular was perfectly happy to work with Geoff.

'Up to now I have therefore kept out of this row, but as things are developing I think I should now let you know that the players are wholeheartedly behind the Committee in the change.'

Contrary to Illingworth's claim in his book, *The Tempestuous Years*, that he didn't instigate the poll regarding the captaincy, Geoff Cope, then the senior professional, recalls being rung up by Illingworth and asked to sound out the players as to whether they wanted a change. Although reluctant to do Illingworth's bidding, Cope complied and found that the overwhelming majority wanted Boycott out. He duly conveyed his findings to Illingworth, who passed them on to the committee. According to Boycott, 'The fact that Illingworth was prepared to issue a letter like that left me in no doubt where he stood and therefore little doubt where I would stand as a player ... Sooner or later, I knew, they would have to get rid of me. I was resigned to further trouble.'

And so was Illingworth, who had to endure a vitriolic campaign, most notably in the letters' column of the *Yorkshire Post*, from many a Boycott supporter, who held him responsible, along with the committee, of gross iconoclasm. In an era devoid of cricketing giants, Boycott bestrode the Yorkshire landscape like a colossus and was admired for his dedication as well as for his sheer volume of runs. The fanatical loyalty that he attracted remained a thorn in Illingworth's side throughout his five years at the helm.

On taking up the cudgels in the spring of 1979, Illingworth found a badly run and faction-ridden club compared to Leicestershire. The management committee, which had replaced the old cricket committee, was too large and unwieldy and some of its members were there for reasons of social prestige rather than a love of the game. Leo McKinstry, in his biography of Boycott, relates the experience of Sid Fielden, the secretary of the Reform Group, who was elected to the committee in 1982. Having told a fellow committee man that he'd been for a walk around the ground to talk to members, the committee man retorted, 'You don't talk to members. Don't you realise that you have joined the most exclusive club in the world?'

'Yes, I know, Yorkshire County Cricket Club.'

'No, the bloody committee.'

There was barely any sponsorship, something Illingworth sought to redress. By using his wealth of contacts, he was able to ring round and gain a number of offers of club sponsorship, including a lucrative £75,000 contract over three years with Berger Paints. He also combined with head coach Doug Padgett to improve the scouting system by speaking at major league dinners and encouraging schools and clubs to send any promising youngsters to Headingley for a trial.

Thinking that the team under Boycott had lacked self-discipline, Illingworth attempted to stamp his authority by starting pre-season a week earlier than previously and placing greater emphasis on physical training. While securing a better financial deal for the players, mainly in the form of win bonuses, he insisted on higher standards in return, not least in dress and appearance.

With eight present and future England players under contract, he felt able to tell the annual club lunch that the squad 'were stronger than any other county'. His optimism proved misplaced since Yorkshire didn't win their first Championship game until 10 July. Some of this could be attributed to the miserable weather, but much of it related to the side's inconsistency as the club's civil war continued to fester. John Callaghan, the cricket correspondent of the *Yorkshire Evening Post*, recalls that at the end of Illingworth's first press conference as manager he said to him, 'I hope I'm not going to have trouble with you. I know you are in Boycott's pocket.' Callaghan explained that he wasn't; he'd merely sympathised with him over his treatment by the committee.

When Boycott eventually signed a new contract before the club's deadline, Illingworth openly speculated whether his acceptance was down to the lack of interest from other counties. Although Illingworth, Boycott and Hampshire took part in a pre-season staged photo linking arms around their shoulders, Boycott's relationship with manager and captain remained fraught. When members of the Reform Group applauded him in the first game at Middlesbrough, Illingworth said 'support was welcome; sabotage we could do without'.

Illingworth's transition to management proved challenging, since he greatly missed playing and when a finger injury threatened Hampshire's participation in the Championship while Boycott and Chris Old were away on World Cup duty, he stood ready to deputise. In the end Hampshire recovered in time, but the mere possibility of Illingworth playing prompted Sid Fielden to write to chairman Arthur Connell deploring it as a retrograde step.

Fielden's intervention failed to impress Illingworth. 'I am not sure what the Reform Group think they are achieving by carrying on like this,' he told the *Yorkshire Post*. 'They were democratically defeated at a special meeting and most of their candidates have been beaten when they put themselves up for election against sitting members. They are doing nobody any good by constantly nagging and criticising.' According to Boycott, Illingworth confronted him shortly after this outburst and accused him of working with the Reform Group against him, an accusation that Boycott strenuously denied.

After his disappointing tour of Australia Boycott had returned to his very best form, standing head and shoulders above his Yorkshire team-mates. On the morning of a crucial Benson and Hedges semi-final against Essex, he told Illingworth he couldn't jog properly because of a slight hamstring strain and Illingworth, assuming he was unfit to play, left him out of the team. Irked by Boycott's public pronouncement that he'd been dropped, Illingworth responded tartly that his presence would have made no difference to a match that Yorkshire lost by three wickets. It was the nearest the county came to silverware in a disappointing season in which they finished seventh in the Championship, three places below their performance the previous year.

Geoff Cope wrote: 'When Illy came, I thought, "That is a good appointment, I like that. I saw him as a cricketer – a fabulous tactician, a very good bowler, shrewd, knowledgeable. But as a manager he still wanted to be playing. We would be struggling at five or six down, needing to get our heads down, and Illy would say, "We were in a situation like this at Leicester and Birky and I went out and got some runs." He said it not once but fairly regularly, "What I did at Leicester." It rubbed. "Illy, you're not at Leicester. You're at Yorkshire, and we need a bit of advice."'

Cope had other reasons to be disappointed with Illingworth. In 1977/78, he'd won his first Test cap on the MCC tour of Pakistan but the following season he was once again suspended because his action was deemed questionable, despite the fact that he'd never been called for throwing. Looking to Illingworth for support, he looked in vain because Illingworth proved most unhelpful. According to Pat Pocock, Illingworth approached him in a Surrey–Yorkshire game and encouraged him to report Cope because his action was so bad; then on 22 May 1979 Illingworth went further, telling the Yorkshire cricket committee that he still wasn't happy with Cope's action, prompting the committee to re-register Illingworth as a player. Later that summer Illingworth told the *Yorkshire Post* that he didn't 'want to clog the second team up with 32-year-old spinners, to try again to satisfy the authorities' and talked Cope into accepting a joint benefit with opening batsman Barrie Leadbeater. Cope wrote, 'Illy made me the offer one Saturday night. Barrie, he said, would probably not play after 1979, and he was getting 1980 as his benefit. I could have 1981 as my benefit. But if I didn't finish up playing, it might not be awarded at all. So, I had to choose between half a benefit in 1980 and the chance of no benefit at all, and he needed the answer first thing on Sunday morning.'

Concerned by all the uncertainty, Cope reluctantly accepted the offer of a joint benefit and, after failing to win a basic contract for the 1981 season, he retired from first-class cricket, a sad end to the career of a talented bowler and affable individual.

During the close season, Illingworth captained an England Past and Present XI on a short trip to Barbados for Worcestershire fast bowler Vanburn Holder's benefit, his first serious cricket for over a year – and serious it was despite the label of friendlies. On losing their second game from a near impregnable position, Illingworth castigated his team, telling Bob Willis and Mike Hendrick that they shouldn't need £10,000 to try hard. Looking back over his first season, he admitted to cricket journalist Alan Lee, that 'After 30 years of playing the game, I find it hard to reconcile myself to sitting back and watching. In fact, with hindsight, I should probably have played for the first part of the season. Geoff Cope had not sorted his action out by then and Peter Whitely, our other off-spinner, was bowling poorly. My experience, both in bowling and in helping John Hampshire with the captaincy, could easily have been beneficial.'

He also acknowledged that not everything had gone smoothly in his first year back. The loss of three successive JPL games in front of large crowds had drained confidence and they'd never regained momentum.

Despite Illingworth's pre-season boast for 1980 'that the squad was 200 per cent better prepared than the previous year', their start proved underwhelming following a quick exit from the Benson and Hedges Cup and the loss of their first six games in the JPL. Depressed by this losing sequence, Illingworth issued an ultimatum to the players: improve or else. Frustrated by Hampshire's defensive captaincy, especially his unimaginative use of the spinners, he began relaying tactical instructions to him from the dressing room via the players, advice that Hampshire often ignored.

Given their erratic form, Yorkshire's one hope of silverware came in the Gillette Cup. Drawn against Surrey at The Oval in the semi-final, Illingworth lashed out at the umpires for starting the delayed game in bad light. Put in to bat, Yorkshire had to contend with the hostility of Sylvester Clarke, one of the game's fastest bowlers, and could only muster 135, losing by four wickets.

Weeks earlier Illingworth revived tension with Boycott by dropping him for a JPL game as part of his youth policy, an omission he repeated in the final match of the season when he also dropped Hampshire as well. According to Boycott, Illingworth was reassuring the press that his future at Yorkshire was secure, when he was telling Jim Laker something very different. 'But Illy was fast causing strife in the dressing room. He referred to Sidebottom, Bairstow, Stevenson and me as the "South Yorkshire Mafia" and seemed to spend as much time manoeuvring as he did managing.'

Disillusioned by all the backbiting and the public insults directed at his family, Hampshire resigned the captaincy at the end of the season. He was replaced by Chris Old, but the change of leadership did little to transform fortunes. In another season blighted by bad weather and injury, Yorkshire failed to win any of their first seven Championship games and won only one of their first five JPL games. Old also found working with Illingworth, who had publicly criticised him for his lack of bottle the previous year, a challenge. 'To start with it seemed fine but I did end up speaking about it to the committee,' he commented. 'If I went away for a Test match, I walked into the dressing room for the next game and I didn't know which players were there, there was no communication.'

When Old was absent, Hampshire and Bairstow deputised until Illingworth, in a bold gesture, asked Neil Hartley to captain the side against Warwickshire at Scarborough at the end of July. Hartley was an intelligent young man who'd captained Bingley to a Priestley Cup and league double when just 19, but he was an uncapped player who'd struggled to hold down a regular place in the first team since his debut in 1978. Hampshire told Illingworth not to appoint him and Bairstow, as a capped player, felt aggrieved to have been passed over. Never one to hold back, he conveyed his frustration to Illingworth in a bitter row in the public bar of the Royal Hotel, Scarborough.

Increasingly convinced that Boycott's presence was detrimental to team spirit, Illingworth left him out of the Sunday side and for a couple of games in the Scarborough Festival on the pretext of pursuing a youth policy, although none of the other senior players were omitted.

Affronted by his omission, Boycott complained in a television interview in York that he'd been treated unfairly by the manager and he would be seeking a showdown with him. His outburst offended Illingworth enough for him to take disciplinary action. Having failed to contact chairman Michael Crawford, who was on holiday in Scotland, he then rang Trueman and Brennan. They agreed with his right to suspend Boycott for allegedly contravening his contract by making unauthorised remarks to the media. The next morning, before Yorkshire's final home game, a furious Illingworth confronted Boycott in the pavilion at Scarborough and told him he would be suspended for the rest of the season. He should pack his bags and leave the ground immediately.

As news of Boycott's suspension trickled out, hundreds of angry spectators lobbied the dressing room and called for Illingworth's resignation. Many of them remained on the field, delaying the start of the match. By the time Boycott made a grand exit to a rapturous ovation from the 5,000 crowd, the Reform Group was busy collecting signatures for a petition demanding Illingworth's resignation, all in full view of the television cameras. It was a sight that finally convinced Hampshire that his future lay elsewhere. 'I was sick to the depths of my soul. This was the end, the last nail in the coffin of Yorkshire cricket as far as I was concerned. I wanted no more of it.'

While the majority of press and public opinion rallied behind Boycott, Terry Brindle wrote in the *Yorkshire Post*, 'The extraordinary thing about Illingworth's decision to suspend Boycott was its severity. In a sense when Yorkshire's record of discipline has been widely criticised, the suspension of a senior and publicly controversial player seems on the face of it a grotesque over-reaction to a relatively technical offence.' What Illingworth didn't know was that Boycott's contract, in contrast to the rest of the Yorkshire team, didn't require him to clear interviews with the club. Had he been on the spot, chairman Michael Crawford later admitted to reporters, he would have advised Illingworth to have taken a more cautious approach to the dispute, but the committee's failure to inform him, Illingworth, of Boycott's special contract was a travesty, according to club solicitor John Bosomworth.

On 17 September, in a day of endless meetings by the various factions at Headingley, the Reform Group presented the committee with a dossier of detailed criticism of Illingworth, while Illingworth and Old spoke of Boycott's divisive influence on the team. After 11 hours of deliberation the general committee agreed that both Illingworth and Boycott would remain at Yorkshire and a sub-committee would be established to investigate the running of the club.

No sooner had an uneasy truce descended than another skirmish arose. To counter the *Yorkshire Post*'s contention that the players wanted Boycott back as captain, the committee made public the fact that Old had conducted a dressing room ballot during the final game of the season. The findings indicated that the majority of players wanted Boycott out and Illingworth to remain as manager, but the decision of the committee to publish the findings further inflamed tensions, as well as eroding their own authority.

The sub-committee under Peter Dobson, a retired accountant, called 32 witnesses, including Illingworth, Old and Boycott. Illingworth declared there was no chance of a team ethos prevailing as long as Boycott was playing for Yorkshire. It was like a cloud descending on the dressing room whenever he returned from a Test. Old went further by suggesting that the committee should get rid of both Illingworth and Boycott, since they appeared unable to work together; he also said that the former had favourites.

When the sub-committee released its report in January 1982 it made uncomfortable reading for all concerned. It concluded, 'The most important single factor on the management of the team and dressing room discipline has been the manager's failure to handle Mr Geoffrey Boycott. The fact remains that Mr Boycott and Mr Illingworth continue to be incompatible and we regret we see little likelihood of this atmosphere improving.

'We have listened to much criticism of the present manager, Mr Ray Illingworth. It has been said that he had too many favourites, that discipline was applied to some and not to others and that the example he set by way of dress on some occasions left much to be desired, thus setting a bad example to the players.'

While the committee agreed to give Illingworth a second hearing on 10 February, their follow-up report nine days later was equally uncompromising. Reiterating the fact that since Illingworth's appointment as manager there had been no marked improvement in results, team spirit or discipline, it recommended that he should be seen by the chairman to have his deficiencies pointed out to him. 'He should be further told that unless these matters are improved during the ensuing year it is unlikely that his contract will be renewed at the end of the 1982 season.'

Yet for all the criticism heaped upon Illingworth, the committee reserved their most damning verdict for Boycott. Describing him as a major obstacle to team morale and unity, they recommended that he should be displaced as soon as possible. Conscious of the growing power wielded by the Reform Group, the committee rejected Dobson's recommendation by honouring both Illingworth and Boycott's contracts. They also set up a sub-committee of Burnet, Trueman and Sutcliffe to help bridge the gap between Illingworth and Boycott. As far as Illingworth was concerned, the failure of the committee to take a firm stand against Boycott left him and others in the lurch.

Old's public declaration that he'd erred in conducting the players' poll and that it had damaged the club's reputation served only to put distance between him and the committee. Increasingly subjected to Illingworth's harsh criticisms, the two clashed bitterly over bowling changes, most notably in the dressing room after Yorkshire's win against the Minor Counties in the Benson and Hedges Cup. 'That's when I realised the manager wanted to captain the side, manage the side and do everything,' Old later recounted. In poor shape and unable to motivate the team as they endured the most wretched of starts, even worse than the two previous years, the captain was warned by Illingworth and Burnet to get a grip or face the consequences. Their patience ran out at Middlesbrough over the weekend of 19/20 June when Northamptonshire twice obliterated the Yorkshire bowling – once in the Championship and then in the JPL – in a performance that Illingworth called embarrassing. He duly relieved Old of the captaincy and told him that the committee had asked him to come out of retirement to lead the side. 'The return of Illingworth will not end the dressing room rows and constant squabbles that have cast so much rot and mildew over the White Rose of late,' reported *The Times*.

'Even Ronald Burnet, another former captain and a major force in the Peace Committee, called it a "desperate remedy for a desperate situation".'

According to Brindle in the *Yorkshire Post*, no admirer of Illingworth, his appointment as team manager had been a serious misjudgement. 'If Illingworth can exert his influence only by captaining the side, what in the name of logic has he been doing for the last four years as manager?' It was a fair question and one that needed a full explanation. In many ways the Yorkshire sides of the 1970s and 1980s continued to live in the shadow of their predecessors. The expectations of press and public alike remained sky high and any failure to live up to these expectations bred fierce disillusion. In addition to criticism from the *Yorkshire Post* – Brindle was close to Boycott – there was constant hostility from the Reform Group, who were never reconciled to Illingworth's appointment as manager. Never one to hold his peace when under attack, Illingworth accused them of elevating the interests of Boycott above those of the team and the publication of his book, *Yorkshire and Back*, which criticised Boycott, only added to the friction.

Even elements of the committee, who resented the diminution of their authority, conspired against Illingworth. John Callaghan recalls being contacted by these people with a request that he run a story to undermine him, but when he asked for names and facts they quickly retreated. Above all, there was Boycott himself and his presence loomed large like Caesar's ghost. While he remained a prince among paupers, his slow scoring placed added pressure on the other batsmen and his fraught relationship with Illingworth did little for dressing-room harmony. It is perhaps no coincidence that the majority of the players most opposed to Illingworth were Boycott supporters.

It should be stressed that the club's continued insistence on fielding a Yorkshire-born team clearly disadvantaged them in an era when every county had two or three overseas recruits, but, equally, many problems were of their own making. A new generation of players, growing up with greater opportunities and interests outside cricket, lacked that uncompromising winning mentality compared to Brian Close's team and they reacted to setbacks with greater equanimity. 'Somehow I had got to make the younger players hate defeat in the way Yorkshire teams of old hated it,' Illingworth wrote after his first year in charge. 'I had to inspire in them that fierce, burning pride in playing for their county – and winning for it – that I had been brought up to believe in.'

When the team was playing away, they might have a quick post-match inquest, but they didn't linger as in times past; instead, they headed for the bright lights downtown, leaving Illingworth to talk over the day's play with journalists David Warner and John Callaghan. According to the latter, Illingworth was a brilliant analyst. 'He read the game so well and if you were in doubt about something in the game, Illingworth would give you a real lecture. I learned so much from him. Nothing escaped his attention.'

Unable to motivate the players to the standards he expected, Illingworth's frustration was compounded by his confinement to the pavilion balcony, where his influence was negligible compared to his presence on the field. One player to frustrate him was opener Bill Athey because of his inclination to give his wicket away with a rash shot; another was all-rounder Graham Stevenson, whose phenomenal talent wasn't matched by the same level of commitment. David Warner recalls an awesome spell of bowling against Northamptonshire at Headingley in 1980, which ended with a whimper. 'He was on for all ten, but he left the field, and we all assumed he must have been injured. But when we got to Scarborough that night and asked Illy, he raised his eyes and told us he'd only gone off to change his shirt.'

A third player to frustrate him was David Bairstow, a gifted wicketkeeper-batsman, and an inveterate trier who wore his heart on his sleeve. He believed Illingworth had been brought back to get rid of his friend Boycott and took exception to him ignoring his own claim to the captaincy on the ground, that he lacked the necessary temperament. 'His time has gone,' Bairstow told John Callaghan to which Callaghan replied, 'He knows more about the game than you'll ever do.'

Yet whatever his difficulties with some of the more established players, Illingworth won the allegiance of the younger ones. According to batsman Kevin Sharp, he was an excellent captain, tactically astute, who got the best out of everyone on the field. His only reservation related to the time he, Sharp, lost form and confidence. Illingworth told him to take a break and return when he was ready, but what Sharp really wanted was some emotional support.

Jim Love, like Sharp, a highly talented young batsman, found Illingworth most helpful and positive. 'He gave you confidence,' he commented. Admiring his ability to work batsmen out, he recalled a game against Leicestershire in 1983 when Illingworth unnerved his team by placing himself at silly point to Brian Davison, a batsman of muscular power. They need not have worried because he caught him off bat and pad immediately.

Another Illingworth man was Neil Hartley who, as previously mentioned, filled in as captain when still an uncapped player. He found him solid, straightforward and very supportive. Even when criticising the team, he expressed himself in measured tones and didn't single out individuals for censure.

In opener Ashley Metcalfe's opinion, Illingworth was the best captain under whom he ever played because of his strategic thinking and understanding of individuals, such as what to say to them if they were out of form. He also respected his candour. Making his debut against Nottinghamshire in August 1983 in place of the injured Martyn Moxon following a minor car accident, he marked the occasion with a century. Complimenting Metcalfe on his performance afterwards, Illingworth said, 'You played really well but I'd promised Martyn I would pick him for the next game.' Naturally disappointed by his words, Metcalfe was impressed by Illingworth's honesty and his loyalty to Moxon.

One youngster who did struggle to realise his potential under Illingworth was Nicholas Taylor, who'd been educated at Gresham's School in Norfolk. According to his father, Ken Taylor, the former Yorkshire opener, his two years with the club were terrible. 'The other players didn't like public schoolboys and he was really given a hard ride.' Blaming Illingworth and coach Doug Padgett in part, Taylor continued, 'They were both men for whom I had a lot of time but I don't think they really made any effort to make Nicholas feel wanted and confident or to sort out the people who were causing the problems.

'He performed quite well on the field but during the second season he was ringing every week saying he wanted to get away.'

When Taylor complained publicly about Yorkshire second XI's failure to give his son the new ball, Illingworth shot back, claiming he'd had it on seven occasions out of 12. 'I feel he has had a fair crack of the whip,' he told the *Yorkshire Post*. 'I just wish parents would keep out of it and let children stand on their own two feet. If every father rings up because his son doesn't have the new ball, we would soon have a real problem.'

Since the beginning of the 1982 season, there had been rumours of an Illingworth comeback and the week before the Northamptonshire game, he'd played for Yorkshire against Zimbabwe, taking a wicket with his first ball and bowling tidily. Defying the march of time, he became, at 50, the oldest captain of Yorkshire since Major A.W. Lupton in 1925, and the oldest official appointment in the game's history. (The only other 50-year-old to have captained was A.N. Hornby, who led Lancashire in Archie MacLaren's absence in 1897.) 'I was still pretty fit,' Illingworth later recounted. 'No weight or anything. The weight didn't vary from 12 stone 10, something like that. I won't say I trained a lot, but I trained enough to stay normally fit.'

After inclement weather decimated his comeback game at Ilford, Illingworth gave himself a long bowl in the draw against Derbyshire. Relying on his age-old guile, he coped with the demands of the first-class game better than most, but while his bowling still commanded respect it lacked the potency of old and wickets proved hard to come by.

Now batting at number ten, Illingworth scored a solid 30 against Worcestershire in his first innings back, and against Derbyshire at Scarborough his 33 helped Yorkshire win a low-scoring game. Under his leadership, they remained unbeaten in the Championship for the rest of the season (they lost one match when he was absent injured) amidst a surfeit of draws and Boycott's prolific batting. According to Mike Brearley, Illingworth's return had enhanced the fortunes of the team. 'As Ted Lester, their scorer, said to me in August of that year, "They're organised now, he's got them together. He doesn't set a field for a bad ball, and the bowlers do better for it."'

In the JPL, Illingworth won his first two games, but thereafter the side lost momentum, winning only one further game. According to John Callaghan, even Illingworth's experience and tactical skill couldn't compensate for the side's lack of consistency and application. 'The hard fact that the committee had to face was that in four years of change things had taken a distinct change for the worse. When Geoff Boycott was removed from the captaincy in 1978, Yorkshire were fourth in the Championship and seventh in the Sunday League, figures which compare favourably with tenth and sixteenth respectively in 1982.'

With Illingworth more approachable once he became captain, his relations with Boycott improved and they even had dinner together on occasions when they discussed the team. 'Geoff's attitude has been splendid all year,' Illingworth told the *Yorkshire Post*, 'and I think he has played more for the side than in previous years.'

That winter, Illingworth led a tour group of England supporters to Australia to watch part of the Ashes series. At 2am on New Year's Eve, a day before the beginning of the final Test at Sydney, he bumped into England all-rounder Derek Pringle, who was returning from a party, in the hotel.

'Why aren't you in bed?' he asked. 'You've got a Test match in just over a day's time.' 'Because it's New Year's Eve and I'm going to be 12th man anyway, as all the talk has been of us playing two spinners,' Pringle replied. 'They keep telling me Sydney will turn.' 'That's as may be,' Illingworth countered, 'but there might be injuries in practice, in which case you'll be expected to play. You need to get off to bed now,' he concluded.

Pringle thanked him for his advice before ordering another beer. He later wrote, 'I was piqued that Illingworth, a hard-bitten northerner with an acute distaste for players he regarded as public-school prats, should be so ready to give me a piece of his mind. Plenty of us had been out later than this for most of the tour, though I didn't tell him that.'

Illingworth continued to lead the side in 1983, a considerable effort for a man of 51, especially in the Championship. In the JPL, his policy of containment reaped its reward, not least his profitable partnership with left-arm spinner Phil Carrick. Against Middlesex at Hull, he gave a masterly exhibition of spin bowling, returning figures of 4-6 off his eight overs, his victims being Clive Radley, Graham Barlow, Phil Edmonds and John Emburey. Thereafter a match rarely went by without a telling contribution from the captain and he ended the season as the league's most economical bowler with 20 wickets at 12.95 apiece.

Winning 11 out of 14 matches, Yorkshire led Somerset by two points on the penultimate Sunday, although the latter with a game in hand seemed the likely winner. In the event they lost unexpectedly to Worcestershire and Yorkshire's two points from their abandoned game against Essex at Chelmsford gave them the title by virtue of a superior number of away wins. 'I never thought I would get such a buzz from winning this competition,' admitted Illingworth. 'But I can tell you it feels, after all the county has been through, as if we have won the Championship and a Test series in one.'

Yorkshire's success in the JPL was more than offset by their form in the Championship, finishing bottom for the first time in their history. Although some of their younger batsmen such as Love, Athey and Sharp didn't quite meet expectation, the main weakness lay in the bowling not helped by injuries to seamers Graham Stevenson, Alan Ramage and Arnie Sidebottom. Dubious about bowling out sides, Illingworth attracted some criticism for his defensive declarations. Against Somerset at Weston-super-Mare, he was so exercised by the threat posed by Viv Richards, who'd been absent through a family illness, that he set the home side a challenging 300 in 245 minutes on a wearing pitch, consigning the match to a draw.

In the Championship, Boycott was once again the pick of the batsmen and his truce with Illingworth lasted most of the summer, until the game against Gloucestershire at Cheltenham on 13 August. On a glorious day and in perfect batting conditions, Boycott scored 140 not out but his turgid display caused consternation in the Yorkshire dressing room. Not only did it take him 347 deliveries, but he also ran out fellow centurion Sharp and ignored Illingworth's instructions to accelerate, a fact Boycott disputed, with the result that Yorkshire missed out on a fourth batting bonus point. Illingworth said little to Boycott that evening while he weighed up his options. 'Are you going to report Geoffrey?' the *Bradford Telegraph and Argus*'s David Warner asked him. 'I can't say,' Illingworth replied. 'You'd better draw your own conclusions.' The next day, the manager referred the matter to Burnet's sub-committee and was told to put it in writing.

The sub-committee met on 19 August and reprimanded Boycott for slow scoring. The decision upset many Yorkshire supporters. The day after the hearing he scored 163 against Nottinghamshire at Bradford, each boundary greeted with ecstatic applause and cries of 'Is that fast enough, Illy?' Incensed by Boycott's reception, Illingworth complained that 'he gets the applause and I get attacked'. When Sid Fielden talked about another petition to reopen the Cheltenham controversy, Illingworth, aggrieved about all the aggravation meted out to him and his family – he was once abused when out dining with them – threatened to walk away there and then. 'I don't see why I should be playing first-class cricket at 51 to help Yorkshire cricket and at the same time have to put up with a constant barrage of attack from Yorkshire supporters,' he said. In a year in which he'd bowled over 400 overs in the Championship and taken 32 wickets at a respectable 29.71, he finally took his leave of the first-class game against Essex at Chelmsford in mid-September. Up against their fiery West Indian fast bowler Norbert Phillip on a sporting wicket, Illingworth was given an uncomfortable farewell, since he was hit on the helmet by a bouncer. Fortunately, he wasn't badly hurt.

On 3 October the Yorkshire cricket committee voted unanimously not to renew Boycott's contract, a move later endorsed by the general committee, and, as a sop to Boycott's supporters, to replace Illingworth as captain with Boycott's ally Bairstow. 'We can go no lower,' commented Burnet. 'The rancorous controversy must end. We must now look to the future and give our youngsters a chance to see what they can do. We realise that Boycott will not be playing during his testimonial year, which is unfortunate, but the situation makes this unavoidable.'

Yorkshire justified Boycott's non-retention by citing the various club luminaries such as Burnet, Sutcliffe and Trueman who didn't support him, yet, according to others, the fault wasn't entirely one-sided. John Woodcock wrote that talk of Boycott's selfishness was valid. 'Yet batting is a selfish business. In choosing the moments when he has preferred not to bowl, Ray Illingworth, for example, has been every bit as self-interested as Boycott when deciding whether or not to attack the bowling.' A similar view was expressed by the cricket writer and broadcaster Christopher Martin-Jenkins. He wrote, 'Boycott is not solely to blame for the cult that has grown around himself, nor has he been handled with much diplomacy or fairness by a manager who did not want him from the start and by a committee which apparently feels it cannot deal with him directly anymore.'

The decision to release Boycott generated a storm of protest from his supporters, who felt he was being held accountable for the deep-seated malaise in Yorkshire cricket. They formed the Members 84 Group calling for his reinstatement and under pressure from the membership a special meeting was held at Harrogate on 21 January 1984, where votes of no confidence in both the cricket committee and general committee were carried, along with a vote to reinstate Boycott.

Although the votes in theory weren't binding, the committee felt compelled to resign and in fresh elections nearly all the establishment, including Burnet and Trueman, were swept away in a landslide of seismic proportions. With the new committee in charge, it was no surprise that not only did they offer Boycott a new contract but they also dispensed with Illingworth's services. Unwilling to continue under the new regime, Illingworth remained in Spain to learn of his fate and when chairman Reg Kirk duly rang him, he merely asked that the announcement be delayed for several days, so that he could inform his daughters on his return home. Unfortunately, the news had already leaked out, much to Vicky's distress when she learned of it on the radio. Recalling these events a few years later, Illingworth commented, 'I suppose at the time I felt a little disappointed in one way because Yorkshire cricket suffered, but, frankly, I had had enough of the Boycott faction, the members and so-called supporters who put one man above the club and all the other people in it. My wife and family were abused and the situation got completely out of control. Looking back, I reckon it was the skulduggery, the scheming and the downright dishonesty that sickened me most.'

Yet, for all the political and emotional capital spent dealing with Boycott and his supporters, the role of manager didn't sit easily with someone of Illingworth's restless temperament. As Brearley wrote, 'Being only the manager must have been purgatory for Illingworth; like having the kid next door play with your train set every day and being condemned to watch the derailments, collisions and general run-down of the assets of a life-long love. And the invitation to lead out the side at the age of 50 must have been an irresistible challenge, to be able to put his cricketing brain to work again and run his own train set.'

According to Boycott, it was soon obvious that Illingworth wanted to control his captains rather than help them. 'He always felt he could do better on the field than they could – and he was undoubtedly right. But that is something which team managers have to come to terms with – the captain is not really supposed to be an extension of the manager's personality. He wanted to lead the side by remote control, and that is simply never going to work.'

Illingworth himself admitted that 'it's hard, from the dressing room, to have an effect. You can suggest something, in an interval, but it has to be done at the right time.'

It was a dilemma that taxed him once again when he became chairman of the England selectors and team manager, and one for which he found no ready solution.

Chapter 11

A View from the Box

IN 1977 Illingworth's life took a turn for the better when he and Shirley bought a two-bedroom apartment at Playamar, just outside Torremolinos, in a complex with swimming, tennis and a restaurant. Granted near-permanent sunshine and a loyal circle of expat friends, they were blissfully happy there, especially when escaping the cold of the British winter. He played competitive golf three times a week at El Parador Golf Club, alias the Malaga Golf Club, close by before adjourning to a small Spanish bar owned by a friend of his thereafter.

Liberated of Yorkshire commitments, Illingworth re-joined Farsley in 1984, playing for them for the next four years in the Bradford League. According to Ashley Metcalfe, he was still their best bowler in his 50s, his control such that he posed few dangers to short leg. That year he enjoyed playing under the shrewd captaincy of Brian Hird and when the latter was forced to relinquish the post because of his wife's illness, Illingworth took over, lifting everyone to new heights with his inspired leadership. Leading a side that contained Yorkshire seamer Simon Dennis and Lancashire batsman Mark Chadwick, when available, they finished second in the first division of the league behind Pudsey

St Lawrence in 1985. After two 'marvellous' years as captain, Illingworth played for one more year before bowing out at the end of 1987 when his arm used to ache from bowling ten overs.

Following his demise at Yorkshire, Illingworth wasn't out of a job for long. Having impressed as a summariser in the commentary box on occasional outings in the past, he was quickly snapped up by the BBC for Test matches and other important games, sometimes for BBC's *Test Match Special*, but mainly for television over the course of the next decade. He also commentated for the BBC on their coverage of the World Cup in India and Pakistan in 1987.

Always his own man, understated and concise – he didn't repeat what the commentators had said – Illingworth was a natural summariser both on radio and television. According to the renowned broadcaster Brian Johnston, who recalled his ability to sniff out a chocolate cake at tea, his dry wit and quick reading of the game gave him a natural authority. His opinion was fully endorsed by fellow commentator Christopher Martin-Jenkins, who called him one of the best summarisers he worked with, and producer Peter Baxter, who recalled his candour and sense of fairness – he would give umpires the benefit of the doubt over a contentious decision.

He brought these same attributes to television, becoming a valuable part of the team alongside presenter Tony Lewis, Jim Laker and Richie Benaud. 'Jim Laker, Richie Benaud and Ray Illingworth were regarded as an unbelievable triumvirate,' wrote Laker's biographer, Alan Hill. 'The alliance of an Australian and two Yorkshiremen carried more than a trace of their origins. They did not get fussed over things or ever go foolishly over the top. All was tight and under control.' According to BBC cricket producer Nick Hunter, 'Ray was able to narrow down tactics, or the way someone was playing, with tremendous clarity and fairness.' In the opinion of commentator Jack Bannister, who took over from Laker after his death in 1986, there was no easier man to work with. 'No need to think how to phrase a question, no need to explain what you, as commentator, want from him as an expert.' He greatly admired Illingworth's analysis of the pitch, the captaincy and individual techniques – he greatly worried about Graeme Hick's weakness against the short ball – especially when dissecting their dismissals. He also proved uncannily accurate in his predictions.

Bannister thought that Illingworth's television involvement played an important part in his nomination for the vacant chairmanship of England selectors because of the respect he commanded from players and umpires, with whom he would converse throughout a Test. He was also a regular, welcome visitor in every committee room on the Test match circuit which must have helped his cause once he became a candidate for the chairmanship.

Yet for all his expertise, he couldn't escape the commentator's curse of the occasional verbal gaffe. In the Edgbaston Test of 1986 between England and India, he said, 'That turned anything from 12 inches to a foot.' At Headingley, in the England–West Indies Test of 1991, there were two. Focusing on West Indian vice-captain Desmond Haynes, who was discomfited by a back injury, Illingworth commented that he wouldn't be allowed a substitute, since he'd come into the match with the injury. When Benaud suggested that perhaps Haynes would be wiser to strain a hamstring, Illingworth replied, 'Good thinking, Richie, but I'm not sure they're all that intelligent.'

Later, in a discussion about the improvement in the sight screens at Headingley, he said, 'Yes, I remember the 1960s when

Wes [Hall] and Charlie [Griffith] used to come at you out of the trees.'

Although Illingworth had to sometimes restrain himself from disclosing his real thoughts, England players thought he was too critical. Allan Lamb took exception to his comment that he was one of the worst England batsmen to play spin following his dismissal to the Indian spinner Anil Kumble at Old Trafford in 1990, and on reaching his century in the second innings he saluted the commentary box.

It was during his time as a summariser and *Daily Express* columnist that Illingworth began his cold war with England's iconic all-rounder Ian Botham. He'd already criticised his negligible contribution as England captain in July 1981, stating in the *Sunday Mirror* that he was 'overrated, overweight and overpaid. He should be dropped.' Relieved of the captaincy, Botham then bounced back in dramatic style with his stupendous performances against Australia that summer, enabling England to retain the Ashes.

They clashed again in the 1983 series against New Zealand when Illingworth criticised Botham's bowling, while Botham, for his part, dismissed the Yorkshire JPL-winning side of that year in disparaging terms.

Their most serious spat occurred in May 1986 following Botham's admission in the *Mail on Sunday* that he'd smoked cannabis. Illingworth declared that the punishment should fit the crime and because drugs was a serious business, Botham should be banned for two years. 'Ian's status does not worry me a bit. He's a great cricketer – there can be no doubt about that even though he has been overrated. But there is not a player born who is bigger than the game. And it's the game's future which is at stake today.'

Even at the end of Botham's 68-day ban, during which England failed to win a game against India and New Zealand, Illingworth remained unreconciled to his recall for the final Test against the latter. 'But what really worries me about Botham is his attitude. It's deteriorated so much that I really don't know whether he is capable of doing it at England level.'

His criticism irked Botham, especially following his triumphant return when he took two wickets in his first two overs to break Dennis Lillee's record of 355 Test wickets, but Illingworth wasn't finished yet. Commenting on Botham's threat to leave Somerset unless they reinstated his good friends Viv Richards and Joel Garner, he wrote, 'If Botham stays, on his own terms, Somerset will be stuck with another Boycott and everything that goes with it.' No club could be held to ransom by one player. Despite provoking a great backlash among its members, Somerset held firm to their original decision and Botham left in disgust to join Worcestershire.

Illingworth continued to question his contribution during England's Ashes triumph in Australia that winter and against Pakistan at home the following summer. He rated the Pakistan side and wasn't surprised by their 1-0 win but was bitterly critical of their gamesmanship during England's ill-fated tour of Pakistan later that year when they fell victim to some questionable umpiring decisions. The flashpoint came in the second Test at Faisalabad when umpire Shakoor Rana, employing some expletive-ridden language, accused Mike Gatting of cheating, which prompted a furious finger-wagging retort from the England captain.

As the game came to a halt following Gatting's refusal to apologise to Rana, Illingworth feared an international plot to deprive England of its influence in world cricket. He said, 'Cricket-wise, Pakistan has always been iffy and Pakistanis, in the main, difficult. Now they've become downright Bolshie. Given a chance, they would trample all over us. If the umpire had told me I was a cheat, I might have said a few things back. It is ridiculous for such an incompetent umpire to accuse Gatting of that.'

Having called for the tour to be abandoned, Illingworth then vented his spleen on the TCCB for their failure to support Gatting. 'How could the TCCB instruct Gatting to apologise unconditionally? Even worse, how could they do that and not press for an apology from Rana?'

Illingworth continued to be a firm supporter of Gatting, even after his botched dismissal the following summer over an alleged encounter with a barmaid, and when he became chairman of selectors in 1994, he contemplated restoring him to the captaincy.

Following the disastrous tour to West Indies in 1985/86, when England's discipline and performance were subjected to a full-blooded bombardment from the tabloid press, the TCCB increasingly recognised the need for an assistant manager to relieve the captain of his growing number of duties. He would have responsibility for the team's fitness, practice and day-to-day discipline, but he would be subordinate to the tour manager and the chairman of selectors – rather like Ken Barrington between 1978 and 1981.

In principle Illingworth was interested in the role and he was all but offered it by TCCB chairman Raman Subba Row at Lord's in July 1986, but his interest soon waned when denied the full-blown powers he wanted. Describing the job as 'little more than a glorified bag carrier', he ruled himself out, much to John Woodcock's relief. 'A good thing, too. Cricket does not lend itself, in the way that football may, to a generalissimo. I very much doubt whether Illingworth, when he was captain of England, would ever have tolerated anyone with the authority that he sought for himself.'

The job instead went to Micky Stewart, the director of cricket at Surrey, who made the position his own after England's successful tour of Australia in 1986/87, leaving one with the intriguing thought of what might have occurred had Illingworth accepted. He later acknowledged that this would have been the ideal time for him to have become manager, since he knew everyone in cricket; instead, by the time he assumed a more powerful role nine years later, he was too old and out of touch with the modern game.

He also turned down the opportunity to coach Leicestershire in 1989 because the salary wouldn't compensate for the loss of his media earnings, and the job went to former Australia captain Bobby Simpson. At a time when English cricket was plunging into chaos it seemed unfortunate that the one man deemed capable of reviving it was confined to the relative obscurity of the commentary box, but further humiliations brought about a volte-face by the TCCB in their efforts to stop the rot. Churchill in 1939, De Gaulle in 1958 and Brearley in 1981 had all been noted for their comebacks. Could Illingworth offer something similar?

Chapter 12

Backseat Driver

WHEN TED Dexter resigned as chairman of selectors in August 1993, following England's disastrous home loss to Australia, the assumption was that his successor would be Mike Smith, the chairman of Warwickshire and manager-elect of England's tour of the West Indies. That certainly was the intention of the TCCB executive committee, but their plans were thwarted by a number of the counties, led by Yorkshire president Sir Lawrence Byford. Riled about being sidelined all too frequently in the Dexter–Fletcher era, they insisted that his successor was democratically elected. At the TCCB meeting in December, the England committee was disbanded and re-organised into two sections – selection and development. A four-man working party was set up comprising A.C. Smith, the TCCB's chief executive, Ossie Wheatley, the former chairman of its cricket committee, and two county chairmen, Duncan Fearnley of Worcestershire and David Acfield of Essex, to draw up a shortlist for the new chairman of selectors.

Engrossed with his media work, Illingworth hadn't given serious thought to standing as Dexter's successor. He had even proposed Boycott for the role in the *Daily Express* in July 1993, but all that changed when Byford broached the matter with him that December.

Flattered to be asked, Illingworth, on receiving an assurance from the TCCB working party that he would have the final say over selection, allowed his name to go forward and began lobbying through the media. Having ruled out potential candidates such as Mike Brearley, Tony Greig and Boycott, who weren't available, the working party presented their colleagues with a shortlist of two, Mike Smith and Illingworth. Although from contrasting backgrounds, they were of a similar age, experience and approach to the game, both former England captains, popular with their players and inclined towards caution. With the counties perceiving Illingworth as the more decisive candidate capable of taking hard-headed decisions and Smith as the establishment choice, the former narrowly won the postal vote 11 to 9.

Informed by A.C. Smith of his success, Illingworth returned from Spain to attend his coronation at the TCCB spring meeting later that week. His appointment, while disappointing to those like Botham who considered him too old and out of touch with the modern game, was broadly welcomed. Ian Chappell thought it one of the best decisions that English cricket had made for some time and the former Leicester-based journalist Martin Johnson told the tabloid media that Illingworth would make their life a dream given his propensity to speak his mind.

The task facing Illingworth was immense. At a time when international cricket had become highly competitive, not least with the return of South Africa from political isolation, England had slipped down the rankings under both of his predecessors, Peter May and Ted Dexter. Since their Ashes triumph in Australia in 1986/87, they'd won only three series compared to the ten they'd lost and had been comprehensively outplayed by Australia in three consecutive rubbers. Confronted with this litany of failure, the press had pilloried both May and Dexter, but while they'd lacked consistency in selection, England's malaise went far deeper than individual misjudgement. Whether it be the decline in the standard of pitches, the amount of cricket played or the detrimental effect of the one-day game, the county system was no longer capable of producing enough Test standard cricketers. (It was to raise the standard of county cricket that Illingworth had long advocated a two-tier system.)

Contrary to the low profile of May and Dexter, Illingworth set out to be a much more proactive chairman. Not only would he watch more cricket, he would take the lead in selection meetings in line with his belief that he was a good judge of a player, and be readily available to the media. After the remoteness and obfuscation of the May–Dexter years this proved highly popular with the press, but Illingworth's refreshing candour often pricked sensitivities. According to Johnny Barclay, who accompanied Illingworth to South Africa in 1995/96 as his assistant, he didn't appreciate how much the press had changed and how the respected cricket writer had given way to a ruthless news reporter who would distort his words to detrimental effect. *The Observer*'s Vic Marks recalls that Illingworth rather enjoyed the theatrics of a news conference and journalists would keep asking him questions in the near certainty that sooner or later he would give them a contentious story or a colourful line.

From the outset, Illingworth put down a marker for his no-nonsense approach. 'I would like to think things will work out with [Keith] Fletcher and [Mike] Atherton,' (the England coach and captain) he said, 'but if they don't, I will have the final say in picking the team.'

Convinced that certain England players lacked pride in representing their country, he stressed a more professional approach to practice and for individuals to take greater responsibility for their actions. Disconcerted by their performance in the West Indies, he publicly rebuked wicketkeeper Jack Russell, all-rounder Chris Lewis and batsmen Mark Ramprakash and Robin Smith, and threatened something of a clearout. He also warned spinner Phil Tufnell that he had to sort out his personal life before he played for England again.

Illingworth's resolve was apparent at his first meeting with Atherton, the 26-year-old captain, who'd taken over from Graham Gooch the previous summer and who'd led a young side to the West Indies. Shunning any pleasantries, he outlined his commitment to a five-man attack, including two spinners where appropriate, and produced a list of 60 players he was keen to look at. 'It was clear to me from the start that whatever vision I had had and whatever plans I had made, would be cast aside,' Atherton later wrote. That vision of a younger group of players, ideally on central contracts, that would put an end to the constant chopping and changing of the side, was in direct contrast to Illingworth's. He hailed from an era when county cricket was king and the selectors picked those heading the averages on the assumption that they had the wherewithal to perform at Test level.

Yet despite their differing outlooks, reflecting the huge gap in age and attitudes – Atherton thought Illingworth mistrusted his Oxbridge background – captain and chairman rubbed along quite well on a personal level, not least on the 1995/96 tour to South Africa where they played a lot of bridge together. Noting Illingworth's tendency to hark back to his playing career as a golden age, Atherton used to enjoy ribbing him about it. On one occasion, while shuffling a new pack of cards several fell to the floor, at which point he remarked to much hilarity, 'First time I've put down anything in my life – I held 500 bloody catches, you know.' On another occasion when the BBC ran some old footage of Illingworth padding up to Sobers and losing his middle stump in the England versus the Rest of the World series, much to the team's amusement, he shot straight back with, 'What you lot might like to know is that I top-scored with 97.' 'We often set him up but he always bounces back,' recalled Atherton.

While Atherton appreciated Illingworth's tactical input during a match, Illingworth in turn admired his captain's prowess as an unflinching opening bat and his strength of character. In his more reflective moments, he wondered how he, Illingworth, would have coped leading England in his mid-20s, especially given the intrusiveness of the modern media. Yet the plaudits never lasted that long because of his doubts about Atherton's tactical ability and his own reluctance to stomach views that deviated from his own. It is true that in selection meetings he proved more flexible than some of his public comments suggested, and he deferred to Atherton on occasions, but if Atherton's man failed to pass muster, Illingworth was quick to point the finger. Prone to criticising his captain in public, most notably during England's 1994/95 tour of Australia, he never seemed to appreciate the demoralising effect of his derogatory comments on individuals, even though he bridled on those few occasions when Atherton fought back. Describing their relationship on the England 1995/96 tour to South Africa, Illingworth later wrote, 'I think he has been great to work with. We have never had the slightest problem about our working relationship, and I couldn't have asked for any person in his role more suited to thinking about the game as I do.'

His account was seriously challenged by Jack Russell, who accused him of treating Atherton like a schoolboy for much of the time and for constantly undermining him in front of the team. 'Yet Athers refused to walk away, despite great provocation. The players were totally on his side, he had all of our respect, yet he didn't appear to force many issues with Illingworth.'

It certainly wouldn't have been out of choice on Atherton's part, but recognising Illingworth's unprecedented powers – he was now manager as well as chairman of selectors – and the need for team harmony, he invariably let sleeping dogs lie.

Fortified by the appointment of his preferred choices as fellow selectors, Fred Titmus and Brian Bolus, the former England opening batsman, Illingworth spent the first few weeks of the 1994 season scouring the country for fresh talent. Those who particularly impressed were the Yorkshire trio of Darren Gough, an ebullient fast bowler, Richard Stemp, a left-arm spinner with a nice action, and Craig White, a muscular all-rounder, in addition to the Bradford-born Steven Rhodes, the gritty Worcestershire wicketkeeper. Although an injury to Gough ruled him out of the first Test against New Zealand, the other three were named in a squad that included only five survivors from the previous Test against West Indies two months earlier. When questioned about the selection of the three Yorkshiremen, Illingworth replied, 'Tell them that when Yorkshire are strong, England are strong.'

With Gooch, an absentee in the West Indies, leading the way with a double century, England won the first Test at Trent Bridge by an innings, but their victory was overshadowed by Illingworth's abrupt dismissal of the team's unpaid chaplain Andrew Wingfield-Digby, the director of Christians in Sport. Although the genial

Wingfield-Digby had been a popular member of the dressing room over the previous three years, Illingworth was rather suspicious of him and considered him surplus to requirements. 'We are not going to be playing tiddlywinks in Australia', he declared, 'and, in my opinion, if the players need a shoulder to cry on, they should not be in the side.'

Embarrassed by headlines of 'Illy bans God', Illingworth objected to the publicity surrounding his ban of mobile phones in the dressing room, a ban fully supported by coach Keith Fletcher, and that of sunglasses, which, he complained, was entirely without foundation.

Days later Illingworth once again found himself in controversy following the omission of fast bowler Devon Malcolm from the squad of 13 to play at Lord's. Restored to the England side at Trent Bridge, Malcolm had bowled poorly and Illingworth, overriding the wishes of Atherton, dispensed with him the day before the Test without any explanation. 'That day was the lowest point of my career,' Malcolm later wrote. 'Getting no support from my captain made it worse, especially after he'd admitted that he wanted me to play.'

He was replaced by debutant Paul Taylor, a left-arm seamer from Northamptonshire, a decision that Illingworth later regretted, since Taylor failed to take a wicket in a game England were fortunate to draw.

England had the better of another draw at Old Trafford, a game in which Gough vindicated his selection with a dashing 65 on his debut, to win an undistinguished series 1-0, but a greater challenge awaited them from South Africa, who were making their first tour of England in 29 years. With the selectors divided over the replacement of Robin Smith, who'd lost form and confidence,

Illingworth, an advocate for Graham Thorpe, gave way to Atherton, who wanted his Lancashire team-mate John Crawley.

In humid conditions, South Africa, led by a century from their captain Kepler Wessels, made 357 and took control of the game by dismissing England for 180. On a soporific third day, they were batting themselves into a near-invincible position when Atherton was caught by the television cameras putting his hand in his trouser pocket, then rubbing his fingers on to the ball before returning it to the bowler. The third umpire Mervyn Kitchen witnessed the incident and informed both umpires, Dickie Bird and Steve Randell, and the match referee Peter Burge. What once would have seemed a mundane procedure now passed for something more serious in light of recent cases of ball-tampering. Two years earlier the Pakistan attack had been accused of resorting to sharp practice as they pummelled the England batsmen with reverse swing, so for England to be associated with something similar proved profoundly embarrassing.

Because Illingworth had been watching the game from the pavilion balcony, he missed the television footage, but alerted to the incident by South Africa coach Mike Procter, he was able to view it on a video in the office of the TCCB's media spokesman Richard Little. When he returned shortly before the tea interval, he relayed a message to Atherton via Gooch at third man to come and see him immediately, which he did. Illingworth asked him to turn his pockets out, and he saw what looked like dust. Atherton told him he often did it to stop sweat getting on the ball when he bowled, a practice he considered perfectly legitimate, since it was simply to soak up the sweat on his hands.

At close of play, Illingworth was about to leave the dressing room to go to the Cornhill hospitality room when word reached him that Burge had asked to see Atherton and Fletcher. Thinking that Atherton had been silly rather than culpable, Illingworth made light of the affair when he discussed it with Procter, little realising the storm that was about to break.

On meeting Burge, Atherton told him that he'd put his hand in his pocket to dry his fingers but failed to mention that he'd used the dirt to dry them, fearing that Burge might misconstrue this as him using an artificial substance to alter the ball. With the umpires Dickie Bird and Steve Randell confirming that the ball hadn't been altered in any way, Burge accepted Atherton's explanation that nothing untoward had occurred.

Later that evening, Illingworth ran into Burge back in the hotel where they were staying. Burge told him he'd exonerated Atherton and would be taking no further action against him. His statement to this effect without revealing what the explanation was infuriated the press, especially given the secrecy surrounding the ball-tampering allegations against Pakistan two years earlier.

With the Sunday papers publishing damning photos of the incident, Illingworth took it upon himself to investigate the matter further. On arrival at the ground at 9.30am, he saw Atherton immediately and when Atherton admitted that he hadn't given Burge a complete explanation, Illingworth took the law into his own hands. Anticipating a punitive sanction from Burge, he acted peremptorily by fining Atherton £1,000 for placing dirt on the ball and £1,000 for misleading the match referee, the stiffest penalty he could impose without submitting himself to the full rigmarole of a disciplinary hearing. He then went to see Burge and told him what he was going to do. Burge replied that had he known the truth on Saturday evening, he would probably have suspended Atherton for two games, but in light of Illingworth's punishment he agreed to take no further action.

As England slid to a humiliating defeat, dismissed in their second innings for 99, Illingworth remained closeted in intense deliberations with the TCCB for most of the day, composing a statement that took ages to finalise. He also told Atherton that facing the press in which he would confess all was the price he would pay for maintaining the captaincy. That press conference duly took place in the players' dining room at the end of the match. With the room overflowing with journalists without any air conditioning on a sweltering evening, the tension was palpable as Illingworth and Atherton entered. When someone complimented Atherton on his ability to smile, Illingworth snapped, 'There's nothing to smile about.'

Sweating profusely, Illingworth read his prepared statement, first explaining why he'd fined Atherton. 'I wouldn't really think Michael has done anything illegal but I didn't want him to have this round his neck for the rest of his life. I have fined Michael the maximum I can on each count; and as far as I am concerned, the matter has been dealt with and is now closed.'

Atherton then recited his *mea culpa* statement, explaining his actions, ending with an apology to Burge and the South African team. In response to a fierce interrogation, led by the BBC's cricket correspondent Jonathan Agnew, he admitted he hadn't given the match referee the full facts. While acknowledging that the television footage looked suspicious, he insisted he'd hadn't tampered with the ball. He pointed out that what he was doing was essentially no different from the action of many bowlers who dried their hands by wiping them on the ground.

When the *Daily Telegraph*'s Christopher Martin-Jenkins asked Illingworth why he'd fined Atherton for something which didn't contravene any law, Illingworth accepted that he might have been a trifle hard but added that they had to be above suspicion. 'Unfortunately, by fining him for the use of dirt the chairman seems to have signalled that he does not share the captain's view of his innocence,' noted Martin-Jenkins.

The next day the press were far from convinced by Atherton's performance and many editorials opined he should resign. It was a view given added credibility by Burge's stinging rebuke of Atherton for withholding information and damaging the image of the game.

Relentlessly pursued by the media as he sought respite in the Lake District, Atherton gave serious thought to his future. He rang Illingworth to see whether he still had his support. Illingworth assured him that he did and guaranteed him the support of the other selectors. He also publicly 'backed him to the hilt', adding that he was still a young man who would learn from the experience.

Buoyed by the support he received from selectors, team-mates and public alike, Atherton resolved to stay put and displayed his resilience with a steely 99 in the second Test at Headingley. His stand of 142 for the third wicket with the reinstated Graham Thorpe proved a double tonic for Illingworth in a drawn game in which the bat dominated over the ball.

Anticipating a quick pitch in the final Test at The Oval, the selectors recalled Malcolm in place of Angus Fraser, who'd lost some of his penetration, and went into the game not only with a four-man attack but also without a front-line spinner. The decision marked a significant departure from Illingworth's principles but, convinced that the pitch would offer the spinners nothing, he went along with his captain's preference for just four bowlers, since that allowed them to play an extra batsman.

In reply to South Africa's first innings of 332, England were floundering at 222/7 before a spectacular counter-attack by Gough and Phil DeFreitas at the end of the second day brought them back into the game.

Concerned about Malcolm's erratic bowling on the opening day, Illingworth made it his business to give him a pep talk on the third morning. He wrote: 'When I saw him, he was sitting in a corner, eyes closed, with the cans on, listening to music. I wasn't too impressed, because I confess I thought he was probably listening to pop music and I was even more determined to roust him.

'I tapped him on the shoulder and when he lifted one can to listen to me, I heard the pop music coming out and said: "You should be listening to *Land of Hope and Glory*." I then had a general chat with him for a couple of minutes about his bowling and attitude and left him to it.'

Whether Illingworth's words had any effect on Malcolm that day only the latter would know, but bowling fast and straight he decimated South Africa's batting with the astounding figures of 9-57, by some way the stellar performance of his career. Set 204 to win, England romped home at a canter to win by eight wickets in what Illingworth called the most positive display of cricket he'd seen from an England side in 30 years.

With a convincing 2-0 series victory in the Texaco games that followed, Illingworth thought that the team had improved substantially during the season, helped considerably by the introduction of Rhodes and Gough and the recall of Thorpe. He also appeared to have won the confidence of Atherton, who appreciated the support he'd received from him both at Lord's, and at The Oval, when Burge had fined him for a mild show of dissent on his first-innings dismissal. 'Raymond saved my job,'

Atherton told *The Times*. 'If he had wanted another captain then, he could have got one.

'As this summer has gone on, my relationship with Raymond has got better and better. The chairman and I are much closer than we were before. I don't hesitate to ring him at home now, if there is something on my mind.' That closer relationship had come at a cost, however, since Atherton's waning authority as captain was less able to combat Illingworth's fixed ideas about who should tour Australia.

Departing from the emphasis on youth from the previous tour to the West Indies, Illingworth recalled both Gooch and Gatting despite their age and lack of agility in the field, a real impediment on the large Australian grounds.

While Atherton supported the return of Gooch, he fought a losing battle over Fraser, one of England's most reliable bowlers who'd struggled somewhat that summer after his 8-75 against West Indies in Barbados earlier that year. Never a great admirer of Fraser, and his lugubrious exterior which concealed a lion-hearted trier, Illingworth opted instead for the raw pace of Kent's Martin McCague, despite the concerns about his fitness. 'The selection of the Ashes squad was the final proof that it was no longer the captain who had the final say,' Atherton wrote in his autobiography. 'Illy was the main influence. After all I'd been through in the previous weeks, I wasn't really in much of a position to argue.

'As for Gus [Fraser], it had nothing to do with friendship. I knew that he could do a job for England in Australia. Illy, for some reason, thought he was a negative influence. Nothing could be further from the truth.' Devastated by his rebuff and without any explanation from either Illingworth or Atherton, Fraser gave vent to his frustration in the *News of the World*, an article that cost him £1,000 from his stand-by fee.

At the end of the season Illingworth went to Spain for a month. On his return he was guest at a Sports Writers' Association lunch in London, where his comments at a question-and-answer format landed him in trouble days before the first Test. Not only did he rebuke Atherton for failing to contact him since England had arrived in Australia, he questioned the number of days off for the squad and belittled Fletcher's role as coach.

Up against a formidable Australian side under the astute leadership of Mark Taylor, England entered the Ashes very much as underdogs, but a feckless performance in the field and a failure to combat the genius of Shane Warne led to a comprehensive defeat in the first Test at Brisbane.

Watching the game at home, Illingworth thought England lacked all-round professionalism and when he flew into Melbourne two days before the second Test he didn't hold back. 'The players have to knuckle down. The one thing people back home won't take is players who don't appear to be giving everything. Sloppy fielding is one example. There is no excuse and I won't accept it.'

After dismissing Australia for 279, England began confidently enough before several unfortunate decisions took the wind out of their sails. Conceding a lead of 67 on first innings, they went into defensive mode and set 388 to win, they subsided meekly to 92 all out.

Chastened by the scale of the defeat, Illingworth couldn't conceal his frustration at the decline of team spirit. 'It's amazing to me in two or three months how things have drifted. It's their jobs on the line, not mine, if they don't do the business.' Concerned about Atherton's negative body language, he called on him to come out of his shell and 'gee up the team'.

Atherton did precisely that because England played with greater resolution in the third Test at Sydney and were unfortunate not to win. Despite his own success with the bat, Atherton felt shackled by the presence of five former England captains – Illingworth, Mike Smith, Fletcher, Gooch and Gatting – and public divisions within the management. In an interview with Peter Hayter, the cricket correspondent of the *Mail on Sunday*, he felt emboldened to speak out and make a bid for greater control over selection. 'Last summer, for instance, I went on to the field with players that I didn't particularly want in the side and that was very hard work. And I don't think I am giving anything away when I say that the tour party is not the one I wanted, full stop.'

Regretting the end of the youth policy that marked his first few months in charge, he claimed that what happened in Australia had shown that 'we should have stuck to our guns'. He also demanded a greater say in choosing the team and questioned the age of the selectorial panel, averring that it should be recently retired Test players in touch with the modern game.

To compound matters, his remarks were sanctioned by manager Mike Smith, who'd taken exception to Illingworth's public criticism of Atherton and Fletcher, another skirmish in the war that had developed between Illingworth and the tour management.

Illingworth returned home after the Sydney Test and watched the final two Tests on television. England continued their rally with a creditable win at Adelaide, only then to capitulate at Perth. Although blighted by injury to leading players such as Alec Stewart, Gough and Graeme Hick, England lacked the necessary resolve and consistency to win in Australia. For Gooch and Gatting, it was one tour too many, the same fate that awaited Fletcher.

From the time of Illingworth's appointment with the purpose of getting things done, his days appeared numbered. They clashed over selection, discipline – Fletcher considered the fining of Atherton to be excessive – and man-management. Aside from Illingworth's failure to show a softer side to more sensitive players like Hick, Fletcher thought that his frustration with the team was born of his failure to understand the lack of talent available, especially among the bowlers. What particularly galled him, however, was the chairman's habit of accepting the accolades when England played well and distancing himself from anything that went wrong.

These differences were exacerbated in Australia when Illingworth not only publicly criticised the tour management, but also cast doubt on Fletcher's role. He wrote, 'But, as a team manager and coach, I reckon he needed to be more outgoing and go out of his way to identify more with individual problems. I was sure we could make more of our players if he did that.' When Smith tackled Illingworth over his lack of support for Fletcher, he would deny the comments, claiming that he'd been misquoted. That said, Fletcher's record of five wins in 26 matches damaged his credibility and in Australia he appeared an increasingly remote figure, unable to motivate the side, a point Illingworth stressed to A.C. Smith at a meeting on his return home, although the question of replacing him was never broached.

In early March Illingworth was asked to attend a special meeting of the TCCB's executive committee at Lord's, two days before the full board meeting, to discuss Fletcher's future. Having given his report on the tour, Illingworth left the meeting early to appear on ITV's *Sport in Question*, at which point he was bitterly attacked by Mike Smith for his public sniping, but Smith was a lone voice in his defence of Fletcher.

With Fletcher's five-year contract terminated, the logical outcome was to offer Illingworth the all-powerful role he'd always wanted. Very late that evening, TCCB chairman Dennis Silk arranged to meet Illingworth at the Regent's Park Hilton, where they were both staying, and offered him full responsibility for the England team, an offer Illingworth swiftly accepted.

At the press conference following the full board meeting, Illingworth said his priority was to restore motivation and team confidence, something he felt capable of achieving. He also gave notice of employing some specialist coaches, eventually deciding on Peter Lever for the bowling and John Edrich for the batting, following his failure to lure Boycott. While this was partly down to finance, it went deeper than that. When Illingworth first approached Boycott in March 1995, he proposed two and a half days of coaching before each Test, for which Boycott would be paid £500 a session. Boycott was interested in the idea but casting doubt about the value of these sessions prior to a Test, because of the limited time available to rectify technical deficiencies, he advocated a 70-day coaching programme over the course of the year for which he would be paid £1,000 a day.

When the TCCB declined Boycott's proposals on grounds of cost, Illingworth tried to persuade him to accept his original idea, but he wouldn't budge, calling it a half-baked scheme.

While some cricket writers thought Illingworth fortunate to be given such control after some glaring failures in policy and personnel in Australia, which he claimed were the fault of others, *The Times* was decidedly more upbeat. 'Illingworth brings with him the cutting edge of pride which every team but England seems now to possess. Our cricketers could learn a thing or two from him and also win a Test or two for him.'

Illingworth's public criticism of Atherton's leadership in Australia and Atherton's defiant riposte exposed a deep rift between the two men. When they met at a secret location on the M62 on 14 March to pick over the bones of the tour, it proved an acrimonious encounter with neither giving ground to the other. Although inclined to keep faith with his captain for the home series against West Indies, Illingworth couldn't commit himself to reappointing him until he consulted his fellow selectors, one of whom, Bolus, had lost out to David Graveney, the secretary of the Professional Cricketers' Association. When they met, Titmus took umbrage at Atherton's attack on the selectors' age, so much so that Illingworth was prepared to consider a change in leadership had they been unanimous, but Graveney was firmly behind Atherton. He suggested that before there was a public announcement Illingworth should meet Atherton again, in the company of the other selectors, to agree clear lines of command in order to avoid any future territorial disputes.

At that meeting on 26 April, Graveney was so concerned by the bad blood emanating from Illingworth and Atherton's respective public pronouncements, he asked them whether they could work together. After both agreed that they could, Illingworth outlined his house rules to Atherton. He, Atherton, would have full control on the field, but he would be expected to smarten up his appearance at press conferences – that included shaving – keep out of politics and refrain from making public pronouncements about selection.

Once Atherton had accepted these terms his reappointment, initially for the three Texaco games and for the first three Tests against West Indies, was a formality. When quizzed about his procrastination in the re-appointment, Illingworth said: 'There were things we had to clear up; it's not a captain's job to go around criticising selectors. If he has something to say, he should say it in committee.' According to *The Times*' Alan Lee, Illingworth, by insisting that the captaincy needed serious discussion and a full interview, was issuing a public warning and demonstration of his influence.

Many considered his influence baleful. The editor of *Wisden* Matthew Engel held Illingworth responsible for the shambolic organisation of the Australian tour and reminded him that he didn't have a monopoly of cricketing wisdom; Botham berated him for his 'disgraceful' treatment of Atherton and city financier Patrick Whittingdale, announcing the end of his firm's £3 million sponsorship of English cricket since 1990, attacked him for his poor man-management.

Although West Indies weren't the dominant force of yore having just lost at home to Australia, their first series defeat in 15 years, their side still contained some world-class players such as Richie Richardson, Brian Lara, Carl Hooper, Curtly Ambrose and Courtney Walsh. In order to allow Alec Stewart to keep wicket and bat in the middle order, the England selectors, rather against Illingworth's better judgement, asked Robin Smith to open, a gamble that failed, since he was dismissed cheaply in both innings.

Inserted in dank conditions at Headingley, England played indifferently throughout to lose by nine wickets. When asked whether he was more worried about the failings of the bat or the ball, Illingworth puffed out his cheeks in contemplation and replied, 'It's about even-Steven to be honest,' a comment that brought a wry smile from Atherton.

Accepting that Smith was better off down the order, Illingworth asked Atherton to approach Stewart to see whether he would be willing to both open and keep wicket at Lord's. Atherton informed his fellow selectors that Stewart was unwilling to do this, at which point they recalled Rhodes as wicketkeeper and gave a first cap to Derbyshire all-rounder Dominic Cork.

When Stewart heard Illingworth comment on his unwillingness to perform the dual role, he denied saying anything of the sort. He explained that, given the choice, he would prefer to open than keep wicket, but he was prepared to do both. 'That is what the chairman wants,' he remarked. 'You don't argue with Mr Illingworth.'

Convinced that Stewart held the key to the balance of the England team, Illingworth was prepared to court controversy by leaving out Rhodes and giving Stewart the dual role. He informed Atherton of his proposal and although rather surprised by the chairman's volte-face he didn't object; nor did the other two selectors when Illingworth rang them two days before the match. Later that evening Graveney began to have second thoughts and conveyed his misgivings to Illingworth at the pre-match practice the following day, but Illingworth wasn't for turning. Not surprisingly, Rhodes was upset at his last-minute demotion, evidence according to the media of Illingworth's autocratic ways. 'Given his history it would scarcely surprise anyone, if aged 61 *[sic]*, he led out the England side this summer,' wrote Alan Lee. 'It was certainly the most controversial decision I have ever made in cricket,' Illingworth later admitted, 'but at least it showed that I was not afraid to back my judgement even in the face of criticism and ridicule.'

As it was his instinct proved correct. Not only did Stewart make useful runs in both innings, he took a match-winning catch to dismiss the dangerous-looking Brian Lara off debutant Cork, whose 7-43 on the final day helped England secure a 72-run victory. It was one of the sweetest Illingworth had known, allowing him to get even with his critics. 'I would like to say to you chaps that some of the muddled thinking turned out pretty well.'

With England's morale on the rise in contrast to the West Indies who followed their loss at Lord's with an ignominious innings defeat against Sussex, Illingworth looked forward to the third Test at Edgbaston. Convinced that English Test wickets should be prepared to home advantage like those in some other countries, he met the six home Test match groundsmen at the beginning of May. He asked them for hard, firm pitches that were bare at both ends to help England's spinners.

Ten days before the Edgbaston Test, Illingworth spoke to the groundsman Steve Rouse, who told him that the pitch would be hard and quick. Shortly after this he asked Warwickshire's chief executive Dennis Amiss to take some grass off, especially at both ends, in the hope it might take spin.

To keep the pressure up, Illingworth asked Titmus to call in at Edgbaston on his way up to Manchester to pick the England team. He reported a 'funny-looking' pitch but didn't seem too concerned in contrast to Illingworth, who on his arrival at Edgbaston two days before the match, found a grassy pitch tailor-made for the West Indian quicks. Shocked by what he saw, he requested instant shaving of the offending areas, an exercise that proved too little, too late.

From the first ball of the match, a loosener from Ambrose that soared over Atherton's head for four byes, England were thrown on to the defensive. Shot out for 147, they then bowled erratically, allowing West Indies to establish a match-winning lead of 153.

Beginning the third day at 59/3, England quickly folded for 89 in the face of some fearsome fast bowling, much to the indignation of the crowd, a number of whom heckled Atherton and Illingworth at the post-match awards ceremony. While Atherton called the pitch diabolical, Illingworth and Warwickshire blamed each other for the fiasco. In response to the latter's claim that they were simply following TCCB guidelines, Illingworth released the official TCCB minutes from the May meeting laying down the objectives for the preparation of wickets. He said he wanted even bounce and didn't get it. 'But I won't be made to look a bloody nincompoop. It's ridiculous to suggest that I, or anyone else, would ask for a wicket with a bounce so inconsistent that it played into the hands of the West Indies attack.'

Deflated but not unbowed by Edgbaston, Illingworth, convinced that the West Indies batting was vulnerable, backed England to bounce back. In a side that contained six changes, Jack Russell returned for the injured Stewart and Hick was omitted for Warwickshire's Nick Knight.

On a true surface at Old Trafford, England did well to bowl West Indies out for 216 and, led by 94 from Thorpe, they secured a lead of 221. With Lara in scintillating form in the second innings, the game appeared to be in the balance before a hat-trick by Cork tilted it in England's favour.

Needing only 94 to win, they slumped to 48/4, in addition to losing Robin Smith with a broken cheekbone, before a feisty 31 not out from Russell saw them home without further loss.

Smith's injury, which ruled him out for the rest of the season, allowed Hick a reprieve. Since his debut in 1991 Hick, although a prolific scorer in county cricket, had never lived up to expectation. Beneath his placid exterior there lay a sensitive temperament manifest in his exclusion from the Old Trafford Test. Before the fifth Test, Hick sought out Illingworth and Atherton for a clear-the-air meeting. Bitterly upset by his omission at Old Trafford and Illingworth's suggestion that he lacked mental resilience, Hick went public with his reservations about the lack of confidence he'd received from the England selectors over the past year.

Pinpointing his predicament with brutal candour, Illingworth told him he had to show the right attitude. 'I think you've got a soft centre and it's because you've had a mollycoddled upbringing. Go out and prove me wrong.'

Taking advantage of a flat Trent Bridge pitch and a West Indies attack without Ambrose, Hick batted gamely to score 118 not out. England made 440 but Lara punished some loose bowling with another brilliant century and they had to battle hard to save the match.

Another placid wicket at The Oval produced a further stalemate, enabling England to draw the series 2-2. Despite criticising Atherton for his handling of his attack at Trent Bridge, Illingworth reckoned his captaincy had progressed nicely because 'he is listening more to me', he said with a chuckle. It was the high point of his time in charge.

Chapter 13

One Man Band

ENGLAND'S TOUR of South Africa in 1995/96, their first there for 31 years, comprised five Tests and seven ODIs, before they travelled to India and Pakistan for the World Cup. The day before they flew out, Illingworth put his managerial authority on the line by announcing the scrapping of the traditional selection committee in South Africa and confirming that he would be taking sole control. He then participated in a discussion about recent selection decisions with Geoff Boycott, in *The Sun*, the implication being that the more inspired ones owed more to his tactical insight than to Atherton's and vice versa, a breach of confidence that could have seriously ruptured their relationship. As it was, Atherton put his irritation to one side for the sake of the team and managed to work constructively with his manager for the bulk of the tour, not least in trying to get the best out of Devon Malcolm.

Since his debut against Australia in 1989, there was no doubting Malcolm's pace and hostility, especially on a quick wicket. When he was on song, he was a match-winner, but, equally, there were many days when he was off key and went for plenty, so his Test place could never be guaranteed.

With Illingworth, his relationship was always tetchy. While popular with his team-mates, Malcolm's stubbornness and failure to act on advice could be frustrating. He never forgot the slight of his public omission from the Lord's Test against New Zealand the previous year and Illingworth's lukewarm compliments after his demolition of South Africa at The Oval. He also resented his general carping about his technical deficiencies, primarily his tendency to fall away to the off side in his delivery stride, thereby losing pace and direction. 'If you started with a blank piece of paper,' recalled Angus Fraser, 'you wouldn't bowl like Devon. I could see what they were trying to do – refine a raw diamond. The question was the manner in which they went about it. Peter Lever [the bowling coach] was a lovely bloke, but Illy was old school. He told you how to improve, rather than working with you.'

Prior to the team's departure, Illingworth wanted Malcolm to work with Lever to iron out these faults, but his plans were stymied by the former's slow recovery from surgery on his knee. As the side flew off, he placed added pressure on his quick bowler. 'At Devon's age [32] he has to accept that this is a make-or-break tour for him. He has lacked consistency all through his England career and if he doesn't do it this time, he is going to find it tough to get back in the side.'

From the beginning of the tour a serious rift developed between Malcolm and the management with the former resisting attempts by the latter to refine his action. Feeling under pressure he let slip at an impromptu press conference, 'I hope I get the support of the manager and the captain this time. You could say it has not always been there in the past.'

Illingworth, like Lever, remained frustrated by Malcolm's failure to heed advice and commented, 'His confidence may be affected by the keyhole operation he had on his knee before the tour. But in the first few nets, he hasn't convinced me he is trying to follow my advice about his action.'

As the only black cricketer on either side at this time of enormous racial and political change in South Africa, Malcolm was seen as an unofficial ambassador for black cricketers. He was mobbed by scores of black youngsters when the England team visited the Alexandra township and was the focus of attention during the tourists' inaugural first-class game in the once notorious Soweto. The occasion was graced by the presence of President Nelson Mandela, who dropped in by helicopter on the opening morning. Presented to the England team, Mandela singled out Malcolm, remarking, 'I know who you are, you're the Destroyer,' alluding to his 9-57 at The Oval. Honoured to be acclaimed by such an iconic figure and to address him on behalf of the England team, Malcolm described it as one of the great highlights of his career. 'I don't believe that Illingworth and Lever understood how emotional all of this was to Devon,' wrote Russell. 'They could have guided him sympathetically through that day, then got his mind attuned to the task in hand, which was to get him fully fit.'

Instead, Malcolm was soon brought back to earth by Illingworth. With time at a premium before the first Test, he withdrew him from the Soweto game on the third day for additional net practice at Pretoria an hour away. When Malcolm protested, saying, 'You can't send me to the nets. People want to see me walking round the ground,' Illingworth replied: 'I couldn't care less about you walking round the ground.' Then, to add insult to injury, Malcolm was publicly ridiculed by Illingworth and Lever at a bizarre poolside press conference at the team hotel the next day following the abandonment of the game. While Lever asserted that

Malcolm had just one asset which was pace, Illingworth, wearing multi-coloured trunks and lying on a lounger, said: 'We hoped Devon would be the leading strike bowler but at the moment he wouldn't frighten you, never mind the South African batsmen. As far as I am concerned, he's now just one of six seamers and we may go into the Test with only three.'

Their comments upset Derbyshire captain Kim Barnett, who said England should be boosting his confidence rather than belittling him, and an editorial in *The Guardian*. The paper wrote, 'What is Illingworth playing at even to allow such a slating of one of his champions, a sensitive man and, for all his venom, a sensitive cricketer who needs to be finely tuned with approbation?' Warned by Illingworth that he needed to raise his game against South Africa A, Malcolm rarely threatened on another lifeless wicket and was omitted for the first Test at Centurion.

England batted first and, led by a century from Hick, made 381/9 declared before incessant rain consigned the game to oblivion. The atrocious weather gave plenty of opportunity for a game of bridge involving Illingworth, Atherton, doctor Phillip Bell and scorer Malcolm Ashton. On occasions he was also partnered by assistant manager Johnny Barclay, who failed to come up to his exacting standards. He wrote, 'Hitherto I had only ever played some very informal bridge. So, I just about knew the basics but no more. I always partnered Illingworth who was unimpressed by my style. "Two rather wobbly spades" I would bid somewhat timidly. He would fix me with a cold stare. And then there was always the post-mortem after each hand during which my technique, tactics and ignorance were exposed in a humiliating burst of wrath – mostly tongue in cheek I must admit but wounding nonetheless.'

Malcolm and the bad weather aside, the tourists were in good heart, helped by the inclusion of the emollient Barclay, the respected Bell as doctor and the popular Wayne Morton as physiotherapist. 'This is the best management I have worked with,' declared Atherton, who had risen in Illingworth's estimation, not least for his resilience under pressure, while Alan Lee wrote: 'There is a cheerful, united feel to this team which has been absent from many recent England sides.'

At dinner Illingworth would hold court with a plethora of amusing anecdotes, mainly about himself. Senior players loved to pull his leg over his playing career, asking him whether he'd ever played at Dover, the scene of his greatest triumph against Kent in 1964. Yet beneath the banter and good cheer of the early weeks, there were those who resented Illingworth's pervasive presence in the dressing room, his blunt criticism and his public undermining of the captain. Darren Gough wrote of his dogmatic views and his aversion to being challenged by the younger players, while Robin Smith felt him out of touch with the game and the players, which didn't inspire confidence. 'They didn't understand that I had very little self-esteem,' Smith later wrote. 'For example, with Ray Illingworth in South Africa before the first Test, I was reduced to tears because of the way they handled me in the nets.'

Despite another unimpressive performance from Malcolm against Orange Free State, he was included in an all-pace attack on a quicker pitch at Johannesburg. On winning the toss, England inserted South Africa but failed to capitalise and trailed by 132 runs on first innings.

Set 479 to win in five sessions, England began the final day in deep trouble at 167/4, but an epic rearguard action by Atherton, ably supported by Russell, denied South Africa the spoils. His

185 not out drew a rare encomium from Illingworth. 'This is not easy for a Yorkshireman to say to a Lancastrian, but that was one of the great innings of all time.' To bat for nearly 11 hours was a monumental achievement. He thought Atherton could play better than Boycott at that age and he hoped his example would rub off on his team-mates.

Boosted by their escape at Johannesburg, the England players were in ebullient form on the flight to Cape Town the next day led by Smith, who stood at the back of the plane next to the bar while Illingworth sat stony-faced in his seat. Smith wrote: 'As I went past Illy, I gave him a playful punch and said, "Illy, we've got to be strong!" He looked at me like I'd just called him a Lancastrian.'

After conferring with the groundsman at Durban, venue for the third Test, Illingworth and Atherton, thinking that the ball might swing more than seam, opted for Essex's Mark Ilott and Lancashire's Peter Martin over Malcolm and Fraser. Another significant change was the ousting of Mark Ramprakash after two lean games with the bat. 'As far as Ramps is concerned, I've done all I can to help him, Illingworth told the *Mail on Sunday*'s Peter Hayter. 'I've tried to talk to him in the dressing room and get him thinking positively but he just sits there staring. I've always been honest with the players. They've got to be honest with themselves. The bottom line is that if players can't take honest criticism from me then they are not strong enough to succeed at the top level on the field. It is dog eat dog out there.'

With the final two Tests taking place over the festive period, the players were joined by their wives and families, an unwelcome distraction as far as Illingworth and Atherton were concerned, given the effect that it had on team spirit.

On a flat wicket at Port Elizabeth, England, despite suffering from some questionable umpiring, had little trouble batting out the final day, leaving the series all square prior to the decider at Cape Town.

Abandoning his recent practice of playing six specialist batsmen, Atherton wanted to go in with five bowlers, a gamble that Illingworth went along with despite his concerns about the fragility of England's batting. Anticipating a lively pitch, they recalled Fraser and Malcolm.

Ever since Illingworth had publicly derided Malcolm prior to the first Test, their relationship had remained fraught, so much so that Malcolm grieved in private, spending long hours on the phone to his wife back home. Despite taking six wickets in the second Test, he was distraught to be left out of the third Test and to hear Illingworth's damning verdict of him in the *Mail on Sunday*. 'Devon hasn't got a cricket brain, that's the problem. Trying to talk sense to him about cricket is very difficult. The annoying thing is if he had worked on our suggestion over his action, he could have two or three years left as an automatic choice for England. Now he never will be.'

He then became the object of Illingworth's ire at net practice on Christmas Day. Intent on saving him for the final part of the session when he could bowl quick to Stewart, Illingworth twice asked him to leave the nets till required and when Malcolm continued to hang about, tutoring a young black bowler and distracting Gough, he let fly at him with some expletives. Barclay wrote that Malcolm touched a raw spot and Illingworth was unable to contain his frustration. 'Malcolm had undoubtedly got it in him to do what Snow had done in Australia 25 years earlier. He had pace but perhaps not quite the class to go with it, and this brought out the darker side of Illingworth's character. It exposed a fierce temper which took some of us by surprise.'

Presented with a lifeless wicket at Port Elizabeth, leaving Malcolm out for the fourth Test made sense, but recalling him at Cape Town was something of a risk given that he hadn't bowled competitively for a month. Winning the toss, England, playing only five specialist batsmen, batted first, but they never recovered from losing Atherton without scoring and were all out for 153.

Their bowlers fought back on the second day, reducing South Africa to 171/9 when 18-year-old Paul Adams, playing in just his second Test, joined wicketkeeper Dave Richardson. Facing Malcolm and the new ball, his prospects looked bleak but Malcolm, in one of his most wayward spells, conceded 26 runs in four overs. By the time Adams was out for 29, the last pair had added 73, shifting the momentum of the match very much in South Africa's favour.

Reeling from the early loss of Atherton that evening, England rallied briefly the next day before Graham Thorpe was controversially run out for 59 after pressure was placed on the umpire to refer his original not-out decision to the third umpire, who gave Thorpe out. His dismissal sparked a wretched England collapse, their last six wickets falling for just 19 runs, and South Africa knocked off the 67 required for victory without loss.

With the match ending in three days, leaving many ticket holders for the last two days with nothing, Illingworth was asked by the local authorities to agree to a one-day game under lights.

Keen to give his burgeoning squad some practice in preparation for the ODIs, he agreed without consulting Atherton, who was fielding at the time. Hearing news of this game over the public address system at the presentation ceremony, a frazzled Atherton lashed out at Illingworth when the England team returned to the dressing room. Illingworth dismissed Atherton's objections then, after a few general side-swipes at the team's performance, he turned on Malcolm, accusing him of costing his side the game.

As he gave vent to his frustration, Illingworth suddenly went purple in the face and started choking, raising fears that he might be suffering a heart attack. He rushed to the sink for a glass of water before storming out of the room, leaving the players dumbstruck. 'It was understandable that Raymond was frustrated at the way we played,' wrote Stewart in his autobiography, 'but he was wrong to take it out on Devon. We were all at fault.' According to Russell, Illingworth's diatribe at Malcolm lost what little respect the players might still have had for him. 'The rest of the tour went rapidly downhill after that.'

Although unhappy with some of the umpiring during the series, Illingworth admitted that South Africa had been the better side. 'But the plain fact is that the batting has been very disappointing and apart from Dominic Cork and Peter Martin the bowling has not been up to scratch.'

The loss of the series at Cape Town and the bitter aftermath badly damaged team morale for the rest of the winter. Malcolm excoriated Illingworth's treatment of him in the *Daily Express*, while Illingworth publicly wrote off Stewart, Smith and Fraser as international players in an interview with Peter Hayter.

With the World Cup in India and Pakistan in mind, England shuffled their one-day side around for their seven-game series in South Africa to give everyone a chance.

Having tied the series at 1-1 at Bloemfontein, England erred by making five changes for the third game at Johannesburg and bowled poorly to lose by three wickets. Their sloppy out-cricket earned them a wigging from Illingworth afterwards. He also vented his wrath on Phil DeFreitas for dropping a catch in the defeat in the fifth game at Durban, his invective littered with profanities.

With so many players out of form, the team continued on a downward slope, getting a 6-1 drubbing, adding to Illingworth's sense of isolation and despondency. According to *The Independent*'s Robert Winder, England's manager cut an anachronistic figure. 'With his floppy hair and well-padded midriff, he didn't look too good in an England jogging top and shorts. "You can get a bit lonely," he told one interviewer, "when you're much older than the players." And that's how he looked, slumped in a chair on the dressing room balcony watching wickets fall.'

He admitted to making too many changes but pointed the finger primarily at the players. 'In the end, too many players cracked under pressure. As a team we could not keep cool when it mattered. Because we batted so badly, we never gave ourselves a margin of error in the field. We have lacked the killer instinct and thrown away matches by being unprofessional.'

The World Cup that followed a month later proved more of the same. While the team's preparations were badly affected by their arduous itinerary and poor practice facilities, they once again under-performed. England lost to New Zealand, Pakistan and South Africa in the first round and were outfoxed by Sri Lanka's innovative tactics in the quarter-final, especially their use of a pinch hitter to provide quick starts during the fielding restrictions. They failed to reach the semi-final for the first time. 'Our entire approach to the World Cup was wrong and we got what we deserved,' wrote Russell. 'We arrived not knowing our best side after all the chopping and changing in South Africa, and we were behind the times tactically. Our team meetings were generally poor in the World Cup. The captain did his best to stimulate discussion, but the edge had gone, and Illy offered very little.'

One of Illingworth's most bitter critics was Dermot Reeve, the innovative captain of Warwickshire, who resented his original omission from the World Cup squad. He wrote in his autobiography, 'By the end of the World Cup, nobody among the England players could take him seriously and we all wanted him out of the job. He was too negative, far too dogmatic and he lacked any awareness of how much the game had changed. I kept hearing that he had a brilliant cricket brain, but I saw no evidence of this.'

As far as Reeve was concerned, the real problem lay in the manager's failure to get the best out of the players. 'There was an urgent need to be cheery and upbeat on tour, but from the moment Illingworth got on the team bus every morning he was moaning – about the traffic, the weather, the hotel, the breakfast. It was all so negative.'

'As a new player I thought I might get a bit of input from Ray,' recalled Neil Smith, the Warwickshire off-spinner, 'but I didn't get anything at all. We had two discussions – one about Fred Trueman and Brian Statham; and the other about holiday homes in Spain.'

One incident that seemed to sum up the players' disillusion took place in the nets. Following England's defeat by Pakistan at Karachi, Illingworth made the relevant point that they shouldn't let bowlers tie them down with line and length. If the wicketkeeper was standing back, they had to use their feet to get to the pitch of the ball, even against the quick bowlers. The slow wickets would neutralise the fast bowlers and they needed to be smacked over their heads more often.

Reeve wrote, 'So, we're in the nets at Karachi and Neil Fairbrother is twinkling down the pitch and depositing the ball for what would have been six in a match. It's going well, this new strategy, isn't it? Well, no actually. Illingworth is tearing his hair out, saying: "What's he doing, the bloody idiot? He'll lose the balls if he hits straight." In the end, Fairbrother got fed up of Illy's nagging and said: "That's it. I'm not batting," and walked out of the nets.

'Illy had discovered we were down to our last batch of balls, and we couldn't afford to lose any. So, there we were, practising a desirable discipline in our attempts to progress in the World Cup and we had to stop because we had run short of cricket balls. And we were supposed to be a professional outfit.'

Barclay recalls that after defeat by Pakistan, the team returned to the Pearl Continental Hotel, the composure shattered by Illingworth, who plunged his left foot into the bathtub without testing the water first. Engulfed by boiling water, he quickly withdrew his scalded foot from the tub and hopped down the corridor uttering profanities. 'The guards, presuming an unwanted intruder had disturbed Illy, ran down the passage wielding their guns while Illy jumped about in agony, dressed only in a skimpy, fluffy white towel. It wasn't a great sight to behold. It came as something of a shock to Muslim guards not used to seeing the human frame so scantily clad.'

Reviewing England's dismal World Cup campaign, Alan Lee called it a devastating indictment of outdated coaching, blinkered methods – no video analysis – and bungled application and held Illingworth chiefly responsible. 'His post as a team manager, however, must be relinquished, for here, as never before, were revealed the shortcomings of putting the preparations and tactics of a modern national team in the hands of a man approaching his pension.

'Illingworth's bank of cricket wisdom is vast, but, in an arena such as this, too much of it was palpably obsolete. As the tournament proceeded, he seemed to sense that he was flailing in the dark and the firmness that has been his strongest virtue declined into woolly management. He would make a point of saying that certain decisions had been left to Atherton and that critical areas of fitness and availability were out of his hands, when plainly they should not have been.'

Illingworth returned home to a chorus of siren voices calling for his resignation. Amiss, the chief executive of Warwickshire, commented, 'We don't believe in the concept of a supremo; the England team needs someone younger, someone just retired from the game, as chairman.' Matthew Engel, the editor of *Wisden*, wrote, 'The manager's job is somewhat more important [than chairman of selectors] if it has a coaching and tactical dimension. What he has to do is get the players on the field, mentally and physically equipped to perform to the best of their ability. In this, Illingworth has conspicuously failed in the past three months.'

Physically exhausted after the winter campaign and recognising the need for a younger man, Illingworth willingly stood down as manager, but resisted the attempts to remove him as chairman of selectors. The instigator of the attempted coup was his old foe Mike Smith, who'd been incensed by his meddling on the 1994/95 tour of Australia and who'd been the only dissenter when Illingworth had been granted supreme power the previous year. He wrote to all the counties explaining why he thought he should be replaced as chairman. 'England have not done well under Ray.

I don't agree with the idea of one man running everything, we need a change.'

The man Warwickshire and Surrey nominated as his replacement was David Graveney, the general secretary of the Professional Cricketers' Association (PCA). Although Jack Bannister, the president of the PCA, warned him about a conflict of interest should he become chairman, especially over player discipline, Graveney allowed his name to go forward, much to Illingworth's indignation. 'What is Graveney's experience for the job?' he asked in the *Daily Express*. 'He never played at Test level for England.'

'Graveney wants to get Botham involved because he says "he doesn't know how to lose". Well, how many Test matches did Botham win as captain of England?'

Later Illingworth told *The Times*, 'It's not been a pleasant week. A lot of knives have been stuck in my back and although I've found out where they came from, that, too, has upset me. Some were from too close to home, even from within our winter tour party, and I find that very disappointing.'

In the event Graveney was forced to withdraw his candidacy for chairman, under pressure from his executive at the PCA because of a conflict of interest, but he continued as a selector. Graham Gooch and Mike Gatting were also elected as fellow selectors replacing Titmus, who resigned out of sympathy with Illingworth, while Bolus, Illingworth's choice, failed to win re-election. They were joined on the panel by new coach David Lloyd, the former captain and coach of Lancashire. Illingworth had originally endorsed John Emburey, the new player-coach of Northamptonshire, for the England job, but when Emburey turned it down, saying he needed more experience, he willingly accepted Lloyd, a man he liked and respected. He did, however, block his move to bring in his arch-critic Botham as an assistant coach, fearing his high-profile presence would overshadow both Lloyd and himself. Speaking to the *Daily Mail* on the opening day of the season, he said, 'Team coach David Lloyd has to do the job himself. It would not be easy with Botham there. We discussed a possible role for Botham but he has been in print in the last couple of days and it hasn't done him any good. Indeed, I have been alarmed by what I have read.' His words disconcerted Botham: 'If only Illy devoted as much time and energy getting the England team right as he does slagging me off, we would not be in this mess.'

Genuinely sensitive to the criticism and distracted by his legal tussle with the TCCB over his book (see next chapter), Illingworth cut a detached, less autocratic figure during his final summer in charge. According to Lloyd, he found him a surprisingly supportive chairman. 'Ray Illingworth had his say, then sat back quietly to hear what others had to say. As often as not, he would allow himself to be swayed to a general view.' He did, however, provoke Gooch with his early-season comment that Yorkshire's Martyn Moxon was the best opener in the country. Whenever Gooch made runs for Essex, he would ask Illingworth, 'Have I moved up the rankings yet?'

For the Texaco Trophy games against India, the selectors dispensed with many of the World Cup squad and were rewarded with a 2-0 win. They continued their good form in the first Test at Edgbaston, a hundred from the reinstated Nasser Hussain setting up an eight-wicket victory.

A broken finger suffered by opener Nick Knight brought a reprieve for Stewart, omitted from the previous game, and his half-century in the second innings helped England secure a hard-earned draw at Lord's.

Another high-scoring draw at Trent Bridge in which Atherton and Hussain both scored centuries ensured England won the series 1-0. There were concerns, however, about Hick's poor form. 'Graeme is a highly complex character,' noted Illingworth. 'He wants to be left alone and work things out for himself. But 35 runs in four Test innings against a very ordinary Indian attack, Srinath and Prasad aside, is hardly working things out.'

They faced stronger opposition from Pakistan, especially their renowned opening attack of Wasim Akram and Waqar Younis and their leg-spinner Mushtaq Ahmed. England's bowling, in contrast, lacked penetration and on a flat Lord's wicket the Pakistan batsmen dominated, especially in the second innings.

Set 407 to win, England began well thanks to a second-wicket stand of 154 between Atherton and Stewart, but once they were both out in quick succession, the rest of the batting folded all too easily, losing by 164 runs. Hick, in particular, had a disappointing match, being bowled by Waqar for 4 in each innings, and paid for his lack of runs with his place.

At Headingley, the failure of England's attack to exploit the helpful conditions on the opening day drove Illingworth to distraction. Pakistan made 441, but with Stewart scoring 170 and Knight 113 they had marginally the better of the draw.

Needing a win to tie the series at The Oval, Illingworth and his fellow selectors faced a familiar predicament – how to play five bowlers without weakening the batting. Although his attempt to drop Russell and give the gloves to Stewart had been resisted at Headingley, Illingworth now prevailed. He also helped all-rounder Chris Lewis get the nod over fast bowler Andrew Caddick, an unfortunate choice since the former not only contributed little with either bat or ball, he was guilty of a disciplinary lapse. Arriving 45 minutes late on the Sunday morning, his explanation that his Mercedes had developed a puncture was rejected by Illingworth and Atherton and he was not only dropped from the one-day squad, he also never played in another Test.

Guilty of erratic bowling, England ceded a first-innings lead of 195 and although Atherton and Stewart raised hopes with an opening stand of 96 in their second innings, they fell away to lose by nine wickets, Illingworth's first home series defeat as chairman of selectors. It was a disappointing end to his 30-month tenure, a 2-1 victory in the Texaco games notwithstanding. 'Being one of the game's enduring characters he will be remembered for reasons other than results,' wrote Alan Lee. 'England won only six out of 28 Tests in his stewardship but drew 13. In the previous comparable period, they had won seven of 29 but drawn only six. The conclusion is that Illingworth did not make England winners but he did stop them losing so often.'

From the perspective of nearly 30 years, Atherton reckoned that under Illingworth's leadership England didn't advance, but nor did they regress. 'It was just a difficult time.' It needed the enlightened regime of Duncan Fletcher, who succeeded David Lloyd as coach in 1999, and the introduction of central contracts, to usher England into the modern era, culminating in their regaining the Ashes in 2005 after 18 years.

Chapter 14

'I Want to Clear My Name'

TUESDAY, 19 June 1996 was the worst day Ray Illingworth had ever known in cricket. It was the day he was fined £2,000 by the TCCB for bringing the game into disrepute after what he considered to be an unfair hearing when he was prevented from putting his own defence.

The rumpus related to his ongoing feud with Devon Malcolm in South Africa. Deemed culpable for England's defeat at Cape Town by both Illingworth and Mike Atherton, a seething Malcolm launched a bitter broadside against his manager on his return home. (He wasn't required for the one-day series.) In an article in the *Daily Express*, he accused Illingworth of victimising him during the tour, adding, 'I have to ask, would this have happened if I had been a white bowler?'

His remarks, described as offensive by TCCB spokesman Richard Little, brought a quick retraction from Malcolm's solicitors that his feud with Illingworth had anything to do with colour, but his climbdown did little to appease the latter. He admitted that he'd felt very upset by Malcolm's outburst and he expected Lord's to punish him for breach of contract, but Lord's, sympathetic to Malcolm's right of reply to Illingworth's criticisms, stalled.

Sensing the drift of the wind after talks with Richard Little and Francis Neate of Slaughter and May, the TCCB's solicitors, on his return from South Africa, Illingworth tried to settle the affair. On his return from the World Cup, he rang Reg Taylor, the chief executive of Derbyshire, to this effect, but when Tony Brown, the assistant secretary of the TCCB, heard of his olive branch he immediately forbade Illingworth from attending any such meeting because the matter was sub judice.

Before Illingworth departed for a week in Spain at the beginning of April, he received a proposed statement from the board that was supposed to close the matter. Advised by Peter Lever, whom he consulted, that the statement was nothing short of a whitewash, he informed A.C. Smith that he wouldn't endorse it unless a couple of changes were made. He wanted to deny he'd sworn at Malcolm and he wanted his accusations to be answered.

Four days later Smith rang Illingworth in Spain to read him what the latter assumed would be a new statement, only to discover that nothing had been altered. He told Smith that if it went out in its present form, he would exercise his right to reply.

When the statement was issued the next day announcing that no further action would be taken against Malcolm over his breach of contract, Illingworth went on the offensive. Dismayed by the vapid response of the TCCB, not least its failure to fully exonerate him from comments made by Malcolm, he insisted on giving his side of the story in his book, *One Man Committee*, written in conjunction with his friend Jack Bannister, the cricket correspondent of the *Birmingham Post*.

The book was originally set for publication in September 1995 when Illingworth's two-year contract was due to end, but when he took on the managerial duties in South Africa the publishers agreed to a postponement to the following June. In an interview with James Lawton of the *Daily Express* to promote the book, he questioned Botham's suitability to be a selector – he lacked the ability to motivate when captain – and reopened his dispute with Malcolm. In serialised extracts from the book, he wrote, 'I think he tends to make too many excuses or gives the impression – rightly or wrongly – that he does not care sufficiently about anything. When he was asked the big question, he sank without displaying any trace of the fight and spunk we were entitled to expect from a strike bowler.'

Illingworth's outspokenness and the timing of his book, which even he accepted was not ideal, caused ructions. Derbyshire, upset at his public criticism of Malcolm, lodged an official complaint at Lord's, while Lancashire, aggrieved by revelations about Atherton in selection meetings, called for disciplinary proceedings against him. In response, the TCCB appointed Gerard Elias QC, the chairman of its disciplinary committee, to see whether Illingworth had brought the game into disrepute for his criticism of Devon Malcolm in serialised extracts of his new book. He said, 'The fact that he is not under contract does not affect the issue. Ray Illingworth is on a committee of the TCCB, and, as such, he is subject to the disciplines of the board.'

A week later Elias reported that Illingworth had a case to answer and summoned him to appear before the TCCB disciplinary committee on 12 June, an unprecedented move against a chairman of selectors. This was welcomed by Illingworth's predecessor, Ted Dexter, who rebuked him for going into print while still in office. He felt that England selectors ought to maintain a low profile.

As the pressure mounted, Illingworth vowed to fight his corner. He thought his comments very fair and constructive. 'Devon Malcolm was under contract in South Africa and broke that contract on returning home. He wasn't punished for what he said and, if I am to face a hearing after exercising the right of reply, that's not right and I will contest it.'

He asked London lawyer Alan Herd to represent him owing to his unrivalled experience of defending players against the TCCB. Because he'd acted for Botham in his recent clash with Illingworth over Illingworth's criticism of him in the *Daily Express*, Illingworth agreed to settle with Botham before Herd prepared his defence for the hearing, postponed till 18 June.

At the hearing, held at the Inner Temple to try and shake off the media, an obsession at all times with the TCCB, Francis Neate spent the best part of two hours outlining the case against Illingworth.

Herd, in contrast, was stopped many times by Elias, the chairman of the panel, whenever he mentioned Malcolm, even though he was the centre of the main charge, treatment which Illingworth thought was very unfair.

Despite a glowing testimonial of Illingworth's qualities from TCCB chairman Dennis Silk, the seven-man panel fined him £2,000, plus a further £500 in costs, for bringing the game into disrepute over his criticism of Malcolm. He was also reprimanded for breach of confidentiality of selection meetings. According to Elias, his punishment would have been considerably stiffer but for his previous record.

The verdict stunned Illingworth, who expected only to be reprimanded for breaking the board's regulations. He called it his worst day in cricket and confessed that he'd become so disenchanted with the machinations of English cricket that he wished he'd never taken the job.

His predicament attracted little sympathy from players who thought he betrayed selectorial confidences or the *Mail on Sunday*'s Patrick Collins, a long-standing critic. He wrote, 'His recent decision to publish a whining, self-justifying, catch-penny book is merely the most recent example of his ineptitude. He really does appear to believe that rules which apply to lesser breeds – players and the like – were not designed to restrict people of his own status.'

The majority of cricket journalists, however, were supportive. The *Daily Telegraph*'s Christopher Martin-Jenkins wrote that the board and their hopelessly muddled style of governance had come out worst and Richie Benaud went further. 'In 36 years of writing and commentating on cricket in England I have seen many good things. But nothing worse than the denigration and deliberate humiliation of Ray Illingworth.' The fine was a travesty and the ridiculous allegation of bringing cricket into disrepute was the choking insult.

At first Illingworth was tempted to resign as chairman and walk away from cricket, but urged on by Titmus and Lever, who threatened to go public about the affair if Illingworth wasn't exonerated, and the support of the general public, his natural steeliness soon returned. 'I have been involved in the game for 45 years or so and I don't want to leave it without restoring my reputation for straight dealing.'

For the appeal, Illingworth dispensed with the services of Herd in favour of Michael Lawrence, a Leeds solicitor who'd acted for him when he'd left Yorkshire for Leicestershire. At their first meeting, Lawrence told him he thought the first hearing had failed to adhere to the principles of natural justice by its unwillingness to cross-examine the TCCB's evidence.

At the appeal hearing at Lord's on 3 September, Lawrence declared that the fundamental issue was the different way in which the TCCB handled the different statements. He accused them of racism in reverse and said they were 'frightened to deal with Devon Malcolm but not frightened to deal with Ray'.

After a five-and-a-half-hour hearing in which both sides were given an opportunity to state their case, the four-man panel of the Cricket Council, chaired by Desmond Perrett QC, upheld Illingworth's appeal. A relieved Illingworth pronounced himself delighted with the ruling. He felt himself fully vindicated, declaring that he didn't want to leave the game with the disrepute charge round his neck. Trying to clear his name had been one of the hardest battles of his life. He and his family had had to put up with vile hate mail from people he'd never met.

As they walked out of the appeal hearing he and Lawrence were handed the TCCB's statement explaining why their own committee's findings had been overturned. Lawrence read the first paragraph and snapped, 'Come on, Raymond, we'll find the press and issue our own statement.' At an impromptu press conference, he launched a withering indictment of the TCCB, declaring that Illingworth had been treated very differently from Malcolm. 'Ray wanted to make peace with Devon Malcolm. But he was told by the TCCB that it would be sub judice. This is absolutely untrue.'

As for Illingworth, he insisted on having the last word. In an interview with *The Sun*'s John Etheridge later that year he said, 'I will believe to my dying day that I was not to blame for the breakdown in my relationship with Devon Malcolm. For me, the problem was Malcolm's pig-headedness, refusal to listen, broken promises and show-boating in the reflected glory of Nelson Mandela.'

Embittered by the racist slurs cast at him, he concluded, 'Despite our disagreements on tour, there still would not have been any real problems if he had not put all his rubbish in print.'

This latest outburst upset Malcolm enough for him to threaten legal action but then, wiser counsels prevailed and, after a year of mutual destruction, the guns finally fell silent.

Chapter 15

'My Island in the Sun'

AT THE conclusion of his England duties, Illingworth retreated to Spain, but retirement or not it was unlikely that he would go gently into the night. He castigated Mike Atherton for his 'lacklustre and uninspiring captaincy' during their tour of New Zealand and later said that he should be axed from England's one-day squad to play Australia that summer. His attack brought a rebuke from David Graveney, his successor as chairman of selectors, who reminded him that he, Illingworth, was always very sensitive to criticism he received from ex-players when he was chairman. As for Atherton, he remarked that he felt ever more secure with the captaincy, but after successive defeats by Australia in 1997 and West Indies in 1997/98 he resigned and was replaced by Alec Stewart rather than Glamorgan's captain Matthew Maynard, Illingworth's choice.

Stewart began well, beating South Africa 2-1 at home only then to lose 3-1 in Australia. Following a heavy defeat in the third Test at Adelaide, which ensured the Ashes would remain down under, Illingworth called the performance 'bloody awful'. 'We have more coaches, managers, physios and even more hangers-on than ever but the results are just as bad. What depresses me most is not the fact that England lose in Australia but that they are laying down and dying.'

He was even more scathing about England's dire performance in the World Cup the following summer, which was held on home soil. 'Every time I try to make the point, I'm accused of being out of touch. But you can't tell me that Boycott, Barrington or Graveney needed anyone to mollycoddle them before they batted. We've gone too soft on the players. If an England batsman needs sports psychologists to help him score runs, we must be picking the wrong people.'

He returned to this theme that winter when England, now under captain Nasser Hussain and coach Duncan Fletcher, lost by an innings to South Africa in the first Test at Johannesburg, destroyed by paceman Allan Donald, who took 11 wickets. 'I don't resent young players a decent wage but when you see them driving around in sponsored cars before they have even been awarded their county caps, it makes you wonder if we pamper them too much.

'In too many cases when players are presented with a chance to work on their technique like Donald, they are too busy attending benefit functions or modelling the latest designer sunglasses. They spend more time working on their golf swing than their technique. If my record as chairman of selectors had been as poor as England's results over the last couple of years I would not have expected to last long in the hot-seat.'

Thereafter England's performances began to improve, bringing a period of relative silence from Illingworth.

In May 1997 Illingworth's award of an honorary degree by Leeds Metropolitan University for his outstanding contribution to Yorkshire and English cricket was denounced by 30 of its academics, who implied he was racist. They objected to his treatment of Devon Malcolm on the tour to South Africa and his response to recent research conducted by Dominic Malcolm, a sports sociologist, that claimed racial stereotyping was channelling the majority of young black players into bowling, a legacy of the colonial period when blacks bowled to their white rulers.

Illingworth said that biological make-up was an important consideration in choosing players. 'A lot of the Asian people are not strong enough to bowl quickly. How many of the Indians have ever bowled quick? Pakistan have had one or two but only in the past few years. They are generally from northern Pakistan where the tribesmen are quite tall and strong. It is a fact that a lot of West Indians, because of their physique and looseness, can usually bowl quicker than white people.'

Claiming that he'd never been accused of racism in his life having played with and against many black players – indeed, his honorary degree from Hull University in 1983 was for 'contributions to racial harmony' – he went ahead and received his degree at Leeds Civic Hall.

In August 2001 Yorkshire planned to invite former prime minister John Major, the then president of Surrey, to open the new West Stand at Headingley, along with the Sir Leonard Hutton Gates, but Yorkshire being Yorkshire, the ceremony couldn't pass without a row. First of all, a powerful group of former players took exception to the gates, designed by local artist Kate Maddison, including a frieze of Sir Leonard batting against a background of Asian women in saris. According to Brian Close, it was 'political correctness gone mad', while Illingworth and Bob Appleyard complained that there were no Asian women in the crowd when Hutton played for Yorkshire.

More serious was the threat of Illingworth, Fred Trueman and Geoff Boycott to snub the opening of the West Stand because of their conviction that Major was an inappropriate choice, since he wasn't a Yorkshireman. Embarrassed by the furore and not wanting the occasion to be clouded with controversy, Major withdrew, leaving Yorkshire president Robin Smith to do the honours in front of Illingworth and the others.

The club's attempt to fuse ancient with modern had rebounded on them, according to an editorial in the *Yorkshire Evening Post*. 'Those who fell, sheep-like, behind the calls of Geoff Boycott, Ray Illingworth and Fred Trueman to have no one but a Yorkshireman open the new West Stand at Headingley, have endorsed a stereotype so many in this county have tried hard to bury. What a wasted opportunity to show how far our Yorkshire game has moved on.'

When Yorkshire had something to celebrate weeks later with their first Championship for 33 years, Illingworth was delighted. 'They're not bad this lot,' he remarked. 'But if we played 'em on uncovered wickets, we'd give 'em an innings start.' Recalling that the 1960s side won six Championships and two Gillette Cups, he continued, 'When this side has won, say, three Championships, we can start to compare. Only the two Darrens, Gough and Lehmann, would get into the '68 side.'

There was a better reception to the next stage of Headingley's redevelopment a year later when Yorkshire, keen to bury the acrimony of the previous year, asked Illingworth, Close, Trueman and Boycott to open the new East Stand. Owing to the combustible relationship between Boycott and the other three, reunions of the 'Gang of Four' were as rare as those of the Beatles, but they put their past differences to one side in the name of Yorkshire cricket. According to Illingworth, the stand compared favourably with any in the country and added, 'It will please me if I hear Bob Willis and Ian Botham say this is a good ground because I am fed up hearing them say Headingley is not a Test venue.'

The goodwill didn't last. The redevelopment programme had left Yorkshire with debts of over £6 million, with the result that Illingworth and other honorary life members, instead of receiving their normal free passes for the Headingley Test, were asked to pay £75 a day for a ticket. The decision predictably provoked anger. While Boycott accused the club of being run like a supermarket, Illingworth said, 'Is that how you deserve to be treated after giving 25 years as a player or manager? What Yorkshire would be better off doing would be using their ex-England players to host corporate and sponsorship events. That's what Manchester United do with massive success.'

Yet whatever his spats with the club, Illingworth remained devoted to it and in 2010/11 he was president of Yorkshire, which he considered a great honour, and although impeded by illness in his second year he carried out his duties with elan. He was also the fourth cricketer to be elected to Yorkshire's 'Hall of Fame'.

On 6 July 2005 there was to be one final meeting of the 'Gang of Four' at Trueman's local pub, The Sawley Arms, near Ripon, where they posed for a group portrait by Trueman's friend, John Blakey, a Leeds artist, to feature in his book, *Portraits of Yorkshire*. Formalities over, they repaired to the restaurant for a hearty lunch, at which they looked forward to the forthcoming Ashes series and compared the leading players of both sides unfavourably with the greats of their era. The reunion was voted a great success and as they bade their farewells, the four agreed to meet again, but it never occurred, since Trueman died a year later, ironically on the day when England were playing Sri Lanka at Headingley.

Illingworth, Close and Boycott were all present at the game and were visibly stunned at the news. 'We played for 20 years together from being no more than boys, and I have lost a great friend and colleague,' lamented Illingworth.

The revival of England's fortunes under Nasser Hussain temporarily silenced the sceptics from Yorkshire, but after their unsuccessful tour of Australia in 2002/03, Illingworth questioned whether Hussain still had the motivation to continue. 'He has made mistakes on the tour. I think he left the party when he shouldn't have left them [a reference to his early flight to Perth to accompany his pregnant wife] and things like that.' Hussain duly resigned mid-series against South Africa months later and was replaced by Yorkshire's Michael Vaughan. Following an innings defeat in his first Test in charge, Illingworth accused Vaughan of captaincy by committee and wondered whether he was a natural leader, a comment that upset many. According to James Lawton in *The Independent*, 'Ray Illingworth, who is considered by some reasonable judges to have been the most astute Test captain England ever had, must some days feel he is now operating in his own private dust bowl. The erosion of his reputation has been relentless over recent years.'

Vaughan quickly showed his mettle and won Illingworth round with a series of spectacular results, including the regaining of the Ashes in 2005.

The following year's home series against Pakistan, comfortably won by England, ended in controversy at The Oval when Australian umpire Darrell Hair, suspecting Pakistan of ball-tampering, changed the ball, much to the tourists' displeasure. Their refusal to take the field after a delay for bad light led to the umpires abandoning the game and awarding it to England, a decision fully supported by Illingworth. He reckoned that ball-tampering involving Pakistan had gone on for years. 'Provided that Darrell Hair was satisfied that the ball was tampered with, he had no option but to take the action he did take. He's a strong umpire and we could do with more strong officials in all sports.'

England's series win put them in good heart for their forthcoming tour of Australia. Illingworth thought Andrew Flintoff's side could retain the Ashes, provided they weren't defeated in the first Test at Brisbane, but poorly prepared, badly led and missing several leading players including Vaughan, they lost 5-0. Branding the side complacent and lackadaisical, Illingworth called for coach Duncan Fletcher's resignation, believing that the players had lost motivation, and within weeks his wish had been granted.

Away from his public pronouncements, Illingworth's main priority, outside his family, was Farsley Cricket Club. For ever grateful to the club for nurturing him in boyhood, he was delighted to be elected its president and help out in many different capacities. At a time when it was struggling financially, he tended to the ground more or less on his own for five or six years. Beginning work at 7am, he watered the square, mowed it and rolled the pitch for senior and junior matches. According to his friend Ron Deaton, the ground looked immaculate, and the pitches were good. David Swallow, who played with Illingworth in the Farsley junior championship side of 1948, happened to be visiting the ground for the first time in years in 2005. He wrote, 'And there was the great man himself, cutting the field and preparing the pitch just as he has done for some years. I wonder just how many former Test and county captains are putting back so much into the game, paying off some of the debt they owe to the club where they spent their formative years.'

Frustrated about the lack of help from club members compared to his youth, when cricketers were expected to help the groundsman, Illingworth told the cricket writer Sidharth Monga, 'Nowadays you have to ask them lads, "Do you think you can put the roller on?" That's a different attitude. To life, unfortunately.'

Even after he was forced to give up the ground because of a bad back in 2010, aged 78, Illingworth continued to help his successor Henry Hinchcliffe, as well as touting for sponsorship, collecting gate money on matchdays, selling raffle tickets and taking out the drinks. Still deriving great pleasure from watching Farsley – he called it 'My island in the sun' – he would happily sit and talk to anyone when not conversing with his circle of friends or helping some grateful youngster with a facet of their game. It was in recognition of his devoted service to Farsley over many years that he received the Sir Leonard Hutton Award for outstanding service to Bradford League Cricket in 2009 from the league president and his good friend Keith Moss.

In an interview with John Fuller of the *Cricket Paper* in 2018, Illingworth voiced his concern about the new expanded Bradford Premier League, which had come into existence two years earlier. Not only did greater travelling impose additional expense on smaller clubs like Farsley at a time of escalating running costs, Yorkshire's insistence on playing Academy games on a Saturday undermined clubs because of the non-availability of talent. Why couldn't they play Academy games on a Friday, he asked? The youngsters would be better off playing for their clubs, where the standard was higher.

Continuing to follow the first-class game closely, he remained committed to county and Test cricket. In one final blast in 2018, he denounced the England and Wales Cricket Board for The Hundred, a professional franchise 100-ball cricket competition, claiming it would lower standards at Test level. 'It's an innovation too far; it's making a mockery of the game and overall standards are not going to improve by shortening matches again.

'There are a lot of Test cricketers who have made a fortune by transferring their skills to Twenty 20, but you don't see many players whacking a few sixes who go on to make great Test players. I know we have to make the game appeal to kids, but you won't see me in a replica shirt at Headingley cheering for a team that doesn't exist yet. I'll stick to watching Yorkshire and England.'

He continued to go to Headingley until the end of 2019 and that year he made his final trip to Lord's, where he rang the five-minute bell on the first day of the England–Australia Test.

During his final years Illingworth continued to derive great pleasure from his family, including his growing number of grandchildren and great-grandchildren. Inheriting their parents' love of sport, both Vicky and Diane Illingworth married sportsmen, Vicky to Peter Philpot, a talented rugby player, in 1983 and Diane to Ashley Metcalfe, the Yorkshire cricketer, in 1986. From the very beginning Metcalfe was welcomed into the family and their simple, down-to-earth lifestyle that revolved around Farsley and sport. In addition to cricket, Illingworth was a member of Woodhall Hills Golf Club, playing off a handicap of ten, and an avid follower of Leeds United and the Leeds Rhinos rugby league club.

Brought up to be clean and tidy, Illingworth kept an immaculate house, adorned with family photos, and garden. 'Whatever he did, it had to be the best,' recalled Metcalfe, and he would spend hours making the lawn resemble Wimbledon or Lord's. When Metcalfe first purchased a house, Illingworth took him to B&Q, bought him a lawnmower and showed him how to use it. Unimpressed by Metcalfe's effort, he told him his lines weren't straight and taking over the mowing himself, he did it to perfection.

Living next door to Diane and Metcalfe in their converted barn in Calverley Lane, he and Shirley proved model grandparents and Illingworth even mastered the complexities of an iPad and the computer to stay in touch with his other grandchildren – Vicky lived in Spain. Yet his devotion to them didn't extend to games of cards, chess and dominoes. A winner to the very end, he offered them no concessions and when challenged by his uncompromising approach, he would reply, 'They've got to learn.' A particular source of pleasure was the cricketing potential of his great-grandson Oliver, who, aged ten, plays for the Farsley under-13s, and his final appearance as a cricketer was bowling to him in the nets.

One of the perils of old age is the loss of friends along the way and following Trueman's death in 2006, Illingworth mourned the passing of many of his former team-mates: Don Wilson, Phil Sharpe, Mel Ryan, John Hampshire and Brian Close. The loss of Close in September 2015 hit him particularly hard. Visibly choked at his funeral at St Chad's Church, Far Headingley, he paid him a poignant tribute afterwards.

'A lot of people say Brian was a hard man and things like that, but really he was a softy at heart you know. He could be hard on the cricket field, but he could do a good turn for anybody and as far as I'm concerned, well he was my best man. We go back a long way. There won't be another like him.'

That same year, Shirley suffered a stroke, leaving her reliant on walking with a frame and undetected with breast cancer during

Covid, she became ever frailer. On failing to get out of bed one day in January 2021 she collapsed quickly and was admitted to hospital, where tests revealed that she was riddled with cancer. After enduring a gruelling time in and out of hospital and in great pain, her family asked that she return home to see out her days. Aside from the devoted care she received from Ray, Diane and Ashley, nurses came in twice a day, and she was given morphine. On the day she died, Ray took her hand and said softly, 'Don't go fighting and fighting if you are in pain. You've had a tough time. Just go to sleep and relax. Let yourself go.'

After 63 years of marriage, losing Shirley was a bitter blow for Illingworth. According to Dickie Bird, you could see the decline in his health. 'He missed her so much. I have never known a couple so close.' Although blessed with good health for most of his life, Illingworth had suffered a heart attack in 2011 and spent four days in Leeds General Infirmary undergoing an angioplasty operation, in which medics widen a narrow or blocked blood vessel. He recovered pretty well but after lockdown, when he couldn't see a doctor, he visited a specialist for a check-up on his knee replacement in November 2020. The specialist said to him, 'You're looking very pale. I think we should do a blood test.' They did one and the next day further ones in hospital revealed an eight-centimetre tumour at the bottom of his oesophagus.

After 30 days of brutal radiotherapy during which Illingworth lost two stone in weight, the family celebrated Christmas. Doctors had put him on a strict diet and advised all food should be liquidised, but he made an exception for his favourite pudding, trifle. 'No bloody doctor is going to make me liquidise my trifle,' he told his family. On 29 November 2021 Illingworth revealed to the world that he was undergoing radiotherapy for his cancer and supported changes in the law over assisted dying. (Under the 1961 Suicide Act, anyone helping a person to take their own life could face up to 14 years' imprisonment.) In an exclusive with the *Daily Telegraph,* he remarked that he would rather end his life than suffer the agony Shirley endured. 'I don't want to have the last months that my wife had. She had a terrible time going from hospital to hospital and in pain.

'I'd rather go peacefully. I believe in assisted dying.

'The way my wife was, there was no pleasure in her life in the last 12 months and I don't see the point of living like that, to be honest.

'But we don't have assisted dying in England yet, so you don't have that option, do you?

'A lot of doctors are against it, but if they had to live the life my wife did in her last 12 months, they might change their minds.'

Later in a more extensive interview with the *Daily Mail* he said, 'If I was well enough and it was during the summer, I'd like to go and watch a bit of a cricket match up there [pointing to Farsley Cricket Club]. Then I'd come back here and go to sleep. I wouldn't want to go somewhere else [such as an assisted dying clinic in Switzerland] to have it done. If that was the only option I would, but we shouldn't have to do that. I'd like to be put to sleep in peace in my own home in Yorkshire.'

He was hoping that a third round of radiotherapy would get rid of the rest of the tumour, commenting, 'I know my time hasn't come yet. I'll see, maybe, another 12 months, but when it does come, I'll know. I'll think, "This is my time." I'm sure of that.'

On 11 December he repeated his views on BBC's *Look North* with a force and conviction that impressed all who heard it. According to Metcalfe, he remained mentally alert and positive until the very end. He recalled that when he took him for his treatment he would be looking ahead to the new season and speculating about Farsley's new signings. Former MCC president Phillip Hodson, a good friend of Illingworth's, since having the benefit of his advice when playing for Cambridge University against Leicestershire, phoned him about this time and they discussed the cricket in Australia. Illingworth asked him about England's new seamer Ollie Robinson and his ability to get bounce off a length. 'He still noted the small details,' commented Hodson.

In his last conversation with Metcalfe, Illingworth said, 'I'm very comfortable. The time is ripe.' On the evening of 23 December, he suffered serious complications with his stomach and was taken to Leeds General Infirmary, where he died the following day, aged 89.

His passing unleashed a host of tributes to a great leader. According to David Lloyd in the *Mail on Sunday*, 'Ray Illingworth possessed as good a cricket brain as there has ever been. When it came to the tactical side of the game, he was a clinical thinker. For players of my generation, he was a wonderful opponent and rightly thought of as a great captain. Someone who went into every detail for the benefit of the team.'

Tanya Aldred in *The Guardian* admired his ability to coax brilliance from tricky customers such as Geoff Boycott and John Snow; and Brian Scovell commented in *The Times* that 'Raymond Illingworth had the leadership qualities to be England's finest captain, and he was adept at handling the popular press.'

At local level the Bradford League wrote, 'Farsley and the Bradford League have been privileged to have seen one of their own achieve so much at first-class and international level. Like those two other greats Sir Len Hutton and Herbert Sutcliffe, who were also born in Pudsey *[sic]*, he has ensured the town is known through the cricketing world.'

At his funeral a month later, mourners lined the streets of Farsley as the cortege left Illingworth's home and took him on his final journey through the village to St John's Parish Church. A cricket bat with the word Grandad was among the flowers that adorned the hearse.

Addressing the congregation, which numbered Yorkshire stalwarts such as club president Geoff Cope, Richard Hutton, Dickie Bird, Martyn Moxon and Craig White, Ashley Metcalfe spoke movingly about his father-in-law.

'Although his sporting career took him all around the world, he never forgot his roots. He was hugely proud to have spent so much of his life in the village he knew as home. He was far more than a cricketer. He was the most caring, generous and supportive person you could ever meet.

'We will never forget Ray or his late wife, Shirley, who sadly passed away nine months ago. It is hugely comforting to know that they will be back together after such a short time apart.'

Illingworth's passing, in the wake of another Ashes trouncing, was all the more poignant, especially since England's captain, Joe Root, for all his personal qualities, lacked the inner steel of his Yorkshire predecessor. Say what you like about Illingworth, Close and their vintage but they knew how to win and their mental resilience gained them the respect of the Australians, and no compliment could be higher than that.

Chapter 16

Ray Illingworth

THROUGHOUT HIS remarkable 32-year playing career, Ray Illingworth remained the ultimate professional who spared no effort in his rise to sporting eminence. A product of Pudsey, that great nursery of Yorkshire cricket, his love of the game was such that he practised at every opportunity be it in the school yard, the street or in the nets. Growing up with Len Hutton as his idol, he would cycle to all the Bradford League grounds throughout the later years of the war to see him play, learning much in the process.

Following a stellar record at school, Illingworth played for Farsley in the Bradford League, aged 15, and gave notice of his burgeoning talent on the eve of his 17th birthday by scoring a flawless 148 not out against neighbouring Pudsey St Lawrence. Absorbing the strictures of Yorkshire's redoubtable coach Arthur Mitchell, he showed that he had the technique and temperament to succeed at the highest level, but even he struggled with the rivalries and cliques in the Yorkshire dressing room of the 1950s. Heirs to a proud tradition whereby winning was taken for granted, Yorkshire's professionals were noted for their single-minded dedication and ruthless one-upmanship. Consequently, with argument and rancour rife, it needed a Lord Hawke or a Brian Sellers at the helm to keep the lower deck in check. During Illingworth's early years, it was the mild-mannered Norman Yardley in charge and his failure to curb the divisive antics of senior professionals such as Johnny Wardle and Bob Appleyard meant a rough baptism for the younger players. Illingworth had the resilience to survive and prosper but the legacy of that toxic environment stayed with him thereafter and not always for the best, since his raw candour could alienate as well as attract.

For all his reservations about Wardle and Appleyard, he learned much about the art of spin bowling from bowling with them, not least the cardinal attribute of accuracy. Resenting any run scored off him, Illingworth frustrated many a batsman to death with his remorseless accuracy, while on a turning wicket he was invariably Yorkshire's talisman.

As with his bowling, Illingworth's success as a batsman was founded on basic principles and an unflappable temperament and many was the occasion that he rescued his side from the valley of despair and guided them towards the sunlit uplands. As the 1950s gave way to the 1960s, so Illingworth grew in stature, becoming the leading all-rounder, tactician and mentor to the younger players. His influence was particularly conspicuous under Brian Close's leadership, his cool calculation tempering his captain's more audacious instincts. Possessing the finest attack in the country, Close's flair for aggression invariably paid dividends and with Geoff Boycott, Phil Sharpe and John Hampshire there to score the necessary runs, Yorkshire won the Championship four times in six years between 1963 and 1968 and the Gillette Cup in 1965.

In contrast to his accomplishments at Yorkshire, which included six doubles of 1,000 runs and 100 wickets in a season, Illingworth's record for England before becoming captain was disappointing, especially on the harder wickets overseas. At a time when the amateur–professional divide was still in vogue, he resented the gap in status between the two groups, especially in Australia in 1962/63, and his inclination to speak out of turn cost him part of his tour bonus and contributed to his irregular appearances for England. 'I felt reasonably all right when Peter May was captain, but from 1959 on I never had a proper opportunity or felt I was part of the system,' he later declared. 'I played a Test then was left out and always felt whatever I did I would not be playing in the next match. That's why I never performed as well at Test level as I should have done.'

He also objected to the feudal regime at Yorkshire and the committee's disregard of the players, not least their lack of a decent wage. Even by the standards of the time whereby no Yorkshire player was bigger than the team, the willingness of chairman Sellers to dispense with Illingworth's services on the outdated concept that the club didn't offer contracts, must rank as one of the most disastrous in its history. The effect on Yorkshire cricket, along with Close's sacking two years later, was calamitous, but for Illingworth it proved a blessing in disguise since it opened up all kinds of new avenues. No sooner had he assumed the captaincy of Leicestershire than the England selectors came knocking at his door, asking him to deputise for the injured Colin Cowdrey.

Drawing on all his experience as Yorkshire's leading tactician and his own boundless self-confidence, Illingworth stepped up with the greatest of ease, quickly establishing himself as a natural leader. Not only did he impress with his tactical acumen and assured man-management, his own performances improved out of all recognition. In contrast to his dearth of runs for England over the previous decade, his ascent to the captaincy gave him greater security to give of his best. Having scored an invaluable century against West Indies at Lord's in his second game in charge, he touched new heights the following summer by averaging 53 against a top-flight Rest of the World attack.

It was this late flowering with the bat, as much as his capacity for leadership, that won him the right to lead England in Australia in 1970/71 over his arch-rival Cowdrey. The decision upset many of the amateur establishment and their allies in the press and set Illingworth on a collision course with his manager David Clark, an amateur of the old school, who placed the wider interests of the game above winning. In their repeated clashes, whether it be Clark's agreement to the Australian board's request for an additional Test to compensate for the abandoned third Test or his objection to Illingworth's angry altercation with umpire Lou Rowan over short-pitched bowling, we see two sets of principles in contention, with Illingworth's professionalism increasingly dominant.

While the MCC establishment supported Clark, Illingworth's win-at-all-costs ethos won him the total backing of his team, Cowdrey aside. As fellow professionals, they appreciated his tactical ingenuity and motivational powers; above all, his concern for their welfare be it better accommodation, more generous meal allowances and fewer obligatory social functions. Keeping any group of disparate individuals together on a gruelling tour to Australia calls for sensitive man-management and Illingworth's treatment of the more difficult characters such as Geoff Boycott and John Snow brought the very best out of them. According to Richie Benaud, 'The Australians had a very high regard for Illingworth's team and a great respect for the tough and arrogant way they went about their cricket.

'They had complete confidence in everything they did. Australian players have told me they had the feeling when

Illingworth's men walked on to the field in that series they knew they were better than Australia. They weren't, but there was no diffidence about their play and certainly there was no diffidence about their leadership.'

Illingworth's triumph in Australia earned him the right to captain England for another two and a half years during which he scored a second Test century against India at Old Trafford and retained the Ashes in 1972. Only during his final summer in charge did his form begin to fade and after England's heavy loss to West Indies in August 1973 he was axed as captain in favour of Kent's Mike Denness. Because of his record of played 31, won 12 and lost five and his Ashes triumph, Illingworth's leadership ranks high in the pantheon of great England captains. Only Douglas Jardine would surpass him among 20th-century occupants on the grounds he was less attritional, although Len Hutton and Mike Brearley would have their supporters. (Close's tenure was too short to make an informed comparison.)

At first sight Illingworth and Brearley's styles of leadership differed markedly, the former a down-to-earth, northern autocrat and the latter a softly-spoken intellectual with a degree in Moral Sciences. According to David Gower, who played under both men, Illingworth was the sterner and more forceful of the two who talked about himself and learned how to get through to people, while Brearley studied relationships. Yet while Brearley consulted more widely, he was equally competitive and could be just as ruthless when it came to taking unpopular decisions. Both were greatly respected for their composure under pressure, their winning mentality and a style of leadership that commanded the undying allegiance of nearly every player to experience it. When asked to compare them, Keith Fletcher, a fine captain himself, thought Illingworth had the edge in tactical acumen and Brearley in man-management

England's loss was Leicestershire's gain because Illingworth could now devote himself fully to making the club a force in the land. Inheriting a side of honest journeymen, he, along with secretary Mike Turner, conducted a dramatic transformation in their fortunes by imbibing them with a winning mentality. Previously without a trophy in their 90-year history, Leicestershire, strengthened by some shrewd acquisitions such as Graham McKenzie, Chris Balderstone and Ken Higgs, won the Championship in 1975. They also won both the Benson and Hedges Cup and the John Player League twice, and in doing so they debunked the myth then prevalent that spinners were an unaffordable luxury in the one-day game.

On his retirement from Leicestershire in 1978, aged 46, Illingworth's reputation stood at its apogee, but thereafter it slipped somewhat as he entered the new world of management for which he was temporarily unsuited. An autocrat of the old school like his nemesis Brian Sellers, Illingworth wanted to control his captain in a way he would never have tolerated himself. 'Never argue with Illy. Illy's always right,' Boycott was told when he first played for Yorkshire, since Illingworth was intractable and disliked being contradicted. Consequently, no clear chain of command emerged and when Chris Old was sacked as captain in June 1982 it was Illingworth himself who stepped into the breach, aged 50, to take over the running of the side. The old tactical nous still held good, not least when Yorkshire won the JPL the following year, but they also finished bottom of the Championship for the first time in their history.

In fairness to Illingworth, the situation confronting him on his return to Yorkshire in 1979 would have taxed any new manager. Ever since the break-up of their great team of the 1960s, the club had struggled, their predicament compounded by their continued adherence to Yorkshire-born players in an age of mass overseas imports and the divisive captaincy of Boycott. While no one questioned his prowess with the bat and his tactical ability, his obsession with his own game did little to foster team spirit. The exact role Illingworth played in Boycott's dethronement in September 1978 isn't entirely clear, but from his appointment nearly a year earlier the potential for conflict between these two strong-minded individuals looked inevitable. Certainly, from Boycott's perspective, and that of his supporters, Illingworth had blood on his hands and the simmering resentment towards him thereafter thwarted him at every stage. 'As I watched him work with captains and players,' wrote Boycott, 'and as I learned more about his dealings with me, I realised that Illy's feel for cricket was infinitely better developed than his feel for people. Illy was as bad a team manager as he was good a captain.'

Illingworth's limitations in management were once again on display when he became chairman of the England selectors in 1994 and manager in 1995. Following a depressing decade in which England had lost their way and players had been hired and fired at random, his appointment was broadly welcomed. Compared to his two predecessors, Peter May and Ted Dexter, who were both depicted as distant figures from a bygone age, Illingworth was seen as a consummate professional in touch with the modern game, a view not entirely grounded in reality. For aside from his age, he was out of sympathy with player power and the celebrity lifestyle.

Reared in a more exacting era, his tough, combative outlook had taken him to the highest rungs of the cricketing ladder and now, in a less deferential age, he continued to adhere to the values of his youth. On becoming chairman, he insisted on having the final say over selection which set him against his youthful captain Mike Atherton, most notably over the composition of the team to tour Australia in 1994/95. His support for veterans Graham Gooch and Mike Gatting proved flawed, as did his preference for fast bowler Martin McCague over trusted performer Angus Fraser.

Following the failures of that tour, Illingworth helped engineer the dismissal of coach Keith Fletcher and became overall supremo with responsibilities for management and coaching as well as selection. It proved a retrograde move, especially on the 1995/96 tour to South Africa and the 1996 World Cup in India and Pakistan, when Illingworth's relationship with the team fractured badly. Out of sympathy with the modern player with their flawed techniques, their lack of resilience and refusal to listen to advice/criticism, Illingworth could be brutally frank about their deficiencies, not least with his captain. On several occasions he publicly upbraided him for his poor leadership and nearly dismissed him on return from Australia in 1995 following Atherton's call to restore the authority of the captain. It said much for Atherton's tact that he endured the constant undermining of his authority with stoicism and continued to work constructively with Illingworth throughout his time in office.

Both as chairman and manager, Illingworth commanded respect for his vast knowledge of the game and many a player could be captivated by his personal reminiscences, but the general impression he left was an unfavourable one. Angus Fraser, Mark Ramprakash, Graeme Hick and Robin Smith were among those who felt demotivated by his barbs, but the greatest casualty of all was Devon Malcolm. Christened the 'Destroyer' after his awe-inspiring 9-57 against South Africa at The Oval, he should have been England's secret weapon on tour to that country in 1995/96, but injury and technical problems with his run-up reduced his effectiveness. Unable to remodel his action to their satisfaction, Illingworth and bowling coach Peter Lever publicly berated Malcolm for his obduracy, criticism that quickly deflated his confidence, much to the detriment of the team. Omitted from three of the first four Tests, Malcolm was recalled for the deciding Test at Cape Town when short of practice and his erratic bowling at a vital stage of the game handed the initiative back to South Africa, who went on to win by ten wickets to take the series 1-0.

Infuriated by Malcolm's performance which he attributed to his failure to cooperate throughout the tour, an emotional Illingworth held him accountable for England's defeat in a diatribe that lost him the respect of the players. Traumatised by his treatment, Malcolm denounced Illingworth in print on his return home, a salvo that was met with return fire from Illingworth in his book *One Man Committee*, an account of his time as chairman of selectors. His disclosure of confidential information from selection meetings and his public criticism of certain players earned him a £2,000 fine from the TCCB, and although he managed to get the fine rescinded the whole episode proved an unedifying end to his time as chairman. Few lamented the end of his tenure and most pundits considered his time in charge as a failure, although his record was marginally better than that of his two predecessors.

According to Atherton, Illingworth's man-management was as poor as Duncan Fletcher's was excellent, while to Keith Fletcher, he didn't understand the modern player. As far as Johnny Barclay was concerned, his career as a manager and coach wasn't a patch on his years as a player when he was at the forefront of the action: 'Failure did not sit easily with Illingworth, and he certainly wasn't used to it. Brought up in the hard and unyielding school of Yorkshire cricket where favours are granted to no one, Illingworth in his prime developed and cultivated the finest cricket brain of his generation: shrewd, thoughtful and very skilful. To be manager of the England team combined with responsibilities as chairman of selectors was too much to ask of him and came too late in his career.'

Undeterred by the march of time and his recent brush with failure, Illingworth returned to his roots – performing invaluable service to his beloved Farsley – still in thrall to the values of his youth and often with good reason. For aside from scoring nearly 25,000 runs and taking over 2,000 wickets – and only nine people have achieved that in the history of the game – he'd claimed all the greatest prizes in cricket, thus assuring himself a special place in cricketing folklore.

Acknowledgements

I'D LIKE to thank the following for sharing their experiences of Ray Illingworth: Jonathan Agnew, Dennis Amiss, Mike Atherton, Bill Athey, Johnny Barclay, Dickie Bird, Jack Birkenshaw, Geoff Boycott, John Callaghan, Stephen Chalke, Geoff Cope, Ron Deaton, Barry Duddleston, Keith Fletcher, Stuart Fletcher, Mike Griffith, Neil Hartley, Robin Hobbs, Phillip Hodson, Richard Hutton, Jim Love, Vic Marks, Mick Norman, Peter Parfitt, Bob Platt, Pat Pocock, Kevin Sharp, Mike Smith, Bryan Stott, Ivo Tennant, David Warner and various readers from *The Cricketer.*

In particular I'd like to thank Illingworth's son-in-law Ashley Metcalfe for all his help and advice.

I'm very grateful to Neil Robinson, the Curator of Collections at Lord's and MCC, and Robert Curphy, the former Archive and Library Manager at Lord's, for all their efforts on my behalf.

I'm also indebted to the unfailing help of the staff at the British Library in Boston Spa, Farsley Library and the National Library of Scotland.

Finally, I'd like to express my thanks to my agent Andrew Lownie; to Bruce Talbot for his copy edit; and to Jane Camillin and Alex Daley at Pitch, along with Duncan Olner, Dean Rockett and Graham Hales for all their efforts on the design, proofing and typeset.

Bibliography

Agnew, Jonathan, *Over to You, Aggers: A Cricketing Odyssey* (London: Victor Gollancz, 1997).

Alley, Bill, *Standing the Test of Time* (Manchester: Empire, 1999).

Amiss, Dennis, *Not Out at Close of Play: My Life in Cricket* (Cheltenham: The History Press, 2022).

Atherton, Mike, *Opening Up: My Autobiography* (London: Hodder and Stoughton, 2003).

Bairstow, Jonny and Hamilton, Duncan, *A Clear Blue Sky* (London: Harper Collins Publishers, 2017).

Barclay, John, *Life Beyond the Airing Cupboard* (Bath: Fairfield Books, 2008).

Barclay, John, *Lost in the Long Grass* (Bath: Fairfield Books, 2013).

Barrington, Ken, *Playing it Straight* (London, Stanley Paul, 1968).

Bedser, Alec, *Twin Ambitions* (London: Stanley Paul, 1995).

Benaud, Richie, *On Reflection* (London: Collins Willow, 1984).

Botham, Ian, *My Autobiography: Don't Tell Kath* (London: Collins, 1995).

Boycott, Geoff and Hotten, Jon, *Being Geoffrey Boycott* (London: Fairfield Books, 2022).

Boycott, Geoff, *Boycott: The Autobiography* (London: Macmillan, 1987).

Boycott, Geoff, *Geoff Boycott on Cricket* (London: Ebury Press, 1999).

Boycott, Geoff, *The Corridor of Certainty* (London: Simon and Schuster, 2015).

Brearley, Mike, *The Art of Captaincy* (London: Hodder and Stoughton, 1985).

Callaghan, John, *Geoff Boycott: A Cricketing Legend* (London: Pelham, 1982).

Callaghan, John, *Yorkshire Cricket Greats* (Edinburgh: Scotsprint, 1990).

Callaghan, John, *Yorkshire's Pride: 150 Years of County Cricket* (London: Pelham, 1984).

Chalke, Stephen, *Caught in the Memory: County Cricket in the 1960s* (Bath: Fairfield Books, 1999).
Chalke, Stephen, Hodgson, Derek and Kendall, Susanna, *No Coward Soul: The Remarkable Story of Bob Appleyard* (Bath: Fairfield Books, 2003).
Chalke, Stephen, *Runs in the Memory: County Cricket in the 1950s* (Bath: Fairfield Books, 1998).
Chalke, Stephen, *In Sunshine and Shadow: The Biography of Geoff Cope* (Bath: Fairfield Books, 2017).
Chalke, Stephen, *One More Run: Gloucestershire versus Yorkshire, Cheltenham, August 1957* (Bath: Fairfield Books, 2000).
Chalke, Stephen, *Micky Stewart and the Changing Face of Cricket* (Bath: Fairfield Books, 2011).
Chalke, Stephen, *Summer's Crown: The Story of Cricket's County Championship* (Bath: Fairfield Books, 2015).
Close, Brian, *Close to Cricket* (London: Stanley Paul, 1968).
Close, Brian, *I Don't Bruise Easily* (London: McDonald and James, 1978).
Collomose, Andrew, *Magnificent Seven: Yorkshire's Championship Years* (Ilkley: Great Northern Books, 2010).
Cowdrey, Colin, *MCC: The Autobiography of a Cricketer* (London: Hodder and Stoughton, 1976).
Denness, Mike, *I Declare* (London: Arthur Barker, 1977).
Dexter, Ted, *85 Not Out* (Shrewsbury: Quiller, 2020).
D'Oliveira, Basil, *Time to Declare* (London: J.M. Dent, 1980).
Fay, Stephen and Kynaston, David, *Arlott, Swanton and the Soul of English Cricket* (London: Bloomsbury, 2018).
Fletcher, Keith, *Ashes to Ashes* (London: Headline, 2005).
Gibson, Alan, *The Cricket Captains of England* (London: Cassell, 1979).
Gough, Darren, *Dazzler: The Autobiography of Darren Gough* (London: Penguin, 2002).
Gower, David, *Heroes and Contemporaries* (London: Granada, 1985).
Gower, David and Wilde, Simon, *An Endangered Species* (London: Simon and Schuster, 2013).
Gower, David, *Gower: The Autobiography* (London: Collins Willow, 1992).
Greig, Tony, *My Story* (London: Stanley Paul, 1980).
Hampshire, John, *Family Argument* (Sydney: Allen and Unwin, 1983).
Hignell, Andrew, *Summer of '64: A Season in English Cricket* (Stroud: Tempus, 2005).
Hill, Alan, *Brian Close: Cricket's Lionheart* (London: Methuen, 2002).

Hill, Alan, *Jim Laker: The Biography* (London: Andre Deutsch, 1998).

Hill, Alan, *Johnny Wardle: Cricket Conjuror* (London: David and Charles, 1988).

Hodgson, Derek, *The Carnegie Official History of Yorkshire* (Leeds: Leeds Met Press, 2009).

Howe, Martin, *Norman Yardley: Gentleman Cricketer* (Cardiff: The Association of Cricket Statisticians and Historians, 2015).

Howat, Gerald, *Len Hutton: The Biography* (London: Mandarin, 1988).

Illingworth, Ray, *On Captaincy* (London: Pelham Books, 1980).

Illingworth, Ray and Bannister, Jack, *One Man Committee* (London: Headline, 1996).

Illingworth, Ray, *Spin Bowling* (London: Pelham, 1979).

Illingworth, Ray, *Spinner's Wicket* (London: Stanley Paul, 1969).

Illingworth, Ray, *The Tempestuous Years 1979–83* (London: Pan Macmillan, 1987).

Illingworth, Ray, *Yorkshire and Back* (London: Queen Anne Press, 1980).

Johnson, Martin, *Can I Carry Your Bags? The Life of a Sports Hack Abroad* (London: Constable, 2015).

Knott, Alan, *It's Knott Cricket* (London: Macmillan, 1985).

Knott, Alan, *Stumper's View* (London: Stanley Paul, 1972).

Lewis, Tony, *Playing Days* (London: Stanley Paul, 1985).

Lewis, Tony, *Taking Fresh Guard* (London: Headline, 2003).

Lloyd, David, *The Autobiography* (London: Collins Willow, 2000).

Lamb, Allan, *Allan Lamb: My Autobiography* (London: Collins Willow, 1996).

McGregor, Adrian, *Greg Chappell* (London: Collins, 1985).

McKinstry, Leo, *Boycs: The True Story* (London: Collins Willow, 2000).

Malcolm, Devon, *You Guys Are History* (London: Collins Willow, 1998).

Marshall, Michael, *Gentlemen and Players* (London: Grafton Books, 1987).

Mosey, Don, *Boycott* (London: Methuen, 1989).

Mosey, Don and Trueman, Fred, *Champion County: Yorkshire CCC 1959–1968* (Skipton: Dalesman, 1994).

Murtagh, Andrew, *Sundial in the Shade: The Story of Barry Richards* (Durrington: Pitch Publishing, 2015).

Norrie, David, *Athers: The Authorised Biography of Michael Atherton* (London: Headline, 1996).

Peel, Mark, *Cricketing Caesar: A Biography of Mike Brearley* (Worthing: Pitch Publishing, 2020).

Procter, Mike, *Caught in the Middle: The Autobiography of Mike Procter* (Worthing: Pitch Publishing, 2017).

Rayner, Stuart, *The War of the White Roses: Yorkshire's Cricket Civil War, 1968–1986* (Durrington, Pitch Publishing, 2016).
Reeve, Dermot, *Winning Ways* (London: Boxtree, 1996).
Robinson, Ray, *The Wildest Tests* (London: Stanley Paul, 1972).
Rowe, Mark, *Brian Sellers: Yorkshire Tyrant* (Cardiff: Association of Cricket Statisticians and Historians, 2017).
Russell, Jack, *Unleashed* (London: Collins Willow, 1998).
Sandford, Christopher, *Tom Graveney* (London: H.F. and G. Witherby, 1992).
Shindler, Colin, *Bob Barber: The Professional Amateur* (Nantwich: Max Books, 2015).
Smith, Edward, *Leicestershire Cricket 1949–1977* (London: Paul, 1977).
Smith, Robin, *The Judge: More than a Game* (London, Vintage, 2019).
Snow, John, *Cricket Rebel* (London: Hamlyn, 1976).
Steen, Rob, *David Gower: A Man out of Time* (London: Victor Gollancz, 1995).
Stevenson, Mike, *Illy: A Biography of Ray Illingworth* (Tunbridge Wells: Midas Books, 1978).
Swanton, E.W., *Swanton in Australia* (London, Collins, 1975).
Taylor, Bob, *Standing Up, Standing Back* (London: Collins Willow, 1985).
Titmus, Fred, *My Life in Cricket* (London: Blake Publishing, 2005).
Tennant, Ivo, *The Cowdreys: Portrait of a Family* (London: Simon and Schuster, 1990).
Trueman, Fred, *As it Was: The Memoirs of Fred Trueman* (London: Pan Books, 2004).
Trueman, Fred, *Ball of Fire* (London: J.M. Dent and Sons Ltd, 1976).
Tubervill, Huw, *The Toughest Tour: The Ashes Away Series 1947–2007* (London: Aurum Press Ltd, 2007).
Underwood, Derek, *Beating the Bat* (London: Stanley Paul, 1975).
Walker, Peter, *Cricket Conversations* (London: Pelham, 1978).
Walters, Doug, *Looking for Runs* (London: Pelham Books, 1975).
Ward, Kirwan, *Put Lock On!* (London: Hale, 1972).
Waters, Chris, *Fred Trueman: The Authorised Biography* (London: Aurum, 2011).
Westcott, Chris, *Class of '59: From Bailey to Wooller: The Golden Age of County Cricket* (Edinburgh: Mainstream, 2000).
Whitington, R.S., *Captains Outrageous? Cricket in the Seventies* (London: Stanley Paul, 1973).
Willis, Bob, *Lasting the Pace* (London: Collins, 1985).
Willis, Bob, *The Cricket Revolution: Test Cricket in the 1970s* (London: Sidgwick and Jackson, 1981).
Wilson, Don, *Mad Jack* (London: The Kingswood Press, 1992).

Newspapers and Periodicals

Bradford Observer, Bradford Telegraph and Argus, Cricketer, Daily Express, Daily Mail, Daily Mirror, Daily Telegraph, Evening News, Guardian, Independent, Independent on Sunday, Leicester Daily Mercury, Observer, Pudsey and Stanningley News, Sun, Sunday Times, Times, Yorkshire Evening Post, Yorkshire Post.

Videos and DVDs

Cricketing Legends: Ray Illingworth, IMDb Pro, 1989.
Cricketing Legends: Ray Illingworth, BBC Video (UK), 1990.
Yorkshire Cricketing Legends: The Ray Illingworth Story with Stephen Chalke, Yorkshire CCC, 2006.

Online Resources

BBC News Online
Cricket Archive – cricketarchive.com
ESPN cricinfo – www.espncricinfo.com
The Cricket Yorkshire Podcast
The Cricket Newspaper – www.thecricketpaper.com
Wikipedia – en.wikipedia.org

Index